D0710592

Design for Preaching

DESIGN
FOR PREACHING

HENRY GRADY DAVIS

FORTRESS PRESS + PHILADELPHIA

Fourteenth printing 1985

Library of Congress Catalog Card Number 58-5749

ISBN 0-8006-0806-2

1889C85   Printed in the United States of America   1-806

Preface

Nineteen years ago, just when I was undertaking to teach homiletics, a young minister drove forty miles to ask me this question: "What do you do to your thought when you preach?" He was keen enough to have noticed that when he or I or anyone else preached acceptably, the sermon as like as not refused to conform to the expected patterns, and handled its material in ways not covered by known rules. He had been taught homiletics in a good theological school. So had I. Yet neither of us could give a satisfactory answer to his question. I knew then that traditional homiletics needed some insight it did not have.

As recently as eighteen months ago another graduate of a good seminary, a man who has himself won distinction as a preacher, wrote to ask me among other things: "What method do you propose to your students as they go about the task of preparing their sermons? Specifically, how does the text come alive from a basic statement of truth about God to the living existential person-to-person relationship?" It is an excellent question, everyone will agree, and a reasonable question to ask. It is fundamentally the same question as the first, and it shows that the really urgent questions about preaching are still unanswered by homiletical theory.

Up to now this man has received no answer. This book is my attempt to answer such questions, for him and those who, like him, are already engaged in the work of preaching, and for undergraduates trying to learn to preach. The answers ought to be the same for both. It is not good that men should start with a theory of preaching too small to go with them all the way. And so my teaching began with a sense of unanswered questions.

My subsequent efforts led me to the conviction that the answers lie neither in the traditional study of homiletical forms as forms, nor in a preoccupation with the vital content of preaching apart from the forms it takes, but in a sharper awareness that content and form are two inseparable elements of the same thing in the design of a good sermon. My effort led me further to understand that, because this is so, there can be no brief, categorical answer to any question about preaching methods, and no useful statement of principles short of a full account of the sermonic process in both its aspects at once.

This book is therefore primarily a description of what takes place in actual preaching, actual sermons. It sets forth no theoretical form which a sermon must take to be a good sermon, since even the most perfect form cannot make a good sermon of shoddy material. The book is rather a report of the surprising variety of forms that do turn up in different phases of sermonic design, and how each reflects and affects the content.

To present a particular method of sermon construction is not my intention, though a writer's own methodology will show in spite of him. But a working method is a thing every man finds for himself, and no book can help him so much as can a living teacher with whom he is working. This book aims rather to furnish a critical apparatus, a basis for discrimination, which can be used with any sound method of working.

With a purpose so definite, if also so narrow, the present volume is no attempt to cover the whole work of preaching. In the writer's opinion, the attempt to cover everything results in failure to give all needed and possible help on the crucial phase of the task, the production of sermons. That at least is my excuse for not covering the minister's life and qualifications, his study, the relation of preaching to pastoral work, or the delivery of sermons—except as good delivery grows out of good preparation of what is to be delivered.

The book did not arise from a restudy and synthesis of existing texts on preaching. It rose from the analysis of many hundreds of sermons of all grades from worst to best, by men of all persuasions, from Jewish rabbis and Unitarians to Roman Catholics and Lutherans, from liberal humanists to fundamentalists, from undergraduate students taking their initial steps to first-rank theologians.

I had to look at them all to find out what the difference is. We cannot be sure what a sermon is unless we know what it might be.

I am indebted, however, to far more people, writers and living persons, than I can name. I have borrowed and stolen, have sucked the blood of thought, from so many that I no longer know whom to thank for what. My special thanks go to the Chicago Lutheran Seminary for the sabbatical leave that made this writing possible in one winter, to my colleagues, Professors Arthur Vööbus and Joseph Sittler, to Dr. Paul E. Scherer, and to more intimate readers and critics, including my daughter Margaret.

Table of Contents

CHAPTER I

Substance and Form

SOCRATES: At any rate, you will allow that every discourse ought to
be a living creature, having a body of its own and a head and feet;
there should be a middle, beginning, and end, adapted to one another
and to the whole?
PHAEDRUS: Certainly.

Plato, *Phaedrus*

Life appears in the union of substance and form. These are the
elementals. To be without form is the void of matter, and it is the
void of thought.

The relation of substance and form in the communication of
thought is the kind of relation that exists between living tissue and
organism. All life, every living thing we know, comes in some
organic form. Every common plant comes with shapes of root and
stem and leaf, of flower and fruit. By these forms we identify the
plant, and apart from the organic structure we do not know the
plant. In fact, every cell in the plant or animal comes with its
own individual form that can be analyzed under the microscope,
and can be drawn or photographed. We cannot have the life without the form.

Every thought likewise comes in some form. We cannot have
a thought without its form. Quite correctly we say that a thought
"takes shape" or "is formed" in our minds. The thought must
take form in order to be recognized for what it is, and it certainly
has to take form in order to be expressed. Expressing a thought
means giving it a form recognizable by another person. Shakespeare has described it as the poetic process, but it is what actually
takes place in every person who thinks or speaks.

And as imagination bodies forth
The forms of things unknown, the poet's pen
Turns them to shapes, and gives to airy nothing

1

A local habitation and a name.
A Midsummer Night's Dream, Act V, Scene 1.

An unformed thought, a thought not yet turned to a shape, is only a vague impression, sensed but not grasped, an airy nothing, until given a local habitation and a name. The local habitation is its embodiment in some image associated with remembered sense experience. That image must have a name, a word, a sound that stands for it. By this process it is given a recognizable form.

The most elemental form thought takes is that of a simple assertion, consisting of two parts, subject and predicate. "Time flies," we say. First we name a subject: time. Then we say something about it, we predicate, we assert that it does something: it flies. This brief assertion is the form of all thought, an organic form with two indispensable members. Intellect, in this its primal deed, takes thing in one hand and act in the other and says, "Let there be meaning."

Subject and predicate, subject and predicate—this is the constantly recurring form of thought, as universal as stem and leaf and as necessary to thought as stem and leaf are to life, essential to all apprehension and expression of meaning. The form is not elementary, but elemental: not elementary in the sense of being childish or easy, but elemental in the sense that it is so basic nobody pays any attention to it. We shall find that we never get away from or advance beyond it.

A man may never have known or may completely forget that this form, subject and predicate, exists. He may pay no attention to this or any other of the forms thought takes. Nonetheless, he constantly gives his thought some form, whether careful and distinct or careless and blurred. Careless form is form no less than strict form. There is no shapeless mass of matter or of thought, except as a way of speaking. A brushpile is not a tree, nor an organism. A brushpile is a mass of unrelated dead branches—like some sermons—but it is not a shapeless mass. The brushpile has a form that can be measured, drawn, painted. There are forms of disorder, as there are forms of order. The difference between chaotic thought and ordered thought is not the difference between no form and form; it is the difference between confused form and organized form. The chaotic talker perpetrates form as surely as the skilful speaker does. The only question is, what form?

A man who ought to know better may choose to ignore the whole question of form; he cannot choose not to deal in form. He cannot avoid the effect which form has, for good or ill, upon all his communication with other people. Neither can he avoid responding to form himself. Like all of us, he will react with indifference to most of the talk he hears. But he will react with interest to a remark like the one a policeman made in traffic court the other day. He said, "This young lady never parks her car; she abandons it." Our interest in that remark is in large measure our response to a form of words.

Our response to form seems to take place at levels of awareness deeper than rational thought, and may never rise to conscious attention. It begins deep down among the intuitive feelings. A man would have a hard time figuring out the reasons why he likes the shape of a certain automobile body. He either likes it or does not like it long before he knows why. Its lines and proportions affect him, do something to him in a quite irrational way. He may never go on to notice what lines and contours, what particular masses and proportions, affect him thus. If he does, it will make little or no difference in his appreciation. The form has already done its work for him. However, the work of a designer of automobile bodies requires him to know exactly what he is doing, to study form and master its use.

The shape of a thought works the same way. A good joke owes as much to its form as to its thought, if not more. The form may not attract attention to itself as form, though in a joke it often does. Yet the joke depends on both its idea and its form, on both together and not on either of them alone. Not the thought alone, but the thought when given particular form, makes a good joke. The hearer feels the effect of the form directly, and need do no

more than feel it; it is not necessary for him either to analyze it
or to account for its effect. But the teller of the joke must be more
deliberate. If he bungles the form, he will not convey the joke.

Likewise, it is not simply the thought of a poem that makes it
a poem. What makes a great poem is a great thought expressed
in just the way the poem expresses it, given just this form. Milton's
thought is great but not peculiar to Milton. Many a poor preacher
has said the same thing in his own way. It becomes an unforget-
table utterance only when said thus:

> . . . "God doth not need
> Either man's work or his own gifts. Who best
> Bear his mild yoke, they serve him best. His state
> Is kingly: thousands at his bidding speed,
> And post o'er land and ocean without rest;
> They also serve who only stand and wait."

This ought to show how foolish it is to suppose that if a thought
is good it does not matter much how it is expressed. The character and dimensions of a thought, its weight, its reach and force,
are either limited or extended by the form of its expression. A
thought does not seem the same when said indifferently as when
said well. When the form is right, form and thought become one.

The only way one can extend or limit a thought, can turn or
color a thought, is by the words used to express it. The only way
one can improve the form is to shape it more exactly to the thought.
Once the right thing is said rightly, there is a feeling of finality
about it, as if it could never be said so well in any way but this.
Thought does not have that feeling of finality until it is said rightly.

Finality and power of expression is no accident, does not come
heedlessly like a gift out of the blue sky, but is the result of careful
effort. It does not happen automatically even to a genius like John
Keats. Remember the first lines of *Endymion:*

> A thing of beauty is a joy forever:
> Its loveliness increases; it will never
> Pass into nothingness; but still will keep
> A bower quiet for us, and a sleep
> Full of sweet dreams, and health, and quiet breathing.

That, of course, leaves muddlers like us in despair. We have to test every word to find how impossible it would be to change one. But it has been no little consolation to me to read that Keats first wrote this opening line—a household word that sticks like a burr in the mind—as follows: "A thing of beauty is a constant joy." Keats' roommate said the line was fine but lacked something. Only after pondering it a long time did Keats exclaim, "I have it!" and write it as it now stands.

Whatever considerations of sound and rhythm and overtone may be involved in this line, the fact remains that the word *constant* did not express Keats' real meaning in this passage. It suggests only a continuing and unvarying joy, while Keats meant an increasing, endless joy. The improvement in this case did result from shaping the words more exactly to the thought. And if John Keats had to do this by hard work, there is hope for any of us who must labor to find the right shape for his thought.

If this is the true relation of form to substance in the communication of thought, there are special reasons why the man who is called to preach must be concerned about the form of what he says. The first reason has to do with the purpose of preaching. The aim of preaching is to win from men a response to the gospel, a response of attitude and impulse and feeling no less than of thought. Since form does its work immediately and at deeper levels than logic, persuades directly and silently as it were, form has an importance second only to that of thought itself.

A second reason is the exceedingly complex nature of the people who hear the Word of God. As he listens, a man may believe, deep down among the lower currents of his being, that divine wisdom and love are speaking to him in this Word. He may feel himself deeply involved in the conflict of life and death, time and eternity. He may feel an intuitive urge toward the gospel and wish he could believe it. Yet at the same time, while all this is going on in the depths of his soul, his rational mind may be picking God's Word to pieces, making all sorts of arguments against it, waging against it a defensive war which at any moment can become an offensive war. It is poor tactics to think we must fight it out with him up where the logical bullets are flying. Indeed, his fight may be with the preacher more than it is with the Lord.

This is one kind of listener. Another man may agree all too quickly and easily with everything that is being said, but down inside him he may be completely unconvinced and unmoved by it. At the top of his mind—as John Baillie expresses it—he may be a believer, but at the bottom of his heart an atheist. A human being is mysterious and awesome to contemplate. The top of his mind and the bottom of his heart may have little to do with each other; a conflict between them may be wrecking him. The easy conformity at the top of his mind may be a mask to hide his heart's treason from himself and others, just as militant atheism at the top of his mind may hide a true believer.

The Word of God is a call to both these persons, to broken and divided selves who stand swaying giddily on the edge of life. It is a call to both mind and heart at once and equally. At such a time, the form which strikes directly and silently below all rational defenses may make the difference between a hearer's redemption and his despair. The truth can reach him best through its imaged forms: beauty and compassion, strength and courage, regret and forgiveness, faithfulness and love, pain and hope. The issue may turn on a single, lean, clean-cut, athletic sentence whose voice fills the dark with echoes. It has been so before now: "Fear not, for I am with you"; "I will not leave you comfortless, I will come to you"; "I know whom I have believed"; "Forgetting what lies behind and straining forward to what lies ahead, I press toward the goal. . . ."[1]

A third reason why the form of his message should be of special concern to the preacher is the character of God's Word itself. The Word of God differs from all our habitual outlooks. It speaks of

[1] The Scripture quotations in this book are from the *Revised Standard Version of the Bible*, copyrighted 1946 and 1952 by the Division of Christian Education, National Council of Churches, and used by permission.

Another, whereas our first and last interest is in ourselves. It declares that Other to be the center of our existence, whereas we make ourselves its center. The Word reveals what we could never discover or guess. It affirms God's uncaused and unconditional love for every man, while the world of nature and culture seems indifferent. It discloses our condition as so wrong and desperate that God must take its deadly consequences upon himself, while our instinct is to vindicate our condition. The Word of God calls us to a way we would not choose to go. It tells us the self we are must die that the self God wills may be born. Yet all the time we are struggling to preserve at any cost the self that is. The Word calls us to a life by trust in him, when we can reasonably expect success only through our own wisdom and power. Its imperative is to be for God and not for self, while our wish is that God may be for us, regardless. It offers us his life and glory, while our dream is always of our own.

Thus the gospel cannot be a way of getting what everybody wants, a formula that can be sold to people by an appeal to self-interest. The gospel cannot become an expedient philosophy which can be made convincing to every sensible person on reasonable grounds. The gospel is meant for everybody, but it cannot become what everybody would like it to be. Whatever does that is something else than the gospel. Paul saw very clearly, at that early date, that what we have to preach, though it is the wisdom of God and the power of God, seems foolish by the standards of intellectual "wisdom" and seems weak when compared with the power of a miraculous "sign" from heaven.

This judgment that the gospel is foolish and weak is an intellectual judgment, our human judgment of what God is saying to us. It is our presumptuous attempt to judge and resist God. Our reasoning about God is never unprejudiced reasoning, our judgment never an impartial judgment. To recognize God changes our whole status, dethrones us and puts Another in the center of our existence where we have always kept ourselves. The question of the existence of God is never an objective intellectual inquiry. In us God meets resistance which must be overcome and defenses that must be broken down. The gospel must win us in spite of these.

How are we to proclaim such a message as this? It should be obvious that the form it takes may make a great difference. If it takes the form of an intellectual argument alone, it is well-nigh certain to fail. If it takes the form of an appeal to self-interest, it is sure to lead back toward self and away from God.

The man who would learn to preach must take note that these large aspects of preaching—intellectual arguments, appeals to self-interest—are matters of *form,* not of the substance of the gospel. These are the forms taken by much of the preaching of our day, but these forms have not dominated preaching throughout Christian history.

If the form of what we say has an immediate and almost automatic power to repel or attract, and to do its work on levels of response that lie below the arguments and counterarguments, then the very nature of the gospel, as well as the nature and condition of mankind, requires us to be concerned with form.

There is no ideal or standard form which every sermon should take. The sermon is not a species with fixed and invariable characteristics, as the form of the violet, the lily, the leaf of the red oak, the twig of the weeping willow is fixed. There is no pre-existent mold into which the substance of thought must be poured in order to make a sermon.

It may be that the concept of a sermon itself is a hindrance rather than a help to the preacher. Perhaps we should never aim at preaching a sermon, at making a kind of speech that falls, with ten thousand others, into a category called sermons. Certainly that should never be our chief aim. We can be very sure that on the day of Pentecost Peter had something else in mind than preaching a sermon. So did Paul at Antioch in Pisidia, and Jesus in the synagogue at Nazareth. It is very certain that none of these began by saying to himself, "Now the time has come to preach a sermon."

That unusual sermon we occasionally hear of, that good sermon which is supposed to break all homiletical rules—generally its preacher is the one who proudly admits that it does—is a fiction. If it is a good sermon, it does not break good rules; it breaks only the unnecessary and artificial rules. Any homiletical theory which fails to show why Peter's sermon on the day of Pentecost was a good sermon, or why this unusual sermon is good (if it is as good as its preacher thinks it), is an artificial theory, not worth the trouble it causes.

Nevertheless, there is a right form for each sermon, namely, the form that is right for this particular sermon. A right form can never be imposed on any sermon. If it has to be imposed it is not right. The right form derives from the substance of the message itself, is inseparable from the content, becomes one with the content, and gives a feeling of finality to the sermon.

When form is rightly used, it seems to be the inevitable shape of the thought, and is then indistinguishable from the thing said; it becomes the thing itself.

Form has its dangers and temptations. The preacher is a human being subject to all the aberrations of other people. There is danger that he too may try to escape the pressure and demands of the gospel by turning himself into a mere manipulator of forms. There is danger that his use of forms may be so calculated that his work will sound contrived and insincere. Too much concern for form with too little concern for content, a too-deliberate use of form for form's sake, is a mark of inferior work, whether on canvas, on the stage, in the concert hall, or in the pulpit.

A preacher, therefore, ought to be a good craftsman, but never a mere technician. He has only so much time for preparation, and it is never enough time. If he devotes too much time to form and too little to content, if he studies the use of form as something apart from content, he may become a rhetorician, an attractive speaker, but he will turn out to be something less than a preacher of the gospel.

This is not the greatest danger, of course, or the commonest failure. A greater danger is that the preacher will be concerned only about the content of his preaching, will never in his life study form enough to begin to master it, and will never become the preacher he has it in him to be. A man determined to preach his best has before him, like any artist, a lifelong struggle with form—to subdue it and make it serve his message.

In some highly gifted men such a mastery of form seems like second nature. They seem never to have to pay any attention to it. In such cases appearances may be deceptive. We must remember that these fortunate creatures have an equal facility of thought. They seem not to struggle with anything. At any rate, a mastery of form does not come to most men without study, much practice, long and patient effort. And even the gifted man does not produce any great work, nor any considerable body of respectable work, without sustained and concentrated application. Many a man with brilliant talent fails to produce anything; he lacks the character to make the required effort.

Let us be realistic. Most students for the ministry, possibly with their heads in the clouds, want to learn an easy way to preach. They are not willing to put forth a tenth of the effort required for excellence in comparable fields. They can give sixteen reasons, some of them being theological reasons, why they should not be bothered about form. It would be hard to find this attitude in serious workers at any similar task.

A young student in an art school would not expect to be able to paint a decent picture without months and years devoted not only to the great paintings of others but also to the how of painting, to the handling of brushes and pigments, to the management of lines, masses, space, light, and color. He would not expect any picture of his to be good until he had tried time and time again to improve its plan, its composition. He would examine every detail critically, and let nothing stand that did not pass the test of his feeling of rightness, not a brush stroke, a tint, or a shadow. He would know that while he is working to get this picture right he is cultivating his own feeling for what is right, is developing that discrimination in the use of forms upon which his whole hope of success must rest.

The young poet knows very well that there is no hope of his becoming a good poet without having acquired a mastery of language, the medium in which he works. A love of words, a taste for their sound, weight, color, and overtones, a lifelong search for images that suggest more than logical abstractions can convey, an ear for the sound, the movement, and the balance of phrases, lines, and stanzas—such things as these are the very stuff of his work, and he knows it. He would not expect to say anything important until he could supply his vision with a fitting embodiment in words.

The young novelist or playwright takes it for granted that his hope of success rests upon his handling of language, of character, action, and plot, the movement and rhythm of life. He knows that if his work is to be true, he must watch with interest the action and interaction of people about him, he must cultivate a taste for their speech, whether formal or racily colloquial, he must look deep into the hearts of human beings with love and understanding. If his apprenticeship should last ten years, and equal Robert Louis Stevenson's in intensity of determination, he would not think it too much.

Only the apprentice preacher dares to think such things as these beneath him, and expects to succeed in his work without knowing anything about how it is done.

This is not a plea for an intensive formal study of rhetoric. Just the same, it is chastening to remember the proud history rhetoric has had, from Aristotle to Brooks and Warren, as the art of communication in language. Many of Christianity's great preachers were rhetoricians before they were preachers, among them Ambrose, Augustine, and Chrysostom. Rhetoric is not equivalent to a blown-up, artificial style. Whately's *Rhetoric* was among the few books Abraham Lincoln studied most avidly, and the incomparably simple force of the Gettysburg Address and the Second Inaugural Address would not be the same without it.

Nor do I mean to suggest that the preacher can withdraw himself from life into some vacuum and practice an esoteric art, as painting and poetry and music sometimes are practiced now. The gospel has to be preached by busy parish ministers. They cannot shut themselves in the study and stay there with the singleminded purpose of becoming creative artists, and they should not if they could. Yet every time they preach, they practice the art of communication in some fashion, however poor, and the practice is poorer than it needs to be.

Fortunately, true art is not something esoteric or "arty." The communication of the gospel, any communication, is an art rather than a science. It is a way of doing rather than a complicated theory of what to do and how to do it. In this, speech is like any true art. Art is skill in doing, controlled by an inner sense of rightness, a sense that is nearer to feeling than to calculation, nearer to intuition than to deliberation. Skill in doing may be helped by study, but basically it must be acquired and perfected by practice. The inner sense of rightness, too, can be awakened and sensitized by a study of theory, and still more by exposure to fine work; but it remains a kind of feeling or intuition.

If a man is called to preach, then, he is called to work in the great art of oral communication, and is called to cultivate all the sense and skill he can. What the preacher does is not done by the manuscript or the page of notes before him. It is done by his body and his voice through the sounds and signs he makes, before people assembled in a room. All preparation, from his youth up, is preparation for that. The Spirit of God, we believe, strives to guide and use him. But both he and the Spirit work against the limits of his skill to communicate, guided by his inner sense of rightness, keen or dull.

The minister must preach out of a busy life, full of hard work. He will not have time to bring every sermon to the perfection of a published poem or short story. But if he lets that fact excuse him for poor work, he is doomed. Having been in his shoes, I understand. But my sympathy grows less indulgent when I hear William

Faulkner speak of his life's work as an agony and sweat of the human spirit, when I know that Bach's cantatas are ours because his contract required him to write new music for every Sunday along with a teaching job, when I remember that Mozart's symphonies and concertos and operas were composed in a life harassed by disappointment, poverty, and sickness, when I recall that Luther and Calvin had to preach every day for long periods, while leading the Reformation and writing its literature.

It takes more than craftsmanship to do a work that lasts, but it does take craftsmanship. And speaking now in terms of craft alone, what the busy man needs is a theory of preaching which is stripped of all nonessential and merely traditional matters, which sticks to the factors that are decisive, and deals with them clearly. If theory is to help him, it must be a clear theory of design, uncluttered with superfluous rules, that can be carried in the mind until it becomes second nature and guides him even when he is not thinking about theory. For the time comes when the preacher, like any artist, must stop thinking about theory. Augustine said that a young man can quickly learn all that rhetoric has to teach him, that he ought to learn it and then no longer bother about it. This is true, as far as the theoretical side of it is concerned.

On the other hand, there is a sense in which no art is ever learned, and surely no man ever felt that he had learned to preach. The permanent benefit of theoretical study is not a knowledge of the rules and laws of form. The permanent benefit is in what the study does to one's inner sense of form and one's skill in using form.

Therefore, the apprentice preacher should study his work in three directions. First, he should read good books on writing and on speaking. If his college work has not included an adequate training in speech, he should thoroughly study a textbook on speaking, and go on to books on writing. He should learn all he can about writing. He should write—anything and everything— in the attempt to bring whatever is significant inside him to expression. He should remember that his common speech and conversation is also self-expression and communication, and make it worthy of what is in him.

This theoretical phase of his study should include literary criticism as well as what other serious interpreters of life in his day, such as novelists, poets, and playwrights, are saying about their work. He should read all this not only as an intellectual adventure, but with the realization that all of it applies to his own work. This theoretical study is basic, but by no means enough.

The beginner should study the sermons of other men, the great ones of an older day, and all he can hear and read in the present. There is no substitute for the study, analysis, and evaluation of actual sermons, lots of them. A man can no more develop his best skill in preaching without having studied the work of great preachers, than he could find his own best way of painting pictures, designing buildings, or writing plays or symphonies without knowing the great works of the human spirit in these forms. The labor of humanity is a continuing enterprise, and the best work rises from previous work.

Moreover, the young craftsman should study sermons not only for their thought and vision, but especially for their craft. Craft is of first importance to him at this stage but is usually the last thing noticed. If he does not like to read sermons, finds them less interesting than other forms of writing, regards them with the contempt they sometimes deserve, let him take that fact as the severest rebuke possible to his profession, and the strongest challenge to him not to go on producing more of the same kind. No preacher would admit that his themes are less vital than those of the novelist. Is there any insurmountable reason why a sermon has to be less stimulating than a novel? With a theme as vital, what but inadequate form could keep it from being as absorbing as a story?

Finally, a man must learn the craft by hard and unremitting practice in his own work. Until he knows it in his own work he does not know it. While he is studying it theoretically, craft is one thing; it has a different look and feel when he tries to use it. Craft does not exist in a vacuum. In every case it has to do with some particular message he hopes to deliver, has to do with its content and its form in relation to each other and to the people to whom he will speak it. Therefore, the formal problems will be different in every separate sermon, since they are always problems of the material itself. There is no hope of learning the craft, then, except by designing actual sermons, and no hope of its being the craft of preaching unless these products are real sermons. The beginner should plunge in and do them as fast as he can do them with care, for every one will be different.

DESIGN FOR A SERMON

A sermon should be like a tree.

It should be a living organism:
    With one sturdy thought like a single stem
    With natural limbs reaching up into the light.

It should have deep roots:
    As much unseen as above the surface
    Roots spreading as widely as its branches spread
    Roots deep underground
        In the soil of life's struggle
        In the subsoil of the eternal Word.

It should show nothing but its own unfolding parts:
    Branches that thrust out by the force of its inner life
    Sentences like leaves native to this very spray
        True to the species
        Not taken from alien growths
    Illustrations like blossoms opening from
            inside these very twigs
        Not brightly colored kites
            Pulled from the wind of somebody else's thought
            Entangled in these branches.

It should bear flowers and fruit at the
        same time like the orange:
    Having something for food
        For immediate nourishment
    Having something for delight
        For present beauty and fragrance
        For the joy of hope
        For the harvest of a distant day.

> To be all this it must grow in a warm climate:
>   In loam enriched by death
>   In love like the all-seeing and all-cherishing sun
>   In trust like the sleep-sheltering night
>   In pity like the rain.

[This is not an attempt at a poem. It is the design of an idea (the first line) and of its development. It is the sketch—the notes, the outline— of a lecture delivered more than once. The lecture is longer than this. But it does not say more than this, nor does it say it better than this— perhaps not so well.]

SUGGESTIONS

Dear Fellow-worker:

Let me take this way of addressing you man to man. Here let me speak of different ways you may look at the whole business of preaching and go about it, of your attitude, your stance before the job.

I hope you will see at once why I ask you to think of preaching as it relates to other high forms of intellectual and artistic endeavor. Simply as a work of man, not to speak of its more-than-human purport, it is akin to writing, music, and other arts. Preaching offers the same full scope to all the gifts of thought and imagination you have in you. In preaching as in the arts, high achievement calls for a lifetime of sustained and dedicated labor, and is worth it.

It is possible, however, that you may regard preaching much more lightly than this. You may think of it as being only a practical necessity of your occupation, useful to others, but not the fullest expression and fulfilment of your own nature and gifts. You may thus start preaching, or trying to preach, far out on the margin of your ability, because your real self is held aloof from it. Then only a fraction of your powers will be engaged in the effort.

This would not make for usefulness, nor for happiness. I should be very sorry to see this happen to you. That is why I hope you will from the beginning remember that, while it may be more, preaching can never be less than a medium for the highest work you have it in you to do—you or any man. Its possibilities are no more fulfilled in the customary unskilful puttering than the possibilities of poetry and music are fulfilled in the sung commercial. If you will bring yourself to think this way about it, you will have taken the first important step in the right direction.

For further reading in connection with this chapter, I suggest that you start, not with works on homiletical theory or method, but with the biography of some great preacher of your choice. Or start with brief biographical sketches of several, such as you will find in Jones (24) **(The numbers refer to entries in the bibliography at the end of the** book), or in some short history of preaching, like Part I of Garvie (8), or pages 1-95 in Smith (14). Longer histories are Dargan (20) and Webber (32).

You could just as well begin with something on the work of preaching in general (not the techniques) like pages 1-23, "The Imperative Call," in Sangster (27). The whole of Section II of the bibliography is on this general task of the preaching ministry.

CHAPTER 2

Footnote on Terminology

Attempting to think together about the intricate processes of thinking, we venture into a world of thought as complex as the world of things and far less tangible, far less orderly. As if thinking about thinking were not difficult enough, we are further attempting to talk together about thinking about thinking.

Since we have to talk about these processes, we are forced to use words, not fresh and precise words, but words worn by long use and confused by inconstant meanings in writings on homiletics. We shall be lucky to avoid getting entangled in our words.

I want to speak as naturally as I can about the technical elements of sermon production. There is never a word that actually describes one of these processes. There is never a group of two or several words that between them describe the process. In every case I am talking about a thing that goes on in the mind but which cannot be accurately described, a concept which cannot be contained within any word or any number of words. To speak naturally, I must not allow myself to be bound to any set of technical words. In every case the thing is important, but the word is not important.

The processes I have to describe seem to me to be more like the organic processes of biology than the mechanical processes of, say, carpentry. That is the first reason why I sometimes prefer to use a word other than the word traditionally used in homiletical writings. A more urgent reason is that the traditional words all have different meanings in different writings. The most compelling reason of all is that the crucial work on a sermon, the work not commonly done well, is more like the work of an architect sketching the plan of a building than like the work of the carpenters, concrete and steel men, and other construction workers, who put up the building.

Concerning my terminology in general let me speak a word of clarification. I hope it is clear that I do not use the terms *substance, form,* and *idea* in the sense they would have for a philosophical idealist. They can mean what they meant to Plato only in a philosophical system that tries to comprehend existence without an adequate theology. The absoluteness and eternity of the idea makes it greater than any god, since the god is a god by participating in the idea of god-ness.

But the truth we preach is not an abstract thing. The truth is a Person. The goodness we preach is not an ideal quality. The goodness is Someone who is good. The truth, the goodness we preach is not a thing that can first be defined and then applied to God, to Christ. The truth, the goodness, is God in Christ.

The love we preach is God himself in Christ. There is no such thing as love—there is only somebody who loves. Love, "this thing called love," does not exist in heaven or earth or any secret corner of creation. It exists only when somebody loves and only in that somebody's act of loving. There is no love, there is only a lover.

Substance

If love is thought of as having *substance,* its substance is God himself. If love is for ever, its eternity is the Eternal. But in order that we might apprehend this eternal Love and Goodness and Truth, it took the form of human flesh and dwelt among us. And in order to speak about it we have to get some idea of it, some incarnation, some vision, image, or plain concept. And any idea we get of it is in the form of a human thought, consisting of subject and predicate. That is to say, truth or goodness or love must take the form of thought to be apprehended and spoken of.

Form

The form is not something that exists apart from the idea that is apprehended and spoken of. Form is not a chalice of fixed shape containing wine today but usable for quite different content tomorrow. I speak of substance and form rather than content and form, because the relation between them is not mechanical but organic. The sermon idea is thought having form, not thought contained within a form that might just as well contain some other thought. The form is the shape of the thought itself, its image in the human mind, its likeness to ourselves.

Idea

A well-prepared sermon is the embodiment, the development, the full statement of a significant thought. Every thought is an idea. But a sermon idea is more than a bare thought. It is a thought plus its overtones and its groundswell of implication and urgency. It has more than the form of a thought; it has the energy, the life force of a thought.

So it seems natural to speak of *the idea* of a sermon. The term is used in that sense in homiletical writings. In many other connections, we use the word constantly in this sense. We speak of "great ideas." We say, "I ran across a good idea." We ask, "What's the idea?" of a sermon, a book, almost anything.

The idea of a sermon, in this sense, is the same thing as is often inaccurately called a subject, or a topic, or a theme. These words do not all mean the same thing, and none of them any longer conveys an exact sense. But this essential feature of the sermon is decisive in its importance. It seems more natural to call it the idea or the thought, but I shall freely call it a theme or a topic when one of those words seems appropriate.

Central Thought

Because a sermon is a developed thought, that thought is central to the sermon. It is more than central, however. It is not merely in a central position in the sermon, with other independent thoughts surrounding it. It is rather one thought catching others up into itself. Yet because it is central to the sermon, I shall at times call it the *central thought*. Because the thought is an idea and the idea is central to the sermon, I shall at times call it the *central idea*. The thing is the same, and the thing is what matters. The words differ, but the words do not matter. I shall feel free to use any that seems best at the moment.

Generative Idea

Moreover, the thought, the idea produces the sermon by the energy, the vitality inherent in it. I shall speak of the *productive thought*, the *productive idea*. The thought generates the sermon. I shall speak of the *generative thought*, the *generative idea*. The sermon is inherent in the thought; the sermon exists in the thought or idea as the plant exists in the germ, the seed. I shall speak of the *germinal thought*, the *germinal idea*. I shall use any of these terms or any other words which seems best at the moment. The productive, generative, germinal relation of the idea to the sermon is the thing that matters; the words do not matter.

Design

To design a sermon is more than to construct it. It must be designed before it can be constructed. Design is seeing and shaping. Construction means to work with a saw and hammer, to make forms and fill them with concrete, to rivet together pieces of steel already shaped. Designing a sermon is more like making a plant grow to the form inherent in it.

So I shall speak of *sermonic design* rather than of sermon construction, but the thing I am talking about can be called construction or planning, and I shall say construction or planning when it seems natural to say that. I shall speak of the *sketch* or the *design* of a sermon rather than of an outline, for it seems more significant and closer to the nature of the work. But if we know the thing we are talking about, it can be called an outline or a plan just as well. It seems more natural to call it a design, because the word *outline* does not necessarily connote true seeing and shaping. But the thing, not the word, is what matters, and I shall freely call it an outline or plan when it seems natural at that place.

Continuity

There is one compelling reason, among other reasons, why I shall not rely on the word outline to designate the plan of a sermon. The conventional outline is a static and visual plan, whereas the sermon can be properly planned only as an audible movement in time. The proper plan of a sermon, then, the proper sketch of a sermon, the proper design of a sermon, is the design of a time-continuity. And so I shall prefer to speak of the *continuity* or the *movement* of a sermon, rather than of its outline.

Complete Idea

An idea is at least a thought. A complete idea is a complete thought expressed in a complete sentence with subject and predicate. An incomplete idea is an incomplete thought, a subject without a predicate. A sermon may be generated by a *complete idea,* consisting of both subject and predicate. But a sermon can also be generated by an *incomplete idea,* a subject without a predicate. I shall speak of complete and incomplete thoughts, complete and incomplete ideas, in this sense.

Predication

To understand what goes on in thinking, we have to get down to the basic elements: the noun, the name of something to be talked about, and the verb, the predicate, what is said or asserted about that subject. It seems to me natural to distinguish these basic elements of thought by the terms used to distinguish them in English grammar. It seems natural to use the word *assertion* to denote the expression of a complete thought, natural to use *subject* for the thing talked about, *predicate* for the thing said about it, and *predication* for the process of saying or asserting something about the subject. The dictionary's definitions of these words include the larger meaning as well as their technical sense in grammar.

Organic Structure

The thought generates the sermon, and the sermon embodies the thought, thus creating not a mechanism but an organism. An organism consists of parts or members in structural and functional relation to one another and to the whole. Knowing this, it seems natural to speak of the parts, divisions, heads, points, of a sermon as *structural* parts, signifying their character as organic elements of a developing idea or thought.

The chief structural parts of a sermon are things said, assertions, thoughts. It seems natural to call them *structural assertions* or *structural thoughts*.

A part is less than the whole, a member is less than the organism. A part, a member is within the whole and contributes to the whole. So it seems natural at times to speak of the structural assertions or structural thoughts as *contributing assertions* or *contributing thoughts*.

Parts, divisions, heads, points, structural assertions, structural thoughts, contributing assertions, contributing thoughts—they all designate the same elements of a sermon. The words are not important, but to preserve the sense of organism is extremely important. And it seems natural, when we are trying to think of the sermon as an organic development of a thought, to speak of its members in organic terms.

CHAPTER 3

Anatomy of the Idea

It should be a living organism:
　With one sturdy thought like a single stem
　With natural limbs reaching up into the light.

What is the man talking about?
What is he saying about it?
What does he mean?
Is it true? Do I believe it?
So what? What difference does it make?

The anatomy of an idea is revealed in the answers to these questions about it. These are the vital questions. The best literary criticism does little more than ask and answer these questions concerning some work of the mind, and if it sometimes includes other questions, it never gets far away from these or stays away from them long. These are the questions a good reader intuitively asks when studying a book, an author, or a system of thought. An intelligent listener, almost any listener, is consciously or unconsciously asking these questions about any sermon he hears.

A student who begins to study sermons by a direct and persistent use of these questions will avoid much waste of time and effort and achieve sounder results than he could in any other way. If he learns to use them in planning and testing his own work, they will be of incalculable benefit to him, for they lead straight to the heart of the matter.

The first two may be regarded as structural questions, that is, they concern the organic structure of the thought. The first points to the true subject, what is actually talked about. The apparent subject may not be the true subject, and the true subject may be far from easy to discover. Yet until the subject is exactly defined, it is not possible either to understand or to judge the value of anything said.

The second question, completely answered, supplies in condensed form the full body of predication, everything the speaker or writer says. What can be truly predicated concerning one subject may be false if said of another. A thing said, or a group of statements made, may constitute an adequate treatment of one subject, but a totally inadequate treatment of some other subject.

These two elements taken together, what is talked about and what is said about it, constitute the organic structure of any developed idea. Neither can stand alone. A group of assertions not attached to a clearly defined subject makes a rambling, pointless harangue—a brushpile. A subject, however important, that is not followed by predication is not a complete idea.

An example may not be out of place. Let us suppose that a man is talking about *what this country needs*. That is not an idea, only a subject one might have an idea *about*. Here is one man's idea (now long outdated) on that subject: "What this country needs is a good five-cent cigar." Now that is an idea, a complete thought, by virtue of its predicate. One could talk at length about that, for it has taken on meaning. A contemporary of ours has a totally different idea on precisely the same subject: "What this country needs is a car that won't run faster than the driver can think."

What is the man talking about? What is he saying about it? These are the structural questions. The three remaining questions I shall call functional; that is, they have to do with the thought's operation, with its purpose to communicate meaning, with its significance, its validity, its consequences. The functional questions are as important as the structural, but in this chapter we are concerned with the structural (we could also call them anatomical) questions.

If a sermon is well designed, these questions can all be answered satisfactorily. If they cannot be answered, the sermon is not well designed, and the questions will show what is wrong with it. Like any sound piece of work, a good sermon is the embodiment of an idea. It is an organic structure of thought, which unfolds from within, according to the anatomy of the idea that produces it.

It may seem childishly simple to say that every sermon consists of only two things: what is talked about, and what is said about it, a subject with one or several predicates. To say it is indeed simple; to act on it must be very difficult, judging by the evidence. A man who has been to college and seminary, a man who has preached for years, can speak as if he never heard of this primary fact. Sometimes he proposes a subject and then wanders away from it. Sometimes he drags in many other things that do not belong to the subject. Sometimes he seems to be talking about several subjects at once, indiscriminately. Sometimes he just talks about this and that and the other in such a way as to create the suspicion that he either has no subject at all or, if he feels one looming at the back of his head, does not himself know for sure what it is.

Such common faults in design, such lack of organization, result from neglect or defiance of these supposedly simple facts. They are deformities of thought, anatomical monstrosities, like a three-headed calf. No overlay of brilliant or witty talk, apt quotations, choice anecdotes, can hide a misshapen body of thought. There is no way to correct these elemental faults of design except to keep pressing the question, "What am I to talk about? What must be said about it?"

To learn to preach, a man must develop his sense of form, his feeling for the shape and organic structure of a thought. This is the first step in learning. To feel the shape and structure of his idea is also the first and chief task in preparing any given sermon, down to the last one a man will preach before he dies. No man ever graduates from this, or gets above it.

A sense of form can be developed and turned into a skill in the use of form. But it can be done only by constant attention to the organic structure of every talk one hears and everything one reads. And this may call for a radical change in the way a student habitually listens and the way he reads.

Most men have the habit of remaining rather passive, of really noticing nothing except the thing that strikes them personally, that is, gets an emotional response of some kind from them. Such a thing is nearly always a detail, a flashing side light, a striking combination of words, an illustration that is pounced on for its own sake, without regard to *what* it illustrates. Such listening or reading magnifies the incidentals out of all due proportion, and distorts what is being said. The real points, the important contributing thoughts, the structural assertions, being stated in general words and less highly charged emotionally, are missed.

The beginner must change that habit by a sedulous attention to the anatomy of ideas. He must stop getting lost in the details and study the essential structure of sermons. For the time being he has to forget about the sentences, the arguments used, the quotations, the human interest stories. He has to stand off from the sermon far enough to see its shape as a whole. Stubbornly he has to ask, "What is the man really talking about, and what are the basic things he is saying about it?" This means that he must learn to distinguish between the organic structure of the idea, on the one hand, and its development on the other. It is like beginning with the skeleton in the study of anatomy.

In his search for the structure a man may get help from the title, if the sermon has one. When there is a title, it may or may not be the subject that is actually being treated. There is always some relation between title and subject, but a title serves its own purpose, and its purpose may not be to announce the subject. Even if the title sounds like a subject, it may not be the true subject. The real subject is very often more restricted, narrower than the title. The preacher in his introduction may announce what he is going to talk about, or he may not. More often than we might think, he does not anywhere make clear what he is talking about. There is no rule about these things, and if there were the preacher would not always follow it anyway. Too often the listener or reader is strictly on his own, our styles in preaching being what they are at present.

(The soundproof walls within which preachers talk to one another about preaching are a dangerous fraud. As I write, the voices of people living and dead keep breaking in upon my inner ear. I hear one of the six most intelligent persons I ever knew, a man who never went past grade school, asking questions I will never forget about my sermons. I hear Mrs. Ambitious and Mr. Wilful. I hear—but the one I will let speak aloud in the following not wholly imaginary conversation is a mild person and a leader of men.)

GEORGE (A young executive): May I break in here, Pastor?

PASTOR: Of course, George. Go ahead.

GEORGE: I hear you nearly every Sunday. I try to follow you. Would you believe that I sometimes fail to understand you?

PASTOR: Can you tell me what the trouble is?

GEORGE: Not exactly. I have a college training, but I'm not a theologian. What you're saying always interests me. But sometimes in what I feel must be your most inspired sermons I don't know exactly what you are talking about.

PASTOR: Am I obscure? Is my language strange, hard to understand?

GEORGE: No, that's the surprising thing about it. I understand everything you say while you are saying it, but I don't see how it connects, what it adds up to. I can feel that you are driving at something, but I can't see what it is. I don't get the point. It haunts me, but doesn't materialize.

PASTOR: Tell me anything you can about it.

GEORGE: I don't know how to put it except to say that I follow what you are saying but don't know for sure what you're talking about. I can go home and tell my wife many good things you have said. But if she should ask me what your sermon was about today, I simply can't tell her. It's embarrassing.

PASTOR: It must be pretty annoying too.

GEORGE: Well, yes, it is. And since I'm already complaining, maybe I'd just as well say all that's on my mind.

PASTOR: By all means. Let me have it straight.

GEORGE: Well, I like to read poetry, and I sometimes have the same trouble with Eliot and Auden and Thomas. When I know what the poet is talking about, his point of reference, what he says is cogent and moving. But as long as the subject is obscure the poem makes no sense, and the effort and research necessary to discover the subject is often more than the poem is worth to me. Do you follow me?

PASTOR: Yes, for I have the same trouble with them. Go ahead.

GEORGE: Now, if I don't know what a poet is talking about, I can lay him down without much disappointment. But you, sir, use a large part of the worship hour, you stand in the consecrated pulpit of our church, and you have to speak to me of matters in which my very existence is at stake. I think I have a right to know what you are talking about, exactly and without having to guess.

PASTOR: I see. I thought the handling of a subject was only a detail of my sermon technique. You are saying that it is a moral issue, a thing that shows respect or disregard for the people who hear me.

GEORGE: Something like that, I suppose, though I had never put it that way to myself. I have sometimes thought it would be a good thing if a minister had to make his case and defend it against the attack of a skilful opponent, as a lawyer does.

PASTOR: I'm sure it would make a big difference.

A well-designed sermon, then, is the embodiment and extension of an important idea, of which the first element is a clearly defined subject and the second element is one or more significant things said, predicates, structural assertions concerning the subject. The contributing predicates are likely to be few, seldom more than six or eight, more often fewer than that. All the rest is development. The volume of the completed sermon is mostly development. The preacher restates his basic points in different ways, explains them, supports them, traces their significance, shares their values with his hearers, in the living process of face-to-face communication.

But the separate and distinct things he says about his subject are few. To answer the question, what is he saying, means to identify all his structural assertions, stripped of all development.

The apprentice must learn to recognize this anatomical, skeletal form of the thought in every discourse he hears and in every printed sermon he reads. Most of his work will be wasted until he learns this.

As with the subject, so in the identification of the structural points, the student lacks any sure guide. A good preacher is more likely than a mediocre one to state his point explicitly and clearly and to put it in a prominent position. But there are other considerations in preaching besides clarity, and the best preacher will sometimes build up his point at length and make it by implication, yet never state it as an explicit assertion. This point may be one of the most important in the whole sermon. It may be something the listener would deny or resist if the preacher asserted it, but will assert it for himself if the implication is weighty and moving. In such a case, the hearer or reader must go beyond the preacher's bare words, must word the point for himself.

Note on the Use of Examples

Before introducing the first of many examples, let me say that every sermon discussed in this book is chosen for one reason alone: it illustrates some definite point of design. These are not models of preaching in either content or form.

To select only models of form would restrict the choice and remove the necessity of discrimination. To select only models of content would restrict the choice still more narrowly. Worse, to be sidetracked by a theological disagreement or agreement would wholly confuse our task of studying design.

To illustrate the most basic points I have selected sermons that are accessible to all students. That is why so many are in Blackwood's *The Protestant Pulpit*. The hope is that our brief examination will be followed up by a more thorough study and criticism of these sermons.

Thus I neither approve nor disapprove of the sermon I use. I neither approve nor disapprove of the preacher. These sermons are for study, not for imitation. There are no perfect sermons, no model sermons. I therefore beg the reader to concentrate all his attention on that point of design which is being discussed at the time. If he does this, he will learn to discriminate for himself, so that he will not need to imitate. If he cannot tell the difference between good and bad, his only protection is to learn to tell the difference.

The Expulsive Power of a New Affection, by Thomas Chalmers[1]

More than a century ago in Scotland Thomas Chalmers preached a sermon which has become so famous that it is found in almost every collection of great sermons. The text is I John 2:15, "Love not the world, neither the things that are in the world. If any man love the world, the love of the Father is not in him." It is a long sermon, about twice the length of the usual sermon today. Yet its idea is single, uncomplicated, and not new. The idea is suggested by the text but not expressed in the text.

What does he talk about? The sermon has one subject, and it is not *love*, which is too big and indefinite for a sermon subject. Nor is it a double subject: The love of God *vs.* the love of the world. Chalmers first narrows love to *new* love. But the subject is not "New love," which is still too big and general. He narrows new love to new love's *power*, but the subject is not "The power of a new love" in general. He narrows the power of a new love to its power to displace, to *expel* an old love. And then at last he knows precisely what he has to talk about, and he comes up with this memorable subject: "The Expulsive Power of a New Affection." There is, however, still another narrowing required by the text, but not indicated in this title. He does not talk about the power of *any* new love to expel any old love. He talks about the power of a new *love for God* to expel the love of the world and the things in it.

[1] *Works of Thomas Chalmers* (New York: Carter, 1830), Vol. II. This sermon is No. 6 in A. W. Blackwood, *The Protestant Pulpit* (Nashville: Abingdon, 1947), p. 50.

That, now, is a true subject; it is precisely what he talks about.
And what does he say about it? What is his predicate? Well, he
does not say a long series of things about it in this long sermon.
His predicate is as single as his subject. He says one all-inclusive
thing about it. He says: "Only a new love for God can expel the
love of the world and the things in it."

Note that this "only" means "nothing else can." Its weight is
negative, and although it is extremely important in the development, its value is merely as a contrast to the positive: A new love
for God does expel the love of the world. A negative is always
a tension within the idea, not a new organic member of the idea.

Here, then, is a sermon idea, that is, a sharply defined subject
and an all-inclusive predicate, something significant talked about
and something definite said about it. "A new love for God expels
the love of the world, and there is no other way to overcome the
love of the world." That is what the sermon says at great length,
and that is all it says. Everything in the sermon adds up to this,
centers in this thought. This is the idea, stripped of all particularity
and reduced to a single generalization. The whole sermon as it
stands is an embodiment, a development of this idea, plus some
practical conclusions resulting from it.

Like any living thought, this one has a form of its own and
an independent existence. It lives and can be carried in the mind.
The embodiment it finds in this particular sermon is not its only possible development, but is only one possible development, the one
Chalmers found for it. The sermon could not exist without this
idea, but the idea can exist apart from this particular embodiment
of it. The sermon does not produce the idea; the idea generates
the sermon.

This is what is called a topical sermon. The terms, topical,
textual, and expository, are used loosely and not at all uniformly
in homiletical literature, and are of limited usefulness. Having a
topic does not necessarily make a sermon topical. A good textual
or expository sermon also has a topic expressed or unexpressed,
a unitary idea, an inclusive subject with one or several predicates.

Chalmers' sermon is topical in two respects. First, nothing but its topic, its central idea, is derived from the text. The idea, in fact, goes beyond the text and is quite independent of the text. Neither the newness of the love nor its expulsive power appears in the text. But the antithesis between love for God and love for the world is expressed in the text, and Chalmers' theme grew out of that antithesis.

The second feature of a topical sermon is that the idea, once derived, is then developed independently without drawing further on the text. This particular sermon could be preached exactly as it is without using the text, though it might not have been born without the text. A sermon is not necessarily unbiblical because it has no text, nor biblical because it uses one.

JESUS' SERMON AT NAZARETH—Luke 4:16-30

Luke gives us a dramatic account of a sermon preached by Jesus in the synagogue at Nazareth, his home town.

And he stood up to read; and there was given him the book of the prophet Isaiah. He opened the book, and found the place where it was written,
"The Spirit of the Lord is upon me,
    because he has anointed me to preach good news to the poor.
He has sent me to proclaim release to the captives
    and recovering of sight to the blind,
    to set at liberty those who are oppressed,
    to proclaim the acceptable year of the Lord."
And he closed the book, and gave it back to the attendant, and sat down; and the eyes of all in the synagogue were fixed on him. And he began to say to them, "Today this scripture has been fulfilled in your hearing [literally, in your ears]." And all spoke well of him, and wondered at the gracious words which proceeded out of his mouth; and they said, "Is not this Joseph's son?" . . . And when they heard this, all in the synagogue were filled with wrath. And they rose up and put him out of the city. . . .

We wish we could have heard this sermon. Well, we have it entire in the form of its generative idea. We have also, in the omitted verses, the important assertions he made concerning the critical issue.

What is Jesus talking about here? He calls it "this scripture," *hē graphē autē*. But his subject is not this text from Isaiah 61 alone. This Scripture is good news—sent by God, authorized by God's Spirit—to the poor, the captives, the blind, the oppressed. It is the gospel of deliverance and acceptance. That is what the Lord is talking about.

What does he say about this gospel? He says: Today it has been fulfilled in your ears. That is the predicate which makes the thought complete, a single predicate. We can be sure that this is what the whole sermon said, at whatever length, that anything in the sermon was not something besides this, but served only to give this a more detailed and explicit form.

What does he mean by "is fulfilled today in your ears"? He means that the gospel of deliverance and acceptance is present and operative here in this synagogue where he is speaking (the sermon spoke directly to the life situation in which both speaker and hearers were involved). He means that as he speaks it God is speaking it and seriously means it now, today (the sermon was in the present tense, not a historical discussion). He means that God's gracious offer of liberation is a fact to be announced, not a perhaps, a possibility to be realized (the sermon was in the indicative mode, not the conditional mode).

Is it true? Our first impulse is to say that here we have a very special preacher, and reverence forbids us to question or debate. Quite the contrary is the fact. Just because of who is speaking, every man must answer in some form of a yes or no. The listeners on this occasion approved the sermon warmly up to this point, and might have gone out the door shaking his hand and praising the sermon, if it had not been for the stinging issue in its tail.

So, what difference does it make? What is at stake here? This: that the gospel is fulfilled "in your ears," that is, for your hearing, your reception, your response, your espousal and commitment, to be operative for you and upon you. And you may miss it, he says, as it has been missed before. You may reject it because it comes in the familar guise of Joseph's son, a physician you will not let heal you and thus validate himself, a prophet unacceptable in his own country. You may reject it as all the hungry widows in Israel rejected it, so that only the foreign widow of Zarepath could be fed by Elijah; reject it as all the lepers in Israel rejected it, so that only the Syrian Naaman could be healed by Elisha. (This point of rejection Jesus perhaps made by implication rather than by explicit statement, trusting his listeners to draw the inference and apply it to themselves. They did!)

It thus appears that we have been told a great deal about this sermon. We have its complete idea before us, so that we can see its whole anatomy and answer all the vital questions about it, not only the structural but also the functional questions. We can feel the force inherent in this idea, and understand the terrific impact the sermon had and the decisive action it produced. We have seen the things that make it incomparably great—enough of them, at any rate.

UNITY

When a sermon is the embodiment of one vigorous idea, when the whole of it becomes simply the elaboration and extension of that idea, then it produces in the listener that concentration of effect which is called unity. That is all unity is: an impression of oneness and entirety, of an ordered relatedness of parts in a whole. Its opposite is fragmentation, partition, disorder.

The effect of unity is never created by pure singleness. It is always a unity achieved out of plurality and diversity, an *e pluribus unum* of some sort. There are always several things which might be separated, coming together in a larger oneness which either did not exist or was not recognized before. It has in it a strong element of surprise, and a gratified sense of achievement.

Unity is not a sort of academic virtue prescribed by pedants for writers and speakers. Unity is a functional character of effective communication. There is no moral or religious or literary law that a sermon must embody just one idea, one subject, or one theme. If there is a reason why it should, it is that two or more subjects treated together or in quick succession simply do not hold a listener, unless they combine into a larger subject; two or more assertions simply do not convince him, unless they are related assertions joined to support a larger assertion. The desire for unity is a law of the listener's mind. It is his own sense of form at work, trying to bring order out of the chaos of impressions. If we do not join our fragments into a wholeness which we see, the listener's mind will force him to make his own combination of our fragments into a total impression that may be very different from our own. This is the imperative reason for unity.

Nothing but a sense of form can do us any good, really. We can memorize a good rule about unity and theme, but it will not help much, until we come to feel how an entire sermon with all its ramifications can be the organic development of a single idea, how a generative idea becomes the substance of a larger form, the sermon.

This book relies on no inflexible rule in such a matter as the theme, or any other matter. But it implores the apprentice preacher to work, from the very beginning, with respect for the elemental facts concerning oral communication, and to cultivate diligently his own inner sense of rightness. Good preaching as it actually exists furnishes exceptions to most mere rules. It does not, in those cases, violate or ignore the principles of communication and of good design; it carries them out in some other way, with a skill controlled by an inner sense of rightness.

That the best sermon is the embodiment of a single generative idea is not a rule but an accurate reporting of fact. It is a fact by no means confined to preaching. An idea of this kind has always created the great novel, play, poem, picture, building, hymn, opera, symphony—any great work of the mind and spirit of man. If the present book should show any signs of life, it will be because of its basic idea: Thought and its expression, content and organization, substance and form, are not two things but one, two inseparable aspects of the same thing.

However that may be, the statement that a good sermon embodies a single idea is not at all peculiar to this book. All homiletical textbooks say it, pay it at least lip service. Many of them lay it down flatly as a rule, even if they afterwards neglect to carry it out in application. If there is anything peculiar to this book it is that I think this principle useful only if carried out persistently in practice—otherwise it is meaningless—and that I believe it brings us closer to the heart of the matter to work with the basic elements of thought than to work with a concept of theme.

One of the most cogent and useful statements of the principle of unity was made by a great preacher, John Henry Jowett. For insight into the craft of a notable workman, every word of it merits the closest scrutiny.

No sermon is ready for preaching, nor ready for writing out, until we can express its theme in a short, pregnant sentence as clear as a crystal. I find the getting of that sentence the hardest, the most exacting, and the most fruitful labor in my study. To compel oneself to fashion that sentence, to dismiss every word that is vague, ragged, ambiguous, to think oneself through to a form of words which defines the theme with scrupulous exactness—this is surely one of the most vital and essential factors in the making of a sermon: and I do not think any sermon ought to be preached or even written, until that sentence has emerged, clear and lucid as a cloudless moon.[2]

Note that this is primarily a way of working, an order of procedure. First one studies his text and amasses his notes. Next he discovers his true subject, what he should talk about. Next he decides what is the all-important, the all-inclusive thing the sermon ought to say about it. This is the idea or theme in substance. But now, at this point, he does the hard but rewarding work of thinking it through and saying it in the fewest and truest words possible. All this he does before he begins to fashion the body of his sermon or any of its parts.

Clearly, if the theme were less than the whole sermon in the form of its generative idea, it would not deserve this primacy, nor

---

[2] J. H. Jowett, *The Preacher, His Life and Work* (New York: Doran, 1912), p. 133. Quoted by permission.

the hard and patient work of thinking it through and bringing it to perfect expression. It would not be something that comes before the preaching or the writing, so that these must wait for it. Neither would the work of fashioning it be the most fruitful as well as the most exacting work ever done on the sermon. But since it is the substance that will take form in the sermon it does deserve this first place in the preacher's workshop as well as in his estimation.

This working method is not the most natural procedure for every man. More, there is many a fine sermon whose whole thought cannot be reduced to a single assertion, hence its theme cannot be stated "in a short, pregnant sentence as clear as a crystal." It is true, however, that if this procedure can be learned, it is for any man the most economical, the most rewarding in proportion to the time it requires. It is also true that even if a given sermon is doomed never to be thoroughly prepared, completely finished, this work on the central thought is the essential work which cannot be left undone without deforming the sermon.

If a sermon is to be preached without notes, or with notes but without manuscript, then no other preparation whatever can be so valuable to the preacher and to his hearers as the idea clearly thought out and brought to scrupulous expression. Even if the preacher has nothing at all but a subject clearly defined, an inclusive predicate and supporting points lucidly and unambiguously expressed, he is better prepared than if he had any kind or quantity of notes without a clear grasp of the central idea.

Attempting to write the sermon before the idea is worked out is perhaps the most dangerous way of all and the most deceptive. A man can extemporize on paper as easily as on his feet. A fully written manuscript is no guarantee of a prepared sermon. It may be as carelessly done as if he got up and spoke without any preparation at all. If writing is a substitute for thinking the idea through, it rather guarantees that the sermon will never be thoroughly prepared.

Some young men, however, seem unable to develop a sermon, unable to find out what they have to say without writing at some length about it. If a man has to write first, let him write. But let him keep looking for the idea while he writes, and let him understand that all his writing is tentative until the idea becomes clear. It may emerge—not impossibly in disguise—on the third or fourth page, sometimes later, perhaps only near the end. It may never be recognized, though it stands there in black and white. When it is at last discovered, everything has to be done all over again, and the hardest part is to throw away all one has written, or recast it as the idea dictates.

This is not an economical way to work. Of course it amounts to the same thing in the long run, provided the run is long enough; provided, first, that somewhere, sometime, the germinal idea does emerge and find lucid expression; and provided, second, that nothing be left standing in the final draft which does not belong to the development and extension of the true idea. It is often a laborious process, but without it the writing is mere improvization.

THE IDEA IN A HYMN

If thou but suffer God to guide thee,
And hope in Him through all thy ways,
He'll give thee strength, what-e'er betide thee,
And bear thee through the evil days;
Who trusts in God's unchanging love
Builds on the rock that naught can move.

What can these anxious cares avail thee,
These never ceasing moans and sighs?
What can it help, if thou bewail thee
O'er each dark moment as it flies?
Our cross and trials do but press
The heavier for our bitterness.

All are alike before the Highest;
'Tis easy to our God, we know,
To raise thee up though low thou liest,
To make the rich man poor and low;
True wonders still by Him are wrought
Who setteth up and brings to naught.

Sing, pray, and keep His ways unswerving,
So do thine own part faithfully,

And trust His Word;—though undeserving,
Thou yet shalt find it true for thee;
God never yet forsook at need
The soul that trusted Him indeed.

Georg Neumark, 1681.

What is it about? God's care of his own.
What does it say? God can be trusted to take care of his own:

One who trusts him he brings through all evils (1)
Anxiety and grief are worse than useless (2)
God can and does work wonders (3)
One who acts on his Word will find it true (4)

What difference does it make? One can take comfort and strength.

Neumark put it all in his title: "A hymn of consolation, that God will care for and preserve His own." Julian, *Dictionary of Hymnology* (New York: Scribner's, 1892), p. 796.

SUGGESTIONS

I know you have a heart to love and hate and feel disgust and admiration, and an imagination to dream and aspire, as well as a brain with which to think. If it seems to you that I am asking you to go to work without these, be assured it is only for a little while. There will be time, and need, for whatever high thought, keen vision, poetry, philosophy, courage, compassion you have in you. It is by these you will preach, and they will set the tone and provide the reach of your preaching.

I only ask you to try this way of working long enough to see for yourself—I mean, to withdraw your attention for the time being from the details of communication, and concentrate it on the basic elements of thought. If you are a beginner, begin that way. If you are already preaching, try this as an experiment.

Do this in the study of actual sermons, not in books about sermons. Section V of the bibliography lists collections of sermons available for this purpose. I suggest that you take not less than six sermons, and that you first state in one sentence what each sermon as a whole says, if it can be stated in one sentence, and then sketch brief answers to all five questions concerning each sermon.

To read how other writers have treated of the sermon's idea, consult the volumes in Section I of the bibliography. Broadus (4) and Garvie (8) call it the "Subject." Phelps (10) and Davis (6) deal with it at length as the "Proposition."

Good books on speaking all treat of this matter in some way. Phillips (62) calls it "the central idea," and his treatment of it has been of great value to me.

CHAPTER 4

The Text as Source

Tell me where is fancy bred,
  Or in the heart or in the head?
How begot. how nourishéd?
  Reply, reply.
    Merchant of Venice, Act III, Scene 2.

It should have deep roots:
  As much unseen as above the surface
  Roots spreading as widely as its branches spread
  Roots deep underground
    In the soil of life's struggle
    In the subsoil of the eternal Word.

Shakespeare's question applies to thought as well as to fancy. A sermon idea is born somehow. Sometimes, though more rarely than we might wish, a sermon idea seems to come of itself suddenly out of nowhere, and to bring the whole sermon along with it, as the idea of a poem or a story does. The seemingly spontaneous birth of ideas in every sort of creative work is an obscure process, fascinating to study. All writers and artists sufficiently articulate about their work have tried to describe it. There is no use in studying it here, for knowing what ought to happen does not make it happen.

The preacher can do other things more useful than this. He can cultivate a due respect for ideas, a just estimate of their worth. He can come to understand that any sermon has to be an idea first before it becomes a sermon, that if he is ever to have sermons he must get them as ideas first, and that the ideas dancing in and out of his head may in fact be sermons trying to be born. He can discover by experience that the superior idea has decidedly feminine traits: it may come when loved for its own sake, but will be coy if wanted only for some other reason—like making a sermon.

A man can learn to invite ideas, and can alert himself to recognize and entertain them when they come. Recognition means catching the idea as it flashes by. Proper entertainment includes sketching it then and there in words on paper, however briefly. The sentence or two of this sketch are comparable to the decisive lines of a first sketch in the painter's notebook. They catch and hold the idea in an identifying form. Unless the lines are set down at once, the idea is liable to be lost, like the pretty girl who smiled at you one night and whom you never saw again.

Ideas which seem to come of themselves may not really do so. What seems sudden and from nowhere may be simply catching up with a man, having stalked him through all the ancient alleys and doorways and subterranean caverns of his life. Such an idea may have been dogging his footsteps for years.

A spontaneous idea of this kind is also likely to be overrated. Such a sudden inspiration is not necessarily more valuable than a conclusion reached by plodding. It may indeed be an enduring new outlook on existence, a new insight into the Word, broader and fuller than any seen before. Or it may be only a novel angle from which to take a trick snapshot of life.

Furthermore, sermons are not usually born along with ideas of this kind or any other kind. There can be no real sermon without an idea, true enough, but there can be an idea without a sermon. The idea and the sermon belong together, but they are not always together. As there must be a plot, with characters and incidents, to embody the idea of a story, so there must be a plan, a movement from thought to thought toward a goal, to give body and shape to the sermon idea. This thought structure seldom comes ready-made with the idea. It has to be fashioned by work, skill, and taste, just as in any creation of the human intelligence. After the "inspiration" —which is what the uninitiated may call the productive idea— comes the hard labor of producing the shapes, patterns, and colors of the picture, the images, lines, and words of the poem, the themes, rhythms, and harmonies of the symphony, and the organic structure and development of the sermon.

Consequently, it makes less difference than might at first appear whether the sermon idea be a sudden flash from the sky or the unconscious, or be slowly and laboriously hammered out in study. Any idea whatever has to meet certain requirements, has to furnish certain incentives to the preacher, if it is to produce a fit sermon from him. If those necessary qualities are in the idea but are not seen by him, he has to find them before his preparation is truly begun. If they are not in the idea, it is not a truly generative idea, no matter how spontaneous it may be.

These are some characteristics which above all others a good sermon idea will possess, and which the preacher will feel in it.

1. *It must be narrow enough to be sharp.* It must come to a point keen enough to pierce the thick skin of the preacher, first of all. The concentration here indicated is a precise answer to the question, "What am I to talk about?"

2. *It must have in it a force that is expanding,* reaching out in different directions, exploding. Or, to take a milder figure, it must be fermenting. The expansion answers two questions: "What does this mean?" and "What must be said?"

3. *It must be true.* Its truth must not be merely conceded by the preacher. He must feel it as a deep persuasion in his very bones. He must answer *yes* to the question, "Is this true?" Only so can it move him, and it must move him to produce a sermon worth his while.

4. *It must be loaded with the realities of the human heart.* It must concern the deep and universal questions: life and death, courage and fear, love and hate, trust and doubt, guilt and forgiveness, pain and joy, shame, remorse, compassion, and hope. Only among these can be found a serious answer to the question, "What difference does it make?"

These are not yet enough. They are simply the qualities that mark the work of our best secular writers. They are not confined to the preacher's peculiar task. These are the tests which the ideas and themes of serious novelists and playwrights must pass.[1] The

[1] William Faulkner, "Nobel Prize Acceptance Speech." Caedmon record 1035 Eugene O'Neill, *Nine Plays* (Modern Library, Random House). Introduction by Joseph Wood Krutch, p. xvii.

preacher is not attempting less than these writers. He is attempting something more far-reaching and more difficult. What twisted sense of values is it which lets us feel that the gospel we preach somehow exempts us from these stern requirements? A sermon-producing idea must first meet all four of these requirements, and then another one:

5. *It must be one of the many facets of the gospel of Christ.* It must be the eternal Love and Goodness and Truth taking shape in some apprehensible human thought. It must be some audible human word fit for his use, through which he may speak. Unless the idea meets this requirement, it may produce a work of art, even a great human utterance, but not a Christian sermon.

Ideas of this character are not to be picked up at random by a superficial attention to the passing show on the page of the newspaper and the television screen. This is not to say it can never happen. An idea can come from anywhere at any time. However, the man who has no better source of ideas than his casual reading and listening—or his association with people either, for that matter —has an inadequate supply of ideas of the right kind. His preaching either runs swiftly and completely dry, or he becomes a purveyor of more or less interesting but ephemeral trivialities.

I do not want to be misunderstood at this point. A perfectly proper sermon idea, even an excellent one, is on rare occasions suggested by something in the news, on the screen or stage, in a personal conversation, in a new book, in a political or social event. It is not the idea's source which condemns the typical pulpit discussion of such a topic, but the idea's poverty in those qualities required to produce a genuine sermon. If the idea meets the requirements, it does not matter where its suggestion came from. If it does not meet them, no source can validate it.

The decisive effect the idea itself has on the sermon must be taken seriously. Nothing is going to come out in the sermon which is not implicit in the idea. A speech consisting of entertainment, moral instruction and admonition, personal prejudices, slanted propaganda, is limited to these because the basic idea in the mind of the speaker is limited in the same way. That and nothing else is what makes the speech wrong for the pulpit. That sort of idea, being no more than it is, simply cannot produce a genuine sermon.

A sermon is poor for one of two reasons. It may be because the idea that produced it really lacks the qualities described above. Or it may be that the idea does actually possess these qualities, but the preacher has not questioned his idea or searched for them, and so they do not come out in his treatment. An excellent treatment of a shoddy idea will not make an adequate sermon; a passable treatment of an excellent idea will.

A beginner is likely to be mistaken about this. He is likely to begin his preparation by working on the detailed material, likely to do all or nearly all of his work on details, with so hazy an impression of his basic idea itself that he never develops a tenth of its power. The master of his craft will do most of his work on the idea in its clear and simple structure, will ponder it long, will come back to it constantly, will search deeply for its true meaning and its divine and human import, will try its power on his own soul, knowing that any work he does apart from this basic idea is wasted.

Where is a man to find one or two proper sermon ideas every week of his life? Most of them in the Bible, of course. His work cannot attain distinction or even worth unless he scorns and rejects unworthy material. If he sets for his ideas such exacting standards as the above, he will quickly exhaust the treasure of wisdom inside himself and turn gratefully to an inexhaustible source. Where else could he find that source?

A book on the craft of preaching cannot undertake to teach its reader theology and exegesis. It must count on his knowing a good deal about both. The little I can say about the church and gospel should not be construed as a substitute for theology, nor what I say about the interpretation of texts as an adequate exegetical theory or art. What I say is only an attempt to show how theology and exegesis become functional in preaching.

The church's instinct to adjust its message to the witness of Holy Scripture, to use the words of the Bible in its preaching, is not the aftereffect of any precise theory or doctrine of the inspiration and authority of Scripture. It is quite the other way around. So certainly has the church known herself to live and move at the spoken Word of God, so irresistibly does she hear that same Word and that same Voice in the Scriptures, that the aftereffect can be nothing less than such a reverence for the Bible as causes her, when she and it are attacked, to affirm its divine origin and truth.

The best young man who finds himself in a pulpit, the man most fit to preach, far from wishing to stand alone, to speak for himself only, to be a law to himself, knows that he stands within the one fellowship whose Head is Christ, that he is called to deliver a message he did not concoct, to proclaim, in whatever way it can best be spoken to his age, the same gospel which has in all ages recalled men from death and brought the church to life. The more intelligent and honest he is, the more keenly he feels this way. He stands where he would not dare to stand unless he had been put there, where it would be sacrilege to speak if he had not been given a message to speak.

Not that piety, reverence, and godly fear are all the equipment a man needs. Having these, he is still but a man. He still has to learn how to do his work, if it is to be well done. Without knowledge, his very piety may betray him.

For example, he is almost too strongly inclined through piety to accept without question the dogmatic rule that every sermon must have a text from Scripture. Weighty reasons have led to the practice of preaching from a text, and the practice is sound. The rule, however, stands alone without the reasons, a sort of fixed convention, almost a fetish. If he follows the rule without knowing why, as he is inclined to do, the very observance often leads him into errors, not the least of which is the comfortable delusion that if a sermon has a text it is sure to be scriptural. A fair amount of the mayhem preachers commit on the Scriptures is chargeable to a blind use of this rule.

Let us assume that a man feels bound to adjust his preaching faithfully to the biblical message. That is not brought about by the mere act of taking a text for every sermon. The crucial question is not whether the sermon has a text attached to it, but whether the Scripture is the source of the sermon or not, whether the sermon says what the Scripture says or not. Many a sermon uses a text but is not derived from the text. The text of such a sermon is not its source; it is only a resource, a tool used in preaching the sermon—used for psychological or literary effect. Every sermon that has a text falls roughly into one or the other of these classes: it uses the text as source, or only as resource.

In this chapter we are concerned primarily with the germinal idea. The question becomes: Does this idea have its source in Scripture? Is it a biblical idea? Evidently, this is not a question of where the preacher met the idea. If he met it somewhere else, he may in the instant it struck him have recognized it as scriptural and remembered the text containing it. Or, perhaps after thought and search, he may find it in Scripture where he had not recognized it before. In either case it is biblical—with the enormously important proviso that, having found its biblical source, he thereafter adjust his thinking to Scripture's real idea, not adjust Scripture's words to fit his thinking. That is to say, he should never use a false or arbitrary exegesis to make the text support his notion. That does not honor the Bible; it flouts and misrepresents the Bible. It is a dishonest use of the Bible as a resource for advancing his own opinion. It would be less irreverent not to use Scripture at all, but preach his idea, if he must, without any text. That would not, of course, be adjusting his preaching to the biblical message, but falsifying the text comes no nearer.

Suppose one has a sermon idea that is incisive, expansive, most convincing, charged with the heart's deep passion, seeming to ring with the good news—the only trouble being that after racking his brain and worrying his concordance the preacher simply cannot find it in the Bible. Here is a text that sounds something like it, but the words he wants to use are a verbal accident of translation, and the original and other versions sound different. And here is a passage that talks all around the idea and seems on the point of expressing it, but closer study reveals that it is really talking about something else. Yet the idea still seems excellent. What then?

The first word is a warning. Can it be that here is a genuine facet of the gospel which is not expressed anywhere in the Bible? It could admittedly be so. The church has not held that there is no gospel outside of Scripture, only that Scripture's word is the validating test of the gospel message.

On the other hand, it is more likely that what we have here is an attractive but purely human bit of religious thinking. Every teacher has witnessed the chagrin of a sincere student on discovering that some line of thought, fashionable with him and his contemporaries, is wholly foreign to biblical speech and thought.

Therefore, before he preaches a thought for which he can find no scriptural authority, the preacher should make doubly sure that it is consonant with the gospel, not a popular perversion. He must remember that there is simply no way in which he can get the Bible's sanction for something the Bible does not really say. The preacher should also remember that he is answerable before God and his hearers for everything he says without sanction. He cannot claim the Bible's sanction and be honest.

The second word is a little more hopeful. If the idea is truly Christian, it need not be rejected. Though it cannot be found in the Bible in so many words, it may still be biblical, and may honestly be preached with biblical sanction. If there is no text that really expresses this idea, we cannot honestly take a text for it. We shall have to use it as an independent topic. But if it is a gospel thought, we can draw each step of its development from a faithful exegesis of some text of Scripture. The result will be that we use several texts rather than one.

This method entails a risk of disunity, and it requires a sure touch, with scrupulous faithfulness in the use of texts, but there is a time to use it. A topical sermon with this kind of development can be quite as biblical as one drawn entirely from a single text, far more biblical than one which draws only the idea from the text, however legitimately, and then develops the thought independently, without further use of Scripture.

We are not in the clear the moment we find an idea in the Bible. We can find almost anything there. The Bible can be used as a resource by anybody for any purpose. There is a rumor in *The Merchant of Venice* that the irreconcilable enemy of God himself can find words in the Bible to use for his netarious purpose. An idea is not a fit idea just because it comes from the Bible.

Special care is needed to assure the gospel content, even when the idea is scriptural. That is not gospel which contains only moral precepts, duty, right principles, spiritual idealism, which does nothing but commend these and enjoin them. All these are justly required of us, but these requirements always catch us short, convict us, kill us; while the gospel offers us life out of this death and beyond deserving. That is not gospel which offers us only a formula with which to create our own good synthetically, for the gospel centers our good wholly in Another than ourselves. The preacher has to develop his sense of the gospel as well as his sense of form. We shall have to return to this later.

The apprentice must learn to make sure that the gospel is in his germinal idea to begin with. If it is not there, it cannot be at the heart of the sermon where it ought to be. The gospel cannot successfully be dragged in later. The last point of the sermon is much too late to begin thinking about the gospel.

(The next voice you will hear is that of an old and troublesome acquaintance who understands me too well for my comfort and reasons with an acuity so completely void of scruple that I am always at a loss to refute his preposterous arguments. He is the kind of man a preacher should have to face but seldom does. Bill has been known to take over my classroom and criticize a sermon from the back seat.)

THE AUTHOR: Who are you?

BILL: I'm Bill Hamartolos.

AUTHOR: Hamartolos? That's a good one! Know what the name means?

BILL: Of course. Bill the Sinner. That's me.

AUTHOR: You needn't brag about it. It gives you no distinction.

BILL: I am different from the popular brands, though.

AUTHOR: Penitent? You don't look it, scowling over my shoulder.

BILL: Not a bit of it. I mean I like church and such places. It's there I see cussedness practiced by experts in its most subtle and fascinating varieties, especially lying.

AUTHOR: I call that a depraved taste.

BILL: I call it esthetics. I know real art when I see it.

AUTHOR: Well?

BILL: What are you trying to tell these fellows?

AUTHOR: That the best they can do is to serve the gospel faithfully. They have been given an official proclamation to deliver. The proclamation is not a thing to be learned and used, but an announcement of the Ruler's intention and what he has done about it, and his offer to do the rest. It is this proclamation itself, or rather it is the Ruler acting in his proclamation, backing up his proclamation, who does what has to be done.

BILL: So they can only publish the proclamation, and anything else they say or do is futile?

AUTHOR: That's about it, but not quite.

BILL: You are wasting your time.

AUTHOR: Why?

BILL: For two reasons. First, they won't believe it. It's against all appearances and all common sense. It seems obvious that everything done in the world gets done by somebody using such knowledge and resources as he has. They won't believe it because they are afraid, afraid nothing will happen unless they make it happen. They can't believe it because that would require them to discount themselves.

AUTHOR: I'm listening. What is the second reason?

BILL: They can't practice it if they do believe it. They are not

the kind of men they'd have to be to practice it. You are talking
to a professional group that includes all kinds. I've watched them
at work. The ministry can show any kind of man you want to look
for; the smooth operator, the self-employed publicity expert, the
dispenser of masculine charm, the dealer in panaceas, the peddler
of false confidence, the exploiter of human misery and need, and
the gambler with other people's lives.

AUTHOR: I'm not writing for any such men.

BILL: Every man has a little bit of these things in him. The
notably successful minister has more than a little. You may be
writing for nobody.

AUTHOR: That could be, but I don't think so. They have the
Bible, don't they? Many of them sincerely try to preach that.

BILL: Yes, and they think they believe it, but it doesn't make as
much difference as you suppose. It's here they practice the most
exquisitely subtle deception on themselves. Even when they think
they are using a Bible idea, as you call it, they bring it out as cold
as an iceberg, as impersonal as a gas bill, as snobbish as a social
climber, as threatening as a blackmailer, as pitiless as a kidnapper,
as calculating as a golddigger, or as tiresome as a recorded commercial.

AUTHOR: You are being very unfair, and you know it.

BILL: Can you deny that all I've said is true?

AUTHOR: No, but I deny that it is a fair picture of the profession. Why don't you admit that many of them do much better than
that, and a few admirably?

BILL: That's not the point. The point is that the Bible can't
guarantee the work of the man. The problem you have on your
hands is not the Bible but the men who use it.

AUTHOR: Quite so. But if the proclamation can do what has
to be done for all men, it can begin by doing it for the men who
publish it, by changing them into the kind of men who can and
will believe and practice the gospel. It has changed lots of them.

BILL: Not enough to furnish a convincing demonstration. It
never will. They won't let it.

AUTHOR: That remains to be seen.

BILL: I'm completely skeptical.

AUTHOR: It remains to be seen.

To understand a text we must question it. We must find what it is talking about and what it is saying. We do not discover that by beginning at once to divide the text. First we try to see it as a unit, to grasp its meaning as a whole.

Let us experiment with a great text which has proved a trap for the unwary, John 8:31-36.

"If you continue in my word, you are truly my disciples, and you will know the truth, and the truth will make you free." They answered him, "We are descendants of Abraham, and have never been in bondage to anyone. How is it that you say, 'You will be made free'?" Jesus answered them, "Truly, truly, I say to you, everyone who commits sin is a slave to sin. The slave does not continue in the house for ever; the son continues for ever. So if the Son makes you free, you will be free indeed."

A fragment of this text has been used many times, not only to sing the praise of liberty and democracy, but also to claim Christ's authority for the assertion that enlightenment of the mind liberates, that is, redeems men.

What is Jesus talking about? He mentions *freedom* and he mentions *bondage*. What does he mean? Bondage to, freedom from what? Is it political? Is it social? Is it intellectual? If not, what bondage and what freedom is Jesus talking about?

He mentions *truth* and *knowledge* of the truth. What is this truth? What is this knowledge of the truth? Is it knowledge of scientific facts? Is it a correct philosophy of life? Is it truth about history and culture? If not, what is the truth Jesus is talking about? What does he mean by knowing the truth?

What does Jesus actually say? He says, "the truth will make you free." But he also says, "if the Son makes you free." Does he mean that these are two different ways to freedom? If not, what does Jesus mean?

Asking more persistently what Jesus actually says, we get this:

"*If* you continue in my word, (then and only then) you are truly my disciples, and (if you are my disciples) you will know the truth, and (if you thus know the truth) the truth will make you free." What does he mean by that? What is "my word"? Who are "my disciples"? What is "the truth" which one knows only by being a disciple? What does it mean to "know the truth"?

Would this be a proper text for an address on the importance of a college education? Have we here the Lord's sanction for telling people that knowledge is liberating? That men are by nature free? That freedom is an inalienable right?

What subject could be used for a Reformation sermon on this text? For a Fourth of July sermon?

Which of the following subjects could, and which could not, be legitimately drawn from this text?

> The Truth That Makes Men Free
> The Heritage of Liberty
> Conditional Freedom
> What is Freedom?
> Knowledge is Freedom
> Education for Freedom

Next we examine a text that looks very easy, almost fool-proof. It is Matthew 22:34-40.

When the Pharisees heard that he had silenced the Sadducees, they came together. And one of them, a lawyer, asked him a question, to test him. "Teacher, which is the great commandment in the law?" And he said to him, "You shall love the Lord your God with all your heart, and with all your soul, and with all your mind. This is the great and first commandment. And the second is like it, You shall love your neighbor as yourself. On these two commandments depend all the law and the prophets."

This text is the perfect booby-trap, because it looks safe but is full of high explosives. It divides automatically to furnish three heads of discourse. One talks—one can always say something— first, about love to God, next, about love to our neighbors, and then, finally, one can pass on to say something about love in general. It is as easy as lying.

It is easy to say that God commands us to love him with a total love, and our neighbor as ourselves. But what is one to say about both love to God and love to man together? What does the undivided text mean? If the subject is love, or the command to love, what is the predicate that completes the thought? What is one to assert concerning this twofold love?

What Jesus is talking about is plain enough. It is the twofold love-commandment. What does he say? About the command to love God he says, "It is the great and first commandment." Next he says about the command to love our neighbor: "It is like the first." But then he adds a remark about both commands together: "On these two commandments depend (hang: *krematai*) all the law—and the prophets." This is the predicate that completes Jesus' idea.

What could Jesus mean by this? That is by no means easy to answer. I am not sure any man knows the answer. I am sure no man is ready to preach on this text until he has wrestled with those words. It is in them that Jesus goes beyond the lawyer's question. In this remark lies the profundity and originality of Jesus' thought. The rest was familiar to the rabbis. To miss this remark is to miss the whole idea. To omit *the prophets,* to speak only in terms of law and duty, is certainly to miss Jesus' meaning.

Because of the difficulty here hidden under the appearance of safety, many misleading sermons have been preached on this text. Not amenable to Jesus' thought, the preacher asserts what he pleases. He merely says we ought to love God and man. He says love is a very good thing, a beautiful thing, a noble thing, and that we ought to have a lot of it. He says love is the whole duty of man. He says that God values us on the basis of our love or lack of it. He says love is the key to successful living. He says that without love mankind will destroy itself. He says love is the supreme teaching of all high religions. And so on.

More often still, a man preaches without having thought his idea through to any completed predicate. Consequently, he makes no explicit general assertion at all. He just talks about love more or less at random. Yet he cannot talk without saying or suggesting something. The more rambling his talk is, the more surely he will say by implication what he never would say by intention. The suggestion will be very much more powerful than any of his explicit assertions.

So what? What difference does it make? What is at issue here? That is what the preacher has not answered for himself. But these are just the questions which the listener has been asking from the beginning. The listener will get some answer from what the preacher says or implies, or he will make one up for himself. He will draw his own conclusions. The over-all implication of many a sermon on this text, even when the preacher has not so intended, has been one of the following, depending on what clues the preacher happened to furnish:

When I love God and my neighbor as best I can, that is all I need to do—I'm good enough then.
    To love is to earn God's favor—it will therefore pay me to love.
    Love is the recipe for an abundant life—it is the way I can make myself successful and happy.
    Love is the only way to avert disaster and save the American way of life—we had all better get busy loving at once, or else!
    Love is the essence of all religions, and the only thing that really matters in any of them.

The pervading implication of the sermon must never be discounted. It is like the hint that is much stronger than a spoken request. It may never be put into words, may simply ooze out through the pores of the sermon. But the pervading impression is the thing which remains when everything else is forgotten. It is what the listener will carry away with him, what he will remember the whole sermon as having said to him.

This stubborn, elemental fact of communication, not some theorist's rule, is the compelling reason why the sermon's basic idea must be worthy of the hearer's deepest regard, why it must be thoroughly worked out and clearly presented. It is, moreover, the reason why it must be true to the sacred text.

SERMON SKETCH: "A Sense of Belonging"

Romans 8:31-39. What then shall we say to this? If God is for us, who is against us? . . . Who shall bring any charge against God's elect? . . . Who shall separate us from the love of Christ? Shall tribulation, etc? . . . No, in all these things we are more than conquerors through him who loved us. For I am sure that neither death, nor life, etc. . . . will be able to separate us from the love of God in Christ Jesus our Lord.

This Paul had something:
    to hold against the worst, the deadliest, the bloodiest that
    life could do to him.

Not just realism—not just courage—not just faith even—

At the heart of his faith:
    Certainty—fully persuaded—"I am sure"—of what?

That nothing can destroy him—defeat him—why?

Because nothing can separate:

A sense of belonging—of being possessed by—of belonging to:

To the love of God—"Who shall separate" from that?

Not just to the love of God, but
at the heart of his faith as a Christian:

To God's elect—chosen—"Who shall bring any charge"
        against them?
    To the new Israel—the church—"us"—"we"

Not just to the elect church, but:

To the love of God "in Christ Jesus our Lord":
    To the redeeming love—dying—risen—eternal—
        triumphant over the worst, the deadliest.

The Christian has this singing, rejoicing, at the heart of his faith, at the heart of his pain—making music of his worst, his deadliest.

This is the sketch of an idea that once came suddenly out of the text, bringing the whole sermon with it, and was set down in a rapturous fifteen minutes—everything that is now here. It was studied, refined, arranged thus, developed, and preached. It has been edited a little for the reader's sake, but not changed in substance or form.

SUGGESTIONS

Perhaps you have already discovered the release and satisfaction of trying to find shapes for the things pent up inside you: things you have suffered, enjoyed, wondered at; the thing that shakes you with a mixture of terror and loathing and pity and a bitter sweetness; the thing you deeply want to say to the men and girls you knew in college; the thing that haunts you in some hymn or poem or text of Scripture.

I suggest that now you begin to sketch such things as these as possible ideas for sermons, as many of them as you can. Build a sermon sketch book, a single page for each idea. Study and test each one against the five questions and the requirements of this chapter. If the right qualities are in the idea, find them. If they are not, discard it. Do not bother just now about any development except such points as come of themselves without your trying. Set down briefly everything that comes, but do not worry about the order at this stage of the work.

Let some of these be ideas deliberately worked out from texts you select for that purpose. I will tell you a professional secret. If you can find out exactly what the text says to you, and if you do nothing but say clearly and cogently what the text says, the sermon will get undeserved credit for originality and freshness. Don't worry about that being too simple! It takes hard study, plus a personal openness, to hear what the text says to you. But if you don't believe what I'm saying, try it.

As further reading about the relation of preaching to the Scriptures, I suggest first an older work, Forsyth (23), especially Chapters I and II, pages 1-72. Then Brown (5), Chapter II, pages 32-61. These readings should be compared with the newer theological emphasis on the Word, as in Nygren (46), Chapters I and II, pages 9-27.

For one of the very best descriptions of how ideas are gotten hold of, read Scherer (28), Chapter 5, pages 142-175.

If you preach on the Epistles and Gospels for the Christian year, or if you wish to see an intelligent plan for the exposition of passages of Scripture, read Baughman (1).

CHAPTER 5

What's in a Subject?

What's in a subject?
  At least: What is to be talked about.
  Always: The limits within which to keep.
  Or more: A hint of what is to be said.
  At most: All that the sermon will say.

Not every proper subject is a sermon subject for every man. What is fertile for one may be sterile for another. In the previous chapter it was said that a sermon idea must be narrow enough to be sharp, must come to a point keen enough to pierce the preacher first of all. The reason is that if it does not wound him it cannot become in him a productive idea, a germinal idea, a generative idea—we have used those adjectives in talking about the idea. And since the whole sermon is just the idea in extended form, the idea must have in it the power to create the larger form.

I trust this does not sound complicated, for it is really very simple. First of all, it is a question of what a man can honestly want to talk about, can feel strongly urged to talk about, to share with a given congregation. It must of course be an idea that he cares about, one that has power to move him.

A broad and general subject like "Faith," for example, simply does not move him. Some special aspect of faith may move him. He may be moved, say, by "the audacity of faith," like the audacity of Peter's walking on the water to meet Jesus. One begins to think how other people have believed daringly, audaciously—and one is off. How do they dare? What do they risk in daring? What does the Lord think about it? What has been accomplished through the audacity of faith? And so on. The idea is fruitful, germinal, productive.

Secondly, there is the question of how much a man can say adequately in twenty-five minutes, how many contributing thoughts he can clothe with meaning and color, with the form and action of experience, so as really to share them with his listeners. One cannot do that with the subject of "Faith" in its full breadth and sweep. If he does it with a single aspect of faith, if he develops only the audacity of faith and puts that where it should be in the whole picture of a believing life, he will be doing very well indeed.

Preaching is more than simply saying what a man has to say. Preaching is communication: not just talking at people, but sharing with them. When I have some important thing to say to someone I care about, I do not simply say it and let it go at that. I talk it out, explain it, develop it, show why it is important to me and what it leads to. Interest in what I am saying and regard for the person I am talking to, both require some development of my thought.

Not many thoughts can be developed and shared in one sermon. If the preacher tries to cover too broad a subject, he will say too much, too many good things, and will not share even one of them with his hearers. When the sermon merely discusses a broad subject without the sharpness and urgency of a keener point, it does not really convey anything of importance to its hearers.

There might be a theological lecture on such a subject as "Faith," but it would not be good if the man tried to cover the whole subject. A single lecture had better be on "The Grounds of Faith," or "The Psychological Effects of Belief," or "The Relation of Faith to Knowledge," or on "Paul's Concept of Faith," or upon some equally restricted subject. There could be a course of lectures, or a series of monographs, or an immense book on "Faith." There cannot be a moving sermon on faith, just faith, or on any other such large subject.

A good preacher may announce "Faith" as the title of his sermon. There is nothing against that, except that it is not a very interesting title. But if he is "good" that day, he will not be lecturing about faith, will not be trying to say all that needs to be said about faith. He will be talking about some special aspect of the subject which moves him at the time. That is to say, his true subject, the thing he actually talks about, will be much narrower than the general topic he has announced.

When a good preacher is so impressed by all aspects of a great topic like faith that he has to preach on all of them, he will preach a series of sermons on the topic, and every sermon will have its own precise subject. I do not mean that these large topics are to be avoided in the pulpit. On the contrary, there is every reason why a man should avoid trivial subjects and spend his strength on the mighty themes of the Christian faith. But any one of these he will find so manifold that he must take it piece by piece.

The neophyte, however, dares what the master workman would not think of attempting. He chooses large and fuzzy subjects which would not make good sermons in the hands of an expert. He does this not because he has more confidence and courage. He does it because fuzzy subjects are easier to come by. They cost less sweat than true subjects.

FORGIVENESS OF SINS. by Harry Emerson Fosdick[1]

This sermon is based on Matthew 9:5, "Which is easier, to say, 'Your sins are forgiven you,' or to say, 'Rise and walk'?"

This sermon is so important in the study of contemporary sermonic design that we shall have to examine it closely, refer to it more than once, and treat it again under a different head. Here we are concerned with it as an example of how a large general topic is narrowed down to make a sermon.

Dr. Fosdick does not attempt to cover a subject as big as forgiveness of sins. He does not talk about the grounds of forgiveness, for instance, nor about the power to forgive sins, nor about the apparent conflict between forgiveness and justice, nor about the divine imperative to forgive, nor about the relationship between forgiving and being forgiven, nor about the eschatological consequences of forgiveness. A different sermon could be preached on each one of these aspects of forgiveness, and every one of them would be on the subject of forgiveness of sins.

[1] Taken from *The Secret of Victorious Living* (New York: Harper, 1934), used by permission. It is No. 23 in Blackwood, *op. cit.,* p. 191.

Nor does he narrow the subject to one of its aspects. He chooses to discuss two aspects of forgiveness: its difficulty, and our need of it. These are two independent aspects, not more closely related to each other than to many another thing that might be predicated of the forgiveness of sins. A man might say that we need forgiveness without discussing its difficulty, or might say that forgiveness is difficult and costly without discussing our need of it. Dr. Fosdick chooses to say two—not one but two different things about forgiveness: that we all stand in need of it, and that it is very difficult and costly.

Thus this sermon has two themes, like the two themes in the first movement of a sonata. The principal theme is explicit in the text: Forgiveness is not easy but difficult and costly. The secondary theme rises from our human condition: Every one of us needs forgiveness for something. Dr. Fosdick develops these themes with consummate skill. He begins not with the principal but with the secondary theme, and the strategy and tact he uses in the first few minutes to help his listeners realize their need of forgiveness is an example worthy of the closest study.

The principal theme, forgiveness is difficult, comes in at paragraph 7. He gives it a full and polyphonic development, occupying the large central part of the sermon: it is easy to condone sin, but hard to take it seriously and still forgive it; it is costly too, for it means self-giving for us and for God. Then at paragraph 25 he returns to the secondary theme, but this time it is heightened and transformed: No sin is ever done with until it is forgiven, and forgiveness is thus our deepest need. The sermon ends on this.

Dr. Fosdick sounds these themes in succession, but he does not combine them. He never brings these two predicates together as parts of a larger aspect of forgiveness. There is no single sentence "as clear as a crystal" which includes them both. Their only unity is that of the subject, and that unity might just as easily include more than the two predicates. It is plain that here we have a procedure quite different from the one recommended by Jowett as quoted on page 37. These two independent predicates could of course be put into one sentence: "Forgiveness of sins is both necessary and difficult." But that is not an effective theme sentence. It lacks the unity and lucidity of "a cloudless moon," and to have used it would have weakened and not strengthened the sermon.

What we have here, then, is not a complete idea to begin with, a unitary subject and a unitary predicate. We have a unitary subject and a dual predicate. As a form, it stands between a subject with one predicate and a subject with three or more predicates. And the narrowing down of the subject, which is what we are here concerned with, is achieved by adding to the subject only two of many possible predicates.

REPENTANCE, by Karl Barth[2]

This sermon, published in English, is on Matthew 11:28, "Come unto me, all ye that labor and are heavy laden."

This seems a strange text for a sermon on repentance, and it would be if he were talking about the topic in general. Here again, however, repentance is not the true subject. The sermon is really talking only about Jesus' *call* to repentance, as it is contained in the text. Barth does not announce the narrower subject nor define it for us. He simply confines his talk to the call of Jesus, what it is and how it strikes us.

Barth's thought is rich, paradoxical, and intricate, as we should expect. It is not the easiest kind of thought to follow. Yet, though the proliferation of the thought cannot be suggested in one short sentence, its limits can be defined in one predicate and in clear language. The idea is not quite as clear as a crystal; the thought is not as clear as the language. Barth would insist that a true thought can never seem so clear as that, because the truth is not crystal clear to our darkened minds. What the sermon says is something like this: *Jesus' call seems unreal because he calls us to reality.* This is not one of Barth's sentences, but it traces the circle within which his thought revolves.

[2] Karl Barth and Eduard Thurneysen, *Come, Holy Spirit* (New York: Round Table, 1933). It is No. 20 in Blackwood, *op. cit.,* p. 173.

The subject, then, is *Jesus' call,* and the predicate: *seems unreal.* Any of Barth's thought is powerful, but the terrific impact of this sermon to a general assembly of churchmen comes from the sharpness of the issue raised by this restricted idea.

It would be unfair and foolish to present this sermon as baldly as this and look no further at it, and it would deprive us of much we can learn from it. Let us go on a little. Barth's development of this idea can be reduced to five distinct contributing points, each one drawn from some part of the text, from actual words of the text. The relation between assertion and text is not plain in a first reading of the sermon. It may have been more clearly indicated by the voice. Here is the thought structure of the sermon with the textual connections indicated:

Jesus calls us to turn to him, to God, to our own hidden, unknown center and source. Repentance is this turning. "Come unto me."

Jesus' call must be distinguished from all other calls including the church's call. "Unto *me.*"

Jesus alone is for all men. "All ye."

Jesus alone seeks us at the point of labor, burdens, failure, wrongness, death. "That labor and are heavy laden."

Jesus alone asks of us nothing but to come. "Come unto me."

Again, these are not Barth's exact sentences, though they are constructed of his words. They are generalizations of the structural elements of his thought, which is what any outline ought to be. They do say in general terms what the sermon in its entirety says. They show the design of the idea's extension, its development.

This sketch also reveals what the sermon in its printed form does not make immediately evident: that this is a *textual* sermon, that is, it draws not only its idea but also its structural elements from the text.

These two examples from Fosdick and Barth show that when a master preacher appears to be dealing with a large subject like forgiveness or repentance, he does not talk about the whole of it, but chooses some more restricted idea which has an immediate and personal urgency for him.

More than a beginner can realize, the quality of a man's work is settled beforehand by his choice of subjects, what to preach about and what not to preach about. Only Barth would have made the unique character of Jesus' call a key to repentance. Only Fosdick would have presented forgiveness in just the way he presents it.

The difference between Rembrandt and Raphael, between John Steinbeck and Somerset Maugham, between George Bernard Shaw and Arthur Miller, between T. S. Eliot and Robert Frost, between Ralph Sockman and Fulton J. Sheen, begins with a decisive difference in their choice of subject matter. Nothing determines the character of a man's work more certainly than this. The perennial question "What am I going to preach about?" is seldom asked as earnestly as it ought to be, and seldom given the considered answer it must receive before a man's work can take on character.

Let me ask the reader to test his own reactions to some general topics too big for sermon subjects.

Take the word "Prayer" for example. It is a word that covers many things, so many that it does not force us to think of any one of them. That is what we mean when we call it an abstract word: its sense is abstracted from various particulars and is therefore apart from anything in particular. It has no definite content.

Notice how impossible it is to think about prayer without having some particular aspect of it come into mind. One cannot hold the attention upon it without giving it more definite content. One perhaps sees somebody kneeling; then it is no longer just prayer; it is a physical attitude in prayer. Or one thinks of somebody making requests; then it is supplication, one among several particular kinds of prayer. One thinks of somebody in the presence of Deity; then it is facing God in prayer. One sees a congregation praying together; then it is corporate prayer.

Every one of these is a particularizing of the abstraction, prayer, and every one is a narrowing of the general topic. "Bodily Attitudes in Prayer," "Supplication," "Facing God in Prayer," "Corporate Prayer"—any of these can be a true subject. Each has specific content, form, and feeling. But "Prayer" as an abstraction cannot be a true subject for a sermon.

Two important conclusions must be drawn from these facts: First, when looking for a true subject, we cannot use so general a topic as "Prayer" without narrowing it down to some more particular aspect of prayer. Secondly, used casually in a sentence, an abstract word of this kind carries no definite meaning; we cannot count on it to convey what we have in mind.

By way of warning, and for study, I shall make three lists of such general topics too large to serve as sermon subjects. The first list consists of technical terms in theology, extremely useful, indispensable for theological discussion among those who know their technical meaning. They are necessary in the study of theology, but will not serve for the pulpit unless restricted. We cannot count on their meaning to our people what they mean to us. Faith, forgiveness, repentance, and prayer would certainly be on this list if we had not already examined them.

Sin	Original Sin
Redemption	Salvation
Grace	Justification
Atonement	Regeneration

The "doctrinal" sermon covering one whole topic of this kind has fallen into disfavor. Properly so; it cannot be a true sermon, but is rather a lecture and a doubtful lecture. However, these terms stand for great realities which must be preached, with or without the terms. Far from being unwelcome in our day, they are the object of keen and increasing interest. A minister who cannot discuss them in intelligible terms will not be able to answer questions his people are urgently asking, much less to preach to their needs. Theological doctrine is warmly welcomed, but from the pulpit it must come as true preaching.

The next group could be indefinitely extended. The first column lists traits or virtues, the second, relations or forms of activity. Such topics as those in the first column are extremely popular with beginners. The word "Christian" is commonly prefixed by way of defending so huge a subject. If the preacher knows what the word *Christian* means in such connection—which he usually does not—it will restrict the topic considerably, but not enough to make it a true sermon subject.

Christian Love	Christian Education
Christian Hope	Christian Marriage
Christian Humility	Christian Community
Christian Patience	Christian Stewardship
Christian Peace	Christian Service

The preacher cannot and should not avoid these topics, of course. He should find several pointed subjects within each one of them.

Finally, here are topics of a kind often announced when the preacher has not made any preparation and does not intend to make any. They are "safe" to use at such a time, since they do not commit a man to talk about anything in particular. He does not have to know what he is going to talk about! He can say anything that comes into his head without obviously wandering from the announced subject!

These remarks apply in some degree to the previous lists as well, and reveal why the large and indefinite subject is popular.

Simon Peter	The Reformation
Paul	Eternal Life
The Church	Mother's Day
The Bible	Conscience
Heaven	The Christmas Spirit

Now we shall examine some sermon subjects in order to see how the subject itself determines the content and the extent of the sermon.

These I shall give are actual sermon titles. In the case of published sermons we know that the title is also the true subject. The titles taken from newspapers and bulletins may not be what the preachers actually talked about. They sound like true subjects, and we shall treat them as if they were.

These subjects are not chosen for excellence or as models for imitation.[3] They are ordinary, run-of-the-mine subjects like those which come into every man's mind, like those we work with constantly.

These subjects are not all alike. Every one of them is chosen because it differs from the others in certain characteristics that affect the sermon. I shall point out those characteristics and name them. We meet with each type again and again in our work.

AN INDEFINITE, FUZZY SUBJECT

THE SPIRIT OF THANKSGIVING (Newspaper)

We begin with our old friend, the too-general topic. This one was announced on the eve of Thanksgiving. As you might know, it was offered by a very prominent and very busy pastor of a big church.

This is a fuzzy subject, not only because it is too general, but also because the word *spirit* is fuzzy. "Spirit," "spiritual"—it is one of the most treacherous terms in the preacher's vocabulary. It cannot be trusted to convey any definite meaning. It is what Quiller-Couch[4] called a "wool-cotton word," what Jowett called a "vague, ragged, ambiguous word," what Rudolph Flesch[5] calls "gobbledygook," what every intelligent listener recognizes as "jargon" or "lingo" or even "cant."

Webster's Collegiate Dictionary numbers fourteen distinct meanings of the word *spirit,* ranging from God himself all the way down to a volatile liquid. In this title it may signify no more than a grateful feeling or mood. Or it may mean a group humor, a complex of sentiments that comes over the crowds at Thanksgiving time, which one may "catch" from the crowd or the season, which puts one "in the spirit of Thanksgiving." Of course it could mean the Holy Spirit who alone makes us truly thankful to God, but we doubt that it means him in this place.

This subject does not show what the minister proposes to talk

[3] See "Note on the Use of Examples," p. 30.
[4] Arthur Quiller-Couch, *On the Art of Writing* (New York: Putnam, 1916).
[5] Rudolph Flesch, *The Art of Plain Talk* (New York: Harper, 1946).

about, and it does not convince us that he knows what he is
proposing to talk about. Much less does it give us or him any
clue to what he should say about it. It is no sort of preparation
to speak.

A subject like this is too easy. A man can set one down for any
occasion without effort, and they are interchangeable: "The Spirit
of Easter," "The Spirit of Prayer," "The Forgiving Spirit," "A
Loving Spirit," "The Spirit of Helpfulness," and so on as long as
you wish. None of them is better than the others, and none of
them is a true subject.

I am not saying that such a subject should never be announced—
as a title. I am saying that if this is all the preacher has proposed
to himself, he has not begun the preparation of his sermon, does
not know what he is going to talk about. He will not know until
he defines his subject more exactly than this.

A NOUN SUBJECT

The Character of Christ, by William E. Channing[6]

Matthew 17:5. "This is my beloved Son, in whom I am well pleased."

This subject can be related to the text, but it probably was not
drawn from this text.

It is a typical noun subject. That is, it has no predicate and it
suggests none. It names what is to be talked about: Christ's
character. It goes no further than that. It is neutral, noncommittal
as to what is to be said about the character of Jesus.

This is not a complete idea, not a complete thought. It is only a
subject, a noun. "The character of Christ" is not a sentence. Speak
those words, "The character of Christ" and then stop. Your
listener will wait impatiently for you to say something about the
character of Christ. He wants you to complete the idea. The
noun stops short of being a complete idea because it is only a
subject and lacks a predicate. A noun can name a thing, but
to say something it must be followed by a verb.

[6] *Works of Channing* (Boston: American Unitarian Association, 1875).
It is No. 7 in Blackwood, *op. cit.*, p. 63.

The difference between a subject and a complete thought is basic to all sermonic design, to all oral communication. It takes only a moment to name and define a subject. The body, the essential content of the sermon consists of its predication, the statement and development of its predicate or predicates.

Let us imagine ourselves in the audience when Channing began this sermon. He has given us his subject. He has spoken the words, "The character of Christ"—and we are waiting for him to complete the idea. Wishing to communicate, he does not keep us waiting more than thirty seconds. In the middle of his first paragraph, a short one, he says of it: "The character of Christ *is a strong confirmation of the truth of his religion.*" That is the complete idea, the central thought of the sermon. The sermon in its totality is nothing but a development of that one predicate.

Now this subject, the character of Jesus, gives no hint of what the predicate is to be. A noun subject, as here identified, never does. This subject might just as easily have quite a different predicate. For example: The character of Jesus wins us to love him; or, The character of Jesus is our highest example. Channing, in fact, mentions both these predicates as possible themes.

Clearly we would have in these predicates two other sermons very different from each other and from Channing's sermon— three totally different sermons on exactly the same subject, the character of Jesus.

The lesson for the student is that the substance of the sermon is in its predication, not in its subject. If he thinks he has a sermon idea when he has only a subject, he is mistaken. If he works out his subject only, he is working at the less important element of his sermon, and he is neglecting the more important element.

"The Character of Christ" is an excellent subject for the kind of sermon Channing wanted to preach. *Character* is strongly emphasized. In English usage its position, its place at the beginning, accents it. *Character* is also the principal word, and *of Christ* is a qualifying phrase subordinate to it. Attention centers firmly in Jesus' character, his human personality. So this subject reflects a certain theological view of Christ. It suggests only his humanity.

The subject states exactly what the sermon is about. Note how the word *character* centers and limits the subject, and is in turn limited by the word *Christ*. Channing will not talk of character in general, human character in its various aspects, but only of the character of Jesus. He will not talk of Christ in general, his teaching, work, or office, but only of his character. Anything outside these limits will be out of place in this sermon and will violate its unity.

A PREDICATING SUBJECT
The Joy of Grateful Living (Newspaper)

Grammatically, this is also a noun subject. It contains only noun elements, no predicate verb. It simply names something: the joy of grateful living.

Rhetorically—or semantically, if you prefer—it nevertheless has the force of an assertion. It suggests a predicate so plainly that it is actually felt. The way in which joy is related to grateful living by the word *of* implies: *there is joy in grateful living.*

Indeed the suggestion of this predicate, "there is," is stronger here than the words themselves would be. Like other forms of the verb *to be, is* is here so readily understood that it would be pedantic to say it.

We shall call this a predicating subject. Since the predicate is understood, its force is operating, and we can therefore consider this a complete idea without straining the truth unduly. We can say that this subject contains the sermon's theme, its central message. "There is joy in grateful living" is, then, the comprehensive thing this sermon will say, and should be all it says.

Joy and *living* are both fairly vague words. *Living* is qualified by *grateful*. The preacher will not talk about living in general, only about grateful living—a sufficiently sharp subject.

Joy is in the emphatic position, and is also the principal word. The prepositional phrase, *of* etc., is subordinate to it. Joy is, however, limited by this phrase. He will not talk about joy in general, only about that joy which goes with grateful living. This sufficiently limits the rather vague word *joy*.

Consequently, in this subject attention centers firmly in joy. The expansive force of the idea is in this word. The sermon will expand the experience of joy, keeping to those forms of joy that rise from gratitude—which must be taken to mean gratitude to God.

This subject was announced by a Jewish rabbi at Thanksgiving. It is a thoroughly biblical idea: "Joy and gladness shall be found therein, thanksgiving, and the voice of melody" (Isaiah 51:3). It is also a central idea in evangelical Christianity. The Christian is one set free by God's redeeming action in Christ and by the forgiveness of his sins, and his life and ethics are his grateful and joyful response. There could be a soundly evangelical development of this idea.

The idea could, of course, be developed in wrong and dangerous ways as well. A preacher could make it mean or imply that our appreciation of all the good things that come to us has in it some virtue or merit that creates joy. That would make it unnecessary to thank God at all. We need thank only ourselves and crown ourselves with joy. All depends on the development.

A COMPOUND SUBJECT

THE CROSS AND THE MEMORY OF SIN, by William N. Clow[7]
I Timothy 1:13. "Who was before a blasphemer, and a persecutor, and injurious, but I obtained mercy."

This subject is drawn from the text, the cross being present in "I obtained mercy."

Here we have three nouns: *cross, memory,* and *sin.* Two of them are tied together by *of* to make a unit, the memory of sin, which we shall for the moment call one noun, since it names one thing.

We shall call this a compound subject, because it consists of two nouns that seem to stand on equal footing and are connected

[7] *The Cross in Christian Experience* (New York: Harper, 1908). It is No. 17 in Blackwood, *op. cit.,* p. 152.

by the co-ordinating conjunction *and*. There might seem to be two subjects. "The Cross" is a topic much too big for a sermon; note that this sermon is one of a series on "The Cross in Christian Experience." Without the cross, "The Memory of Sin" could be the subject of a good psychological lecture, but not of a Christian sermon.

If there really were two subjects, that would be a fault but not an uncommon fault. Too often a preacher talks about two or more subjects in succession without relating them as parts in a larger whole. In that case we get two or more sermonettes spliced together, with a lack of unity and effectiveness.

The subject before us, however, is a genuine compound subject, and that is quite a different matter. Here *cross* and *memory of sin* limit each other, and the real subject is the relation between them, how they affect each other, especially how the cross affects the memory of sin. There will be no talk about sin except as it enters into memory, and no talk about any memory but of sin. There will be no talk about the cross except as it affects the memory of sin, and no talk about remembered sin except as affected by the cross. The exact subject is: *How* the cross affects the memory of sin, the difference it makes.

The expansive force of this subject is not in *the cross* and not in *the memory of sin*. The expansive force is in the relation indicated by this conjunction *and*, in the unspoken *how*, in the effect the cross has. That is what Clow expands to make the sermon.

This subject is also mildly predicating. It implies that the cross does make a difference. The sermon is an enumeration and development of different ways in which the cross makes a difference in the memory of sin.

The sermon is a series of predicates, the first being: "The cross *takes the sting out of* the memory of sin."

Clow does not put his whole thought into one inclusive predicate. This is another sermon, like Fosdick's, whose whole theme cannot be stated in a single clear and effective sentence. Clow simply defines his exact subject in the form of a question: "How does the cross . . . affect the memory of sin?" Then he speaks his first predicate, and he is on his way.

The whole sermon is one unified idea, and could have been put in one predicate. He could have said it all as follows: The cross makes a great healing difference in the memory of sin. But that sentence is too general to be effective and, instead of adding to the sermon's force, it would have weakened it.

There are other kinds of compound subjects. In the following, what predicates are suggested, and where does the expansive force lie?

"Slavery or Freedom"   "Convicted, Not Condemned"

A QUOTED SUBJECT
THE SACRIFICE OF THANKSGIVING (Bulletin)

The announcement did not identify this as a quotation from Scripture. Anyone familiar with the Psalter will recognize it as Psalm 116:17, "I will offer to thee the sacrifice of thanksgiving, and call on the name of the Lord."

This subject is a direct quotation from the Bible. It is all to this minister's credit that he was in the grip of Scripture at Thanksgiving. There is no reason to doubt that this particular man knew exactly what he was doing and that he preached a good sermon on this subject. If he expounded the meaning of the quotation, he certainly did.

But that is just the point. This subject is chosen to show that a direct quotation of Scripture is by no means a foolproof subject for a sermon. The temptation to use scriptural words is both insidious and strong, for the simple reason that it is easy. Anybody can set down a phrase of Scripture, whether he knows what it means or not. It does not insure his having prepared his subject.

To preach the sacrifice of thanksgiving in its true sense the preacher will have to change his people's whole idea of what a sacrifice is. This biblical phrase will sound strange to them as a subject for Thanksgiving. The thing meant may be known to them as "thank-offering." They would not naturally call it sacrifice.

The word *sacrifice* is ambiguous in current usage, and the sermon must take pains to clarify it. Sacrifice, to most people nowadays, means giving up or depriving ourselves of something that is or might be our own, which we would have liked having—just that: depriving ourselves.

Hence, if the preacher talks carelessly about sacrifice, many of his listeners will understand it to mean: "We ought to be thankful to God, whatever it may cost us"; or, "Giving thanks to God is good for us, no matter what it costs"; or, not impossibly, "It will cost us plenty to be properly thankful."

In the Bible sacrifice means something offered back to God in glad acknowledgment that everything we have and are is his. It centers in God, not in ourselves, and the feeling of being deprived is the least part of it. A proper sermon on "The Sacrifice of Thanksgiving" will proclaim this idea in some form.

The lesson is that a quotation of Scripture as a subject is attended by no less risk than one devised by the preacher. He will have to study the biblical words as hard as his own. In most cases he had much better formulate the subject in his own words.

A FIGURATIVE SUBJECT

SONGS IN THE NIGHT, by Charles H. Spurgeon[8]
Job 35:10. "But none saith, Where is God my Maker, who giveth songs in the night?"

This is another quotation from Scripture, but that is not why this subject is chosen. It is also a figurative subject.

The figure of speech is in the text itself. In fact, the complete idea of the sermon is in the text, both subject and predicate: "God giveth songs in the night."

The figure is a compound metaphor. The "night" is not the dark shadow on the side of the earth opposite the sun; the night is human trouble, the Christian's trouble. The "songs" are not melodies; the songs are the glad recognition and praise of God.

[8] *Sermons,* Second Series (New York: Sheldon, Blakeman, 1857). It is No. 12 in Blackwood, *op. cit.,* p. 114.

"Songs in the night" means the praise of God in time of trouble. This is about as good as any literal statement of the subject would be, but how much less it says than "Songs in the Night"!

Observe the power of a figure. In paragraph three Spurgeon sketches the things he means by "night": sorrow, persecution, doubt, bewilderment, anxiety, oppression, ignorance, and so on. Try to bring these and all like things together in a single abstract word that expresses their pressure on the soul, and the emotions they arouse. I tried it above and got only the lame word *trouble*. Can any literal or abstract term express it half as well as calling it "night"?

What do "songs" mean in this sermon? It is still more difficult, it is impossible to catch all that in a single literal term. "Praise" is the word he uses most frequently, but nowhere in the sermon does Spurgeon attempt a literal statement of all that "songs" means.

Throughout the sermon he uses both the metaphors. He says "night" and "songs," and he wisely relies on the figures to convey his meaning. They convey a great deal more than his rational meaning; they convey an experience of the things he describes.

The very sophisticated modern may, when reading this sermon, be surprised to find himself moved, unwillingly, by this florid rhetoric of a hundred years ago, so different from our tastes of the moment. Can we imagine what it would do to this sermon to reduce it to literal statement? The sermon would simply evaporate.

At times a preacher will frame a literal subject from a figurative text, at other times a figurative subject from a literal text. The main thing here is to let ourselves feel the power of a figure of speech.

The power of a figure does not depend on florid rhetoric. "Design for a Sermon" on page 15 is a metaphor used without reliance on rhetoric. Phillips Brooks has two famous sermons on figurative subjects: "The Fire and the Calf," No. 13 in Blackwood's *The Protestant Pulpit,* and "The Candle of the Lord," in Macartney's *Great Sermons of the World,* p. 513.

A COMPLETE IDEA
GOD CARES
I Peter 5:7. "Cast all your anxiety on him, for he cares about you."

> God cares:
> We have his assurance that he does.
> It does not seem to be true.
> There must be either anxiety or trust.
> Which shall it be?

Since this is not a mere subject, but a subject and predicate, a complete thought, we cannot use it to illustrate what is in a subject. It is put here only for comparison. We shall come to it later.

A complete idea can be used as the title of a sermon. Then the procedure in preaching it should be different. One does not have to define a subject and then add a predicate or predicates to it. The two structural questions are already answered: What to talk about and what to say about it. The sermon moves immediately into the functional questions: What does it mean? Do we believe it or not, and why? What difference does it make? What is at issue here?

There are other kinds of subjects than these we have examined. We have looked at what we called an indefinite or fuzzy subject, a noun subject, a predicating subject, a compound subject, a subject quoted from Scripture, and a figurative subject.

These are not traditional types of subject. This is only an attempt to point out and deal with the central feature of each kind and the problems it raises. Nor do I mean to propose this as a typology of subjects. Our purpose has been to see how much can be in a subject, to see how decisive a right or wrong subject can be for the entire sermon, and to gain some experience in analyzing subjects that should point the way toward skill in their management. If this treatment makes the subject seem simple, I am glad, for it does not remain a simple matter.

The true subject, how one defines for himself the exact thing he is to talk about, is the primary factor in sermonic design. Consider two points of evidence in support of that statement:

Preparing a sermon for a special occasion is that simple (?) task of finding the right subject matter and molding it to the exact shape in which it can most profitably be developed.

What is more, most of the newer types of sermon structure in contemporary homiletical writings are in reality only different ways in which the true subject is conceived. For example, a "life-situation sermon" is simply one whose true subject is a problem rising out of life. An "analogical sermon" chooses to talk about the likeness of one thing to another. The true subject of a "categorizing sermon" is its categories. And so on.

SUGGESTIONS

You can see that a sharp definition of the actual subject is the key to the real character of the sermon. For instance, read Sangster's (12) lively and helpful discussion of the "faceting" sermon, pages 87-92, and you will see that this is a matter of the exact subject. He chooses to talk about a certain facet of a text or idea, and the result is a tightly organized sermon on that phase of the subject. The facet is the true subject.

For further reading on the subject matter, the substance of preaching, read Garvie (8), Part III, Chapter II, pages 378-392. Read Jowett (25), Chapter III, "The Preacher's Themes," pages 75-109. On the way the content of preaching changes, read Thompson (49).

I wish I could see the subjects that are taking shape in your sketchbook. Do you have to re-examine them in the light of this chapter? Are there some you will have to discard? Some you can improve by redesigning them? Is there a really good one there, or one you feel has the makings of an excellent one?

Is there another that seems too much for you at this time, one you can't manage but can't forget? That is probably the most important one in the lot. Most of the easy solutions are specious; most ready explanations do not explain; they are cocksure pretense that the insoluble mystery and wonder is solved. You will be lucky not to escape from the mysteries. If you cannot get this unmanageable subject ready to preach for ten or twenty years, it is still the kind that shows you are a man.

You would need to review your sermon ideas for a year or five years to learn how your choice of subject matter sets its stamp on your output. But you can be aware now that it does determine the quality of your work. You can understand that if you are to preach your best, you must work hard and continuously here at the source, the ideas themselves, with more concern for them than for developmental details such as illustrations and so forth. These matters of secondary importance get nearly all the attention of the mediocre preacher. I hope they won't get all of yours.

Let me suggest that you become very critical about the range of your ideas, the grooves in which you habitually run, your favorite subjects, your prejudices, your enthusiasms, and your dislikes; and, contrariwise, that you deliberately seek for wider views. It may be a humiliating experience, but there is growth and satisfaction in it.

CHAPTER 6

The Expanding Thought

It should show nothing but its own unfolding parts:
Branches that thrust out by the force of its inner life.

The idea that is to generate a sermon comes, then, somehow from somewhere into the preacher's mind and just as certainly into his feeling. It may come well formed and lusty, or it may be nebulous and wavering. In either case the task is not so much to give it form as to find, or rather to feel, its own true form, its native and inherent shape. To recognize this fact and learn to work with it is the first step toward creative skill. A sense of form is primarily an ability to feel the form of an organic idea—not to create a form for it, and surely not to impose a form upon it.

As the form is inherent in the idea itself, so also the energy to move the preacher and expand into a significant communication is inherent in the substance of the idea. Look again at the qualities of a good s mon idea as they have been described: it should be concentrated, expansive, true, human, evangelical. These may sound like ideals—like qualities it would be well for the idea to possess if it can, but which it can do without if it has to. But they are not mere ideals. Actually, these are not ideal but functional qualities; the idea must possess them in order to be generative. The power to move first the preacher and afterwards the listener, the power to engage the heart, the imagination and will, resides in these qualities, and a subject which lacks them is not a good sermon subject.

Good preaching begins with finding such ideas; preaching cannot become good without good ideas to begin with. The trouble with a too-general subject is that nobody really cares much about it, neither the people nor the preacher. Power to expand is generated by compression. Conviction of truth is derived from relevance to the human struggle. Nothing short of the gospel is worth a place among the ardors of the human spirit. A person engaged with less than these—in the pew, the pulpit, or the study—is puttering with trivialities that should not enlist his greatest powers and *cannot.*

We have now reached the point where we must examine the process by which the idea expands into a sermon. It is a difficult point for many a beginner. He may have what looks like an impeccable idea, but having said it once he is through and can seem to go no further.

This process of expansion is also a difficult thing to study, for it is a life process, an action of the mind. We must therefore feel it taking place before we can begin to see how it takes place. To analyze it and try to describe it may help somewhat.

The idea begins with a subject at the very least. If it is a noun subject like "The Character of Christ," expansion takes the form of one or several predicates added to the subject. There may be one all-inclusive predicate, such as "The character of Christ is a strong confirmation of the truth of his religion." Then it is this whole assertion that expands, especially its key word *confirmation.* The entire sermon simply develops and illuminates this one statement.

If one's study of a subject like "The effect of the cross on the memory of sin" does not result in one all-inclusive predicate, then the key word of the subject, in this case *the effect,* expands into a series of assertions describing different effects the cross has.

If the subject is a predicating subject like "The Joy of Grateful Living," then the whole suggested assertion, "There is joy in grateful living," especially its key word *joy,* will expand just as if the predicate were explicitly stated.

We could say that all three of these forms are expansions along the line of the structural questions: What shall be talked about? What must be said about it?

However, the really powerful force of an idea often follows other lines. It may follow the lines suggested by the different parts of the text or context. If the subject is central to the text, it will illuminate the details of the passage and will in turn be illuminated by them, resulting in a true exposition of the text.

Often the beginner, by main force and diligent labor, blows up his idea into an artificial shape, when all the time the lines of its natural expansion lie there unnoticed in the text. This is misdirected effort, zeal not according to knowledge.

Above all, the idea is ready to expand along the lines marked by the functional questions. When a man feels unable to go further than the bald statement of his idea, let him get a pencil in his hand, paper before him, and do two things:

First, let him search this passage of Scripture again (I assume he has already studied it exegetically, consulted commentaries, and made notes of his pertinent findings). Let him now write down what every part of the passage contributes to his subject, changing the subject itself if it proves not to be the right one.

Then let him begin to ask himself, What does this idea mean? Do I, do my hearers believe it? Why or why not? What difference does it make if it is true? What are its consequences to me and my listeners? Let him press these questions, and let him write down every answer that comes to him, expressing them as succinctly and as well as he can, not bothering about their order. If he does this, he will soon know whether he has a sermon or not.

In this way a body of significant material is accumulated, out of which the sermon will be made. It is not yet a sermon, though all the important assertions may be there. It waits for that moment when it all congeals, crystallizes, when the idea gets up on its feet, as it were, finds shape, movement, and direction, decides where it is going.

Now this expansion can take place only when a man is working with some specific idea. Insofar as what happens is right for that particular idea, it will be peculiar to that idea and will not serve as a model for work on any other sermon. For the time being, sense and skill exist exclusively for the service of this very idea and no other. For that matter sense and skill have no existence at any time apart from their service to some definite idea.

This statement of the case is somewhat disturbing, but it is true. It means that no sound homiletical method exists until it comes into being in actual work on a given text or theme, and it also means that no method is ever sound unless it is right for the particular text or theme with which a man is working at the time. This fact greatly increases the difficulty of studying the process by which an idea expands into a sermon.

Furthermore, no man can show you, my reader, this process at work in you. I can only let you look on over my shoulder and see it at work in me. It is a highly personal process. No two men react to the same subject in exactly the same way. I can only describe what happens to me. Sometimes you may react as I do, sometimes differently. But the only way you can ever come to understand the process is to become acquainted with it as it takes place in you.

Consequently, the rest of this chapter has to be an experiment in which the reader watches me at work on a specific sermon, while I try to show him what happens to me and how the work is done.

Before we begin, let me repeat that only an idea that comes alive in the preacher has power to expand into a living sermon. Speeches can of course be knocked together with a saw and hammer. There is always much lumber of moral and religious platitude lying around—prose, verse, stock anecdotes, glittering generalities, all over the place—kites in the wind of fashionable thought. A man can cut, splice, and nail it together exactly as he would build a doghouse.

Our experiment will demonstrate the saw and hammer method first. We have to see them both to appreciate the difference. I shall use a passage from Matthew's version of the Sermon on the Mount, near the end, 7:15-23.

"Beware of false prophets, who come to you in sheep's clothing but inwardly are ravenous wolves. You will know them by their fruits. Are grapes gathered from thorns, or figs from thistles? So, every sound tree bears good fruit, but the bad tree bears evil fruit. A sound tree cannot bear evil fruit, nor can a bad tree bear good fruit. Every tree that does not bear good fruit is cut down and thrown into the fire. Thus you will know them by their fruits.

"Not every one who says to me, 'Lord, Lord,' shall enter the kingdom of heaven, but he who does the will of my Father who is in heaven. On that day many will say to me, 'Lord, Lord, did we not prophesy in your name, and cast out demons in your name, and do many mighty works in your name?' And then will I declare to them, 'I never knew you; depart from me, you evildoers.' "

Thousands of sermons of all kinds have been preached from this passage. If a man is merely on the hunt for subjects he might use in a pinch, he can find a number of them in a few minutes. It is all too easy. A quickly made list will be different for each man who tries his hand at it. Each will catch the things that appeal to him, especially those which get an emotional reaction from him. Here is a list that was made a little more deliberately, though still within an hour.

False teachers ("prophets" equals teachers)
False teachings
Harm done by false teachings
Hypocritical teachers ("Sheep's clothing")
Exploiters of the church ("ravenous wolves")
Character and its fruits ("good tree" equals character)
How to judge people ("by their fruits")
Doing *versus* saying ("not every one who says . . . but he who does")
Unexpected judgment ("many will say . . . then will I declare")

Only one of these subjects, the first, is so general as to be unusable without further restriction. Begin thinking about false teachers and see what happens. False teachers—is it false teachings or false persons? Purveyors of untrue teachings, or dishonest purveyors of teachings that may themselves be sound? To turn in either of these two directions is to restrict the subject. The mind automatically narrows its view until it gets to something compressed enough to spring back, to send out branches, to expand.

False teachings, then. The action of the mind is automatic. I cannot hold *false teachings* steadily at the center of attention for a half minute without the mind working with it, turning it, shifting the view, moving in some direction. I try it, and this is what happens:

I think of certain false teachings that I know. I recall one or two of them and ask what others there are.

I think of the harm done by false teachings and begin to note one or two kinds of harm and ask what others there are.

I may, however, take some other direction, such as the question, What makes a teaching false? How is it to be judged false or true? Then I begin looking for tests of truth.

Anything may happen; something is certain to happen. The point is that if attention is kept steadily focused on a subject, the mind will begin at once either to expand it or to narrow it down to one of its sharper aspects that has relevance and force.

Whatever a brilliant talent might make of them, these are not good sermon subjects. They are all, except perhaps the last one, doghouse subjects, sawed out of the text. Every one of them is apparently related to some words in the text, but none is central to the real meaning of the passage.

A speech can be constructed on any of these subjects with a saw, a hammer, and nails, and the lumber of platitude. The text need not be thought of again. An ordinary man's memory, reinforced by a choice quotation and two or three interchangeable illustrations, will be sufficient. With a little logic and imagination, a speech can be "worried into being," as Robert Frost calls it. A living sermon, of course, can no more be worried into being than can a living poem.

Yet even these subjects have some expansive force. Take any one of them, concentrate on it, do not let the mind wander from it, and it will begin to branch out into definite things that should be said in discussing it. Set each of these things down in as few words as will accurately express it, and one gets the contributing assertions with which to develop it into a talk or address, if not a sermon.

For example, take "Character and its fruits," perhaps the most popular subject in the list. The idea is that *conduct is the result of character,* as the fruit is a product of the tree. When I concentrate on this subject, there are three things which almost say themselves:

> *Character determines conduct;* the tree bears the fruit.
> *Conduct reveals character;* the fruit identifies the tree.
> *The good life is not simply doing, it is being;*
> to produce better fruit one must become a better tree.

Many a discourse on this topic says no more than that. Indeed, an organic development of this idea can hardly say more than that. These are the natural branches of the thought, the limbs of the tree. The discourse can do nothing but expand the idea, can say nothing but what is drawn out of the idea. If the resulting product is not a genuine sermon, it is because the idea is not a sermon idea in the first place.

"Character and its fruits" is a subject for a moral admonition, but not for a gospel sermon. There is no good news in it, only the operation of immutable psychological and moral law. An atheistic moralist could deliver this discourse as convincingly as a Christian minister. A Christian moralist can of course give its detail the color of Christian ethics. But he cannot lug the gospel in at the end of this discourse without breaking its unity and weakening the force of his original argument.

Moral admonition has a legitimate place in the Christian pulpit, but it is not the central place. The law is also to be preached as well as the gospel. But pity the people whose preacher does not know the difference between law and gospel. For law, Paul reminds us, works death, and life is through promised grace. And if it is by law, it is no more by promise.

In addition to its theological inadequacy, this thought, "Conduct is the result of character," fails to qualify as a generative idea. It is not an idea that stirs me to the bottom of my deepest concern. It is a "safe" idea, as its approval by all moralists shows. We have heard it said by very important persons, we assent to its correctness, but we do not deeply feel it or care about it. It is a stereotype, a cliché. Everybody knows it is true, and nobody sets any store by it.

Exactly what are we doing when we preach that character determines conduct, that conduct shows character, that goodness is
not simply doing something but being something? It is not likely
that we are expressing a deep conviction of our own. We are
parroting. We are contriving a speech. We are saying what we
would like to feel, what we think we ought to feel, what we think
is expected of us, being admirable young men and preachers
besides.

The result is sentimentality, that is, expressing "appropriate
sentiments" instead of real feelings. It is no genuine communication, for we ourselves are not in it. Such preaching is like cheap
religious art, the saccharine picture of Jesus, and is created in the
same studio. Such preaching is like poor verse, the mawkish piety
of religious doggerel.

Such preaching is meretricious, that is, like the *meretrix,* the
prostitute, it earns the customer's favor or his money or both by
giving what he expects in a way he likes. It is like the pictures
painted or the books written from no deeper desire than to capture
the mass market.

The sinfulness of sentimental and meretricious preaching is its
insincerity. Its poverty is that it leaves out the truth of the
preacher's own heart. With his very doubt and rebellion he can
do much better than this, not to mention his own love and
compassion.

What is this passage from Matthew about? Prophets? A prophet
is more than a teacher. A true prophet is one sent from God who
speaks God's message for God to his people. Every prophet may
in some sense be a teacher, but not every teacher is a prophet.
Not every good man is a prophet. Not every teacher of truths is
a prophet.

This text is about false prophets. It does not mention true
prophets by name. Where is the true prophet in this passage? If
he is here, he is the sound tree, the fig tree, the grapevine, the one
who does the Father's will. But if the tree and vine mean the

true prophet, they do not mean simply the good man, and Jesus is talking about prophecy, not about character.

If the sound tree means only a man of sound character, if the will of the Father means only righteousness, then there is no reference to the true prophet anywhere in this passage. Then Jesus has changed his subject without warning; he started talking about false prophets but now suddenly means bad men. But if this is so, Jesus switches back to false prophets with the question, "Did we not *prophesy* in your name?" And if "I never knew you" is the rejection of a bad man, not the rejection of a false prophet, then Jesus has once more switched the subject from false prophets to bad men.

The inference is clear. Jesus is talking about false prophets throughout the passage. The bad tree, the thorn and thistle, the man he never knew, mean the false prophet, not simply the rotten character. The sound tree, the fig and grape, he who does the Father's will, is the true prophet, not simply the righteous man. We are getting a different subject entirely, not righteousness but prophecy, not the fruit of a corrupt life but the fruit of a false message.

As the fruit of the grapevine is the grape, so the fruit of the prophet, by which he is known as true or false, is his prophecy, his message. The will of the Father for the prophet is that he faithfully deliver the message God is sending to his people. The best man who is not a true prophet is a wild growth, however healthy and beautiful. He is a thorn or thistle in the Lord's planting, a bad tree which will not be let grow.

It is clear that we have here an idea struggling to be born and already expanding faster than we can contain it. The essential things have been getting themselves said before we were ready for them.

What general thing does the whole passage say about the false prophet? It says "beware." Does everything the passage says come under that warning? Yes, it does. The whole passage is warning; there is not a syllable of reassurance, nothing but warning, stark and unrelieved. Whom is Christ warning? Those people to whom the prophet is coming, those who hear the prophet speaking.

Let us try to say it then: *The Lord warns his people that the man in the pulpit may be a false prophet.*

How shall we design this sermon? What are the different lines of force along which the idea is expanding? How can we organize the various things it is saying? What does it mean? Is it true? What difference does it make?

And here, before we can go further, we must know the kind of hearers we shall speak to. The sermon will take one form if addressed to people who sit in the pew and listen, and another form if addressed to men who stand in the pulpit and preach.

If we ask what this warning means and what difference it makes to the congregation, the thought will expand in a certain way under pressure of the text itself. We shall have to find what dangers a false preacher exposes his listeners to and the issue with which this situation confronts them. The subject will be: *the danger of listening to preachers,* however we may state it.

For the purposes of this book we shall let it take form as a sermon to an assembly of preachers. That is the way it was actually born, the situation in which it was preached. The general title, "False Prophets" might serve. A more exact one would be "The Perils of Preaching." But I actually talked about *the perilous situation of the man in the pulpit.* This is the way it expanded:

> The Lord warns his people that the man in the pulpit may be a false prophet; he makes the preacher listen to that warning.
>
> The only certain thing about the preacher is that he does come in sheep's clothing.
>
> He may be a good man but a false prophet; nothing but his message can vouch for him.
>
> True prophecy differs from human speech not in quality but in kind; it is of a different species.
>
> The man in the pulpit:
> Resists the Spirit who commands him to prophesy,

Constructs rational defenses against the Spirit,
Claims to speak and act in the Lord's name,
Thinks he is doing the Father's will.

In all this he is just like the many who are rejected.

The true preacher trembles before:
The stern, negative warning of Christ,
The mystery of that kingdom he may not be in,
The absolute, uncompromising Will he risks not doing,
The holy Love he can serve but cannot emulate.

It is well that we have to hear this warning; it leaves the issue
as the Lord put it.

This sketch shows the design of the sermon as it took shape in my mind under pressure of the text. It is an attempt to say in the most condensed form possible what the passage is saying as it applies to the preacher, to say what it means, why it may be true of him, and what difference it makes concerning him.

The subject, false prophets, is restricted to a particular preacher, to this very man in the pulpit speaking to the Lord's people— to me as I stand here. It is this restriction that gives the idea its urgency, its sense of perilous responsibility, and its expansive energy.

To be sure, much has happened to a basic idea before it reaches the stage marked by this sketch. It had to be clarified. All the many things that were trying to get said had to be condensed and generalized as contributing thoughts commensurate with the reach of the idea and conveying its urgency as far as possible. These various assertions had to be separated and distinguished from one another, so that duplicates and subordinate assertions did not confuse and obscure the principal ones. And, finally, they had to be arranged into an ordered continuity suitable for communicating the message.

This is not a preliminary sketch then. Rather it is something like a final design of the sermon. In fact, this sketch is a stage in advance of the actual writing out of the sermon. A fully written manuscript is not the final stage in the preparation of a sermon for oral delivery. Rather it is only an incident, one step in the preparation. Writing, even when preceded by a careful sketch, is not the last step. If done without a careful sketch, writing may be only a kind of extemporizing.

There was a preliminary sketch, but it was not like this sketch. The substance was all there, but it changed form, underwent revisions, acquired new directions and new proportions in process of writing. As nearly always happens, the thought grew to new dimensions and produced new elements of form to contain the new dimensions. The design can be improved greatly after a first writing is done.

The sermon as it was actually written is given below. It is not offered as a model. There is no model sermon and no faultless sermon. If you compare the written sermon with the above sketch, you will see that, though it embodies the idea, the written sermon is far from a perfect embodiment either in clarity of specific statement or in its continuity. You may also agree with me that the idea is clearer in design and easier to grasp with the mind in the sketch than it is in the written sermon. The sketch is in some respects an improvement on the manuscript, in my opinion.

This does not mean that a full sketch is better than a completely written sermon, or that writing is unnecessary. I do not know how a man can hope to improve his work without seeing exactly what he is doing down to the least detail, and I do not know how he can see what he is doing unless he writes out word after word everything he intends to say. I am not saying that a well-designed sermon in sketch form is better than the same sermon fully written. I am saying that the design is the basic thing and that a good design without a manuscript is better than a complete manuscript without design. Every teacher has seen both of these things more often than he has seen the best thing of all, namely, a well-designed sermon completely written in clear and appropriate language.

Here, then, is the form this idea took in one man's mind as he wrote. The sermon is printed to show how the thought expanded in all its parts one after another, forming the details of a more or less complete expression.

FALSE PROPHETS
Matthew 7:15-23

This text stops us preachers in our tracks, and makes us listen while the Lord talks to our people about us. Take warning, he says, Stop, look and listen! He cautions our people: Danger ahead! Road unsafe! Travel at your own risk! "Beware of false prophets, who come to you in sheep's clothing." Beware of this very man who stands in the pulpit before you, dressed in the clothing the sheep wear. He may be a false prophet, a pseudo-prophet, a fake. What he says to you may be dangerous and destructive falsehood.

The only sure thing about this man in the pulpit is that he does come in sheep's clothing. Whether plain black robe or cassock and surplice, he wears the vestments of the church; he shows "the outward fellowship of signs." These vestments are no guarantee whatever of him or of anything he shall say. They may be the marks of a genuine calling. On the other hand, they may give him just the venerable disguise, the feeling of assurance he needs to carry off his imposture convincingly.

He comes saying, "Lord, Lord," but the Lord may never have known him, may have to reject him at last, and say: "Depart from me, you evildoer." That is what will happen not to a few of those who say "Lord, Lord," but to many of them, according to the text. This man may be one of the many, not one of the few.

He comes speaking in the name of the Lord, but the Lord may have no control over him and no influence on what he says. He has said an ordination vow, hands were laid on him, the Holy Spirit was invoked. But he may have no notion who the Holy Spirit is; he may never in his life have met the living God face to face; he may believe that inspiration is an ancient mysterious process long since withdrawn into the dark shadows where his dream-god sleeps. This man may be entirely original, may have nothing to say that is not his own. He may be a false prophet. The only certain thing is that he comes in sheep's clothes, saying, "Lord, Lord." He may be a wolf. He may feed on the flock, not feed it.

"You will know them by their fruits," the Lord says. "Are

grapes gathered from thorns, or figs from thistles?" If the Lord's
figure is true to his meaning, the primary question is not whether
this man in the pulpit is a good man or a bad man. That is the
secondary question. The primary question is whether he is a true
prophet or a false prophet. Many a good man, many an intelligent
and gifted man, many an extremely "nice" man is no prophet of
any kind. Many a good and sincere man has turned out to be a
false prophet. True prophecy and manhood grow on different
roots. If the true prophet is a grapevine, the false prophet is a
thorn bush, that is, he belongs to a different species.

It is not moral character the Lord is talking about. As concerns
character, a rotten thorn bush cannot so much as produce good
thorn blossoms and thorn fruit, and a rotten grapevine of the finest
variety cannot produce good grapes. But it is far more funda-
mental that the healthiest and most vigorous thorn bush in the
world cannot produce grapes, not any grapes, not the poorest
grape that ever grew; while if the sickliest vine makes shift to
blossom and ripen any fruit at all, it will be a grape, and not a
thorn seed.

Just as these thorns and grapes are not different fruits on the
same tree, so right preaching and false preaching are not different
degrees of excellence in the same kind of talking. The most perfect thorn bush in the world is a bad tree in the vineyard of the
Lord, and, for all its loveliness of alien bloom, God's fire will
have it. If the trees and the prophets cannot be distinguished by
the dress they wear and the health they show, then they must be
distinguished by the fruit they produce. "You will know them by
their fruits."

The man in the pulpit trembles to hear this, but the Lord's
meaning is unmistakable. As the botanist completes his identification of a species by examining blossom and ripe fruit, you will
know the true from the false prophet by what he produces.

If the grape is not the proper fruit of the thorn, if the downy
thistle seed is not the proper fruit of the fig tree, what is the proper
fruit of a prophet? Is it not his prophecy? Is it not by what he

preaches that you will know a true prophet from a pseudo-prophet? And what makes a true prophet? Is it not that men shall hear God speak through his mouth? Thayer defines the word *prophet* in the New Testament as "One who, moved by the Spirit of God and hence his organ or spokesman, solemnly declares to men what he has received by inspiration, especially future events, and in particular such as relate to the cause and kingdom of God and to human salvation." Is not this what Christ means by a prophet? The fruit of the prophet is his message. The fruit of the true preacher, by which he is known from the false, is the gospel of God in its specific nature; and the gospel has a nature as specific as that of the grape.

The man in the pulpit cries out in anguish, being but a man. And he says: "Oh let me not feel the burning eyes of God upon me while I'm speaking! Let me not hear the unutterable groaning of God's restless praying Spirit! Let me speak only by the familiar Holy Ghost, the comfortable, neighborly spirit who always encourages me to say what I believe! Let me nurse no delusion of prophetic grandeur, no false hope of inspiration! Let me simply use the Bible that lies undisturbingly on the desk, whose words mean what I want them to mean, and come at my call like well-trained dogs! Torture me not with a prophet's vision! Compel me not to reason of righteousness and judgment to come! Let me be humble and please God! Let me be mild and please my people! Let me talk respectfully of the ancient days when God was still in reach and prophets and wolves were both real! Let me interpret this text historically and believe that Jesus is not talking about me but about the scribes and Pharisees! Let me be timely and talk to the interests and needs of this hour about things I understand!" So says the preacher, being but a man.

The man in the pulpit, being also a college graduate, is able to defend himself against the Lord's Spirit. He says, "Is not this text found in that famous Sermon on the Mount which everybody knows is simply the ethical teaching of Jesus? Do not the context and the words of Jesus both show that he is speaking of ethics?

'Not every one who says to me, Lord, Lord, shall enter the kingdom of heaven, but he who does the will of my Father who is in
heaven.' Surely that means ethics. Not the empty profession, but
the doing of God's will, brings one into the kingdom. Surely it is
God's will that I speak in his name. Have I not spoken in his
name? I have spoken for God, of the things of God, in the Lord's
name. And if that's what prophecy is, have I not prophesied in
his name? God's will has been done. And have I not already
entered the kingdom?"

The man in the pulpit elaborates his defense: "Surely it is God's
will that the demons be cast out of me and others, that unremitting
struggle be waged against evil in all its forms and all its strong-
holds. Have I not struggled against evil in his name, and won some
victories, too? Have I not cast out some demons, at least, in his
name? Has not God's will been done in this, not perfectly, but as
well as could be expected of imperfect people? And have I not
entered the kingdom?"

The man in the pulpit points with thankful pride: "Surely it is
God's will that things get done in his name, that churches be built
and parishes extended and budgets met and the hungry and home-
less and sick cared for and the gospel preached to the poor and
all life called to the obedience of God. Have we not done this in
his name? The church is not perfect, but is it not a fact, though
often overlooked, that we have done many mighty works in his
name? And have we not entered the kingdom?"

What is wrong with the logic of this defense by the man in the
pulpit? Not much that we can see—which makes more terrible
the Son of Man's warning that before God's judgment it will not
stand up, that in the face of these very things we are doing in
his name, he may have to declare to us: "I never knew you; depart
from me, you evildoers." Surely he can't mean us! There must be
some mistake! Look who we are!

If we cannot see anything wrong with this defense, then we
can be sure that we are disciples and partners of this false prophet

in the pulpit. We join him in his protest and his question; we tremble before the same judgment as he.

Who is this Christ, so stern and implacable in his demands, so little like the gentle, idealistic Jesus to whom we are accustomed? What is this kingdom that is not anything we can do, at whose narrow gate all that men desire and strive for must be laid down; where even the wish for all that men strive for must be laid down? Who is this Son of Man, so little like the reassuring and gracious teacher from Galilee? Who is this Preacher who, in the best style of bad homiletics, closes his Sermon on the Mount with a whole chapter of harsh negative notes, hard conditions, warnings, denunciations, with scarcely a word of comfort? He speaks of dogs and of swine that trample holy pearls under their feet, of hypocrites plucking at splinters in other people's eyes, of faithless people who give bread to their children but expect only stones from God, of a gate so narrow and a way so hard that the many never find it. And in the very last sentence of the sermon, the noise of a house crashing before the wind and the flood!

Is this the way into the kingdom of God? What does he mean by throwing the impossible, perfect love of God up to me, and damning all the compromises that are my only possibility? Is that, and nothing less than that, the will of God which we must do? Must God be everything, and I nothing? Must he have all the glory, and I no private victory at all?

What if the answer were "Yes, God must be all in all and must have everything, not in the empty piety of a phrase, but in real and dreadful fact"? What if he—this shadowy Figure of our religious imagination—what if he should stand there alive and be the God we have imagined? What if his will is nothing less than that he be God to us always and everywhere and in everything, not as a pious theory but as a desperate, inexorable fact? What if his kingdom is nothing else and nothing less than that it be this way with us here, now?

This will of God which is not my will, and not my mental picture of his will! This good and gracious will of God which "is done indeed without our prayer," but is never yet quite done by me, though I pray daily that it may be! This kingdom of God which is not my ideal of the good life, and not the Utopia of human dreams! This kingdom of God which "comes indeed of itself without our prayer," yet never quite gets to me, or gets me completely in it, for all my praying! This impossible, intolerable love of God! This unreasonable, holy, unconditioned, seeking and redeeming love, before which every human affection must confess itself a prostitute out for her own price! What if the way were as narrow as this? What if there were no other way at all but this?

If this should be the way it is, what could the man in the pulpit do? Well, for one thing, if he does not want it this way, he can get down out of the pulpit, can't he? Is it too much for God to ask that if a man comes into the pulpit he come through this narrow gate and by no wider or easier way? It seems too much to us of course. We shall continue to smooth and pave a broad way into the pulpit. And the Lord's people will continue to need the warning.

For the false prophet will not get down out of the pulpit. That would be more like the action of a true prophet. Almost every true prophet would get out of it, if God would let him. It is well, then, that the Lord stops us in our tracks and makes us listen while he warns our people against us. It is not too much for him to ask that we take what he says seriously. That is the least we can do, but we can do that.

SUGGESTIONS

I am sure you see that there is no way you can work at your sermon idea except to find a form in which to express it, and no way to improve the idea but to improve the form.

In its primary form your idea may be only a thought in a single sentence. When you begin to question your idea, especially when you question the text and it together, it will expand into definite things to be said, things from which your plot, your plan will be constructed. It is not a plan yet, and there is no advantage in hurrying on to make a definite plan. There may be a disadvantage. While everything is still fluid, the substance can expand freely. Once there is a plan, it tends to harden the substance and limit its expansion.

Homiletical literature will not give you much assistance in regard to this process of expanding the thought. The literature takes you too quickly to the types of sermon structure. But this expansion is the process of making sermons, and anything you read about sermonizing, short of types of structure, applies to this work.

I suggest that you read general discussions of sermonizing. For instance, there is Newton (9). In this book a number of leading preachers discuss their method in reply to two questions: 1. What is the best way for the preacher to approach the modern mind? 2. How do I personally prepare my sermons? The replies are somewhat sketchy, but there is the advantage of seeing a number of men at work.

A large part of the homiletical literature of this century in America has been produced by the Lyman Beecher lectureship at Yale University. Baxter (2) has arranged, under different phases of the sermonic process, important things these lecturers have said about each of these phases. Baxter's outline of sermon technique is not complete in its coverage. Also, the remarks of the lecturers are so short we often wish they would say more. They give only a few hints. But you will learn much by a careful use of the index and table of contents of this book.

CHAPTER 7

Functional Forms: Proclamation

As surely as God is faithful, our word to you has not been Yes and No. For the Son of God, Jesus Christ, whom we preached among you, Silvanus and Timothy and I, was not Yes and No; but in him it is always Yes. For all the promises of God find their Yes in him.

II Corinthians 1:18-20.

What he (Paul) says is this: "The promise of my coming was my own and I gave that promise from my self; but the preaching is not my own, nor of man, but of God, and what is of God it is impossible should lie." "Mistrust not then what is from Him, for there is nothing of man in it. . . ." And first indeed he contends for the articles of the faith, and the word concerning Christ, saying, "My word" and my preaching "has not been Yes and No"; next, for the promises, "for how many soever be the promises of God, in him it is always Yes."

Chrysostom.[1]

Before we can go further in our study of the details of sermonic design, we must stop to consider the chief purposes of preaching. Several times already we have had to distinguish between a true sermon and other forms of discourse, between the gospel and moral-religious thought. The distinction became sharp in the preceding chapter. In subsequent stages it will influence our estimate of all forms, for form has no existence apart from substance, and in preaching no form is good which does not perform a proper function.

A functional form is a form taken by a thing the better to accomplish its purpose. In our day, the concept of functional form has taken on new importance, has been affirmed as the dominant principle of good design. There can be no doubt that in creative hands it has been fruitful. Witness the objects in a contemporary kitchen, bathroom, or living-room, as compared with similar objects of thirty years ago. Witness the new as compared with old automobile bodies, or the new public school buildings,

Homily 3 on the passage above from II Corinthians. *Nicene and Post-Nicene Fathers*, XII, p. 289.

factories, and grocery stores. New designs demonstrate the soundness of the assumption that a thing to be beautiful requires no added ornamentation, no imposed esthetic pattern, but requires only that it frankly be itself and do its work with simple strength and grace.

Unfortunately, the principle is not always in creative hands, and what designers work with is not always functional form. "The fullest possible statement of the subject with strictest economy of means," someone has put it, and that is functional form in the true sense. But functional-*ism* as a style, a new style distinct from all older styles, is a different matter entirely. That is no longer functional form, is no longer "form following function." Rather it is form following a new style, and we are back again where we started, in the old grooves we were trying to get out of. If a thing is made to look "functional" or "modernistic" or even "modern," it becomes as deadly an imitation as if it were made to look Georgian or Gothic. And so it is with poems, music, plays, sermons. Modernity in art or in preaching is no insurance against the sentimental and the meretricious.

The functional form of a sermon is the form that sermon takes the better to accomplish the definite purpose for which it is preached. More correctly, it is that form which almost automatically results from the intention to accomplish a given purpose. To an incalculable extent form does follow function in preaching. That is, preaching takes the different forms it takes in our day as a result of many felt but often unclarified purposes, not conscious or deliberate purposes.

The forms of which we are speaking in this chapter are not styles of preaching like the new styles in furniture which the salesman is trying to sell. They are forms resulting from the most important among the recognized purposes of preaching.

What is the function of preaching, or what are the most important among its functions? This book cannot undertake a comprehensive discussion of that question. But it is impossible to give the most elementary answer without looking deep into the question.

I must assume that the student of preaching in the middle of the twentieth century knows that he has to preach in the intellectual and cultural climate of his day, knows that climate to have changed radically in the last forty years, knows that a changed and tragic outlook on mankind and history makes the romantic Victorian optimism strangely irrelevant, and calls for a rethinking of the very purpose of preaching. The student must further be credited with knowing the light a revived and deepened theology throws upon the human situation.

In some ways our world of 1956 is farther removed from the world of 1910 than it is from the world of 1500. As an example, vivid but not unique, I submit a sermon from the early 1920s.

Only thirty years ago, in the aftermath of the First World War, a famous American preached and published a sermon under the title "There Go the Ships," a quotation from Psalm 104:26. It is a paean in praise of ships, ships that have carried liberty and modern democracy—Paul from Troy to Philippi, Augustine as a missionary to England, Columbus to America, the Pilgrims to Plymouth Rock, Carey to India, and battleships and merchant ships to make the world safe for democracy in the First World War. Finally and climactically, there go the ships of war to be destroyed in the agreement to disarm and end war. (It was happening then, under Harding. The sermon was nothing if not "timely.") This sermon said that hate and jealousy sank with those ships, that hate was dead, that there was no longer any room in the world for a prophet of evil, that the voices of pessimists were like the low growling of thunder after the storm is over. The last sentence of the sermon ended, of course, with the lyrical cadence of Tennyson's "Locksley Hall": "The Parliament of man, the Federation of the world."

This mood seems more strange to us, farther away from us, than Calvin or Luther, than John Donne or Bernard of Clairvaux, than Augustine or the Apostle Paul. The sermon breathes that optimistic humanism which believes that mankind is free because men ought to be free, believes that the human venture is inevitably moving toward a perfect society because that is where it could go and ought to go—since nature, or God, or both, intended man for a perfect society, there will surely be one soon. This preacher sees man as enslaved only because he does not know what freedom is or does not will to be free. He believes that since man is the maker of his own slavery he can, by knowing and willing freedom, become the maker and master of his own destiny. He believes that mankind is certain to make its destiny glorious. This is the optimism that sings in "Locksley Hall."

In contrast to this mood is not only Christian theology, but contemporary humanism itself. The secular humanism of our day is not optimistic but tragic. It sees no purpose in the natural universe, but only blind indifference to all human desires and hopes. It sees no Spirit kindred to man's spirit above him. Man is alone, unaided, friendless, in a nature that knows him not, whose pitiless mechanism seems hostile to everything men cherish. The human spirit makes itself noble by the courage with which it hews its ideals out of intractable circumstance and holds them in the face of certain ultimate extinction. This humanism has no "Locksley Hall" to quote, but its prose at its best sounds like the chorus of a Greek tragedy. To many of our contemporaries it is more movingly real than most preaching.

"Locksley Hall" was published in 1843, before Darwin and long before Freud. Nevertheless, it voiced an evolutionary optimism much older than itself, which is by no means dead, though rudely shaken by the events of the twentieth century. However, in that same decade, the 1840's, there were other voices that today sound more grimly prophetic, voices speaking of human bondage, not of freedom. It was in this decade that Henry David Thoreau from Walden Pond looked at the comparatively placid life of his New England neighbors and said:

I have travelled a good deal in Concord; and everywhere, in shops, and offices, and fields, the inhabitants have appeared to me to be doing penance in a thousand remarkable ways. . . . I see young men, my townsmen, whose misfortune it is to have inherited farms, houses, barns, cattle, and farming tools; for these are more easily acquired than got rid of. Better if they had been born in the open pasture and suckled by a wolf, that they might have seen with clearer eyes what field they were called to labor in. Who made them serfs of the soil? Why should they eat their sixty acres, when man is condemned to eat only his peck of dirt? . . . I sometimes wonder that we can be so frivolous, I may almost say, as to attend to the gross but somewhat foreign form of servitude called Negro Slavery, there are so many keen and subtle masters that enslave both North and South. It is hard to have a Southern overseer; it is worse to have a Northern one; but worst of all when you are the slavedriver of yourself.

It was in this same decade that Karl Marx and Friedrich Engels wrote and published the *Communist Manifesto,* with its portentous words, "The proletarians have nothing to lose but their chains."

The optimistic diagnosis of the human condition captured the churches and the preachers, especially those of America. The "social gospel" was one form of it, the "new theology' was another. On the whole, this preaching was an apology for man, whereas Christianity calls for a radical change in man. On the whole, its faith centered in man, whereas Christianity centers its faith in God alone and declares that he only is to be trusted. In this preaching "religion," like the Bible, was commended as a technique by which a man can become master of his life and fate, whereas Christianity says that the one thing man can never be allowed to do in God's universe is to become the master and maker of his own life, by any means whatsoever.

In using the past tense, I do not intend to suggest that evolutionary optimism is dead. But from the destructive madness of our century, one good at least has come: that we can see more clearly, if we will, the demonic forces at work in us as individuals and as groups and as nations, the sin and death from which we can in no wise set ourselves free. We can see that although we might be free and blest by trusting in God—since he would have us free and blest—it is far more likely that in further defiance of him we shall destroy ourselves than that we shall finally hear and obey him. We can see more clearly, if we will, the precarious thread by which we hang.

The functions of preaching cannot be intelligently stated in any smaller context than this. The answer of historical Christianity is clear; there need be no doubt what it is. It has pleased God, who somehow unaccountably loves mankind, to save men, to save the race from self-destruction if men will let themselves be saved, or, if they will not, still to save out of the destruction as many as will acknowledge and trust him. Since by "wisdom" men neither know him nor their own safety, it has pleased God to save them by his own wisdom, which looks to men like foolishness, the "foolishness" of what he commands men to preach: Jesus Christ and him crucified.

As Christian theology sees it, the crucifixion of Christ is humanity's attempt to destroy God, and no thanks are due humanity that it did not succeed. The cross is the place where the Parent stands for the children's sake to absorb into himself their all-destroying fury. The cross is a point chosen in time and space where all the evil in time and space—every shred of which is a defiance of God—can be concentrated into one visible decisive action against him. The cross is the wisdom of God to choose this point, to make this attempt manifest, and to defeat it. The cross is the power of God to absorb the ignorant blind rage of humanity into himself and avert its deadly consequences.

(For the identity of the person who now interrupts me, see page 49. For the reason why I let him speak, see page 28.)

BILL HAMARTOLOS: Your "ignorant blind rage" is pretentious, I think.

AUTHOR: "Sneaking malice" then.

BILL: That's better.

AUTHOR: The ignorant blind rage and the sneaking malice that attempt to dethrone and destroy God are attempts to destroy mankind as well, and they succeed in destroying men.

BILL: No fooling! Is that a Christian view?

AUTHOR: Yes.

BILL: Could you document it?

AUTHOR: Yes.

BILL: You could never guess it from what you hear in church.

AUTHOR: That's too bad, if it's so.

BILL: It touches me off, starts me speculating.

AUTHOR: What about?

BILL: About the increasing concentration of power in the hands of a single individual.

AUTHOR: Let's have it.

BILL: Ahead of us, perhaps very soon, there is coming another point of time and place when power to destroy the whole human race will be in a single person's hands. One man before a switch or lever can act to obliterate a race he could neither create nor preserve. Is there any good reason to doubt that somebody will throw that switch?

AUTHOR: I'm afraid not.

BILL: Then for the third time the fate of all living things and all unborn generations to come will be decided by the act of one.

AUTHOR: Third time?

BILL: The first was in the Garden of Eden, remember?

AUTHOR: Of course—the first Adam.

BILL: Thanks for reminding me of the phrase. Yes, in that moment a race that is sure its first Adam could not sin for all, a race that is sure its second Adam could not die for all—that race will perish utterly by the act of its last Adam, and so end as it began.

AUTHOR: There would be a sort of poetic justice in it, you mean?

BILL: There will be a delightful irony.

AUTHOR: A ghastly irony!

BILL: It's delicious! "He that sitteth in the heavens shall laugh; the Lord will have them in derision."

AUTHOR: If he were like us, he might laugh.

BILL: I expect a wry smile at least.

The nature and purposes of preaching have been subjected to a critical reappraisal in the first half of the twentieth century. It began and acquired force first in Europe. It arose within the church itself, is the church's own re-examination of its message and the manner of its publication.

Such a re-examination was an inevitable consequence of the church's experience in times of confusion, oppression, resistance, and war. Christian leaders in Europe have reported that in the times of supreme testing the church had to learn again something it had forgotten: how to read, preach, and hear the Word as God's Word. Preaching had been only a kind of religious discourse, a "sacred oratory." One of them said, "We found we had only been presenting .considerations about the gospel. We had not been presenting the gospel itself as God's message." The church, they said, had been only practicing a religion; they had to learn again to live, actually to exist from day to day, by God's Word through faith. The Word was all they had left. They did live by it, and it did not fail them. And only when everything else was gone did they learn how to preach it.

This reappraisal of the nature and purposes of preaching has moved principally through two channels: a revitalized theology, and intensive biblical studies, especially studies in the New Testament.

The impact of Karl Barth and his group reached America with the publication of Barth's *The Word of God and the Word of Man* in 1928. Barth has said that his whole theological study began as a marginal note on preaching. All the theologians who have followed Barth, and likewise all his opponents, have assumed that one chief function of theology is to bring the church's preaching under critical scrutiny.

One result of New Testament scholarship has been a sharp distinction between the proclamation of the gospel and moral and religious teaching or exhortation. C. H. Dodd's *The Apostolic Preaching*, first published in America in 1937, produced something like a sensation in homiletical circles. Dodd said that early Christians would not recognize as proclamation of the gospel much of the talk heard in our pulpits. He said that preaching in the New

Testament sense was not the same thing as delivering moral instruction or exhortation. He reminded preachers that, "While the church was concerned to hand on the teaching of the Lord, it was not by this that it made converts. It was by *kerygma,* says Paul, not by *didache,* that it pleased God to save men." [2]

It is necessary to state at once that, while this distinction between *kerygma* and *didache* is true as regards the New Testament, and while preachers cannot afford to overlook it, yet insistence on the distinction in homiletical writings since 1937 has produced not only some gain but also considerable confusion. It is true that only proclamation of the gospel is called preaching in the New Testament. It is true that the New Testament writings point to this *kerygma* alone as the means by which God is pleased to convert and save men. But books and lectures on preaching have sometimes implied that, in consequence of these facts, no preaching is legitimate in the church's public ministry in our day except that which meets the New Testament test of *kerygma,* both in content and in form.

This conclusion does not follow, for several reasons. The first has to do with the very word *preaching.* In the New Testament this word meant only the proclamation of the gospel in its technical and therefore restricted sense, while *teaching* and *exhortation* were used to designate other legitimate forms of speech used in the church's ministry. Teaching and exhortation were not called preaching, but they were used in the New Testament church, and they were considered both legitimate and necessary. With us, however, the word *preaching* is not so restricted. It is used to cover all forms of speech in the public ministry of the church, and in that ministry proper teaching and exhortation are of course included.

In the second place, the ministry of the Word has other purposes in addition to that of converting non-Christian persons into Christians. After becoming Christians, they still need to grow in knowledge, in faith, and in practice. They need to be built up in their

[2] C. H. Dodd, *The Apostolic Preaching* (Chicago: Willet, 1937), p. 8.

lives with Christ and one another. If the church in New Testament times understood that converts are made by *kerygma,* it understood as clearly that Christians are equipped and sustained by Christian *didache.*

In the third place, the congregation faced by the preacher in our day differs from the assembly of Christians in New Testament times. We need not idealize the early church to understand how different it would be to speak to a small, compact, and perhaps secret group in which every person present was a believer and confessor of Christ—and every one knew it might easily mean death to be a confessor. To such a group a man would not speak of Christ in the same way as he would speak to a congregation containing not only believers but half-believers, nominal adherents, indifferent persons, and unbelievers.

If the New Testament refers to preaching, in its technical sense, as something ordinarily done in contact with people outside the church rather than in the assemblies of the church itself, the reason is found in the rather special character of the Christian assembly. If the New Testament commonly uses the words *teaching* and *exhortation,* rather than *preaching,* to designate forms of speaking within the assembly of believers, it does not thereby assign them a lower place than preaching, but it does indicate that *kerygma* and *didache* have different functions to perform in the total ministry of the Word.

At any rate, the student of preaching in our day should be aware that the work and message of the preacher have to face not only the judgment of an indifferent and unbelieving society outside the church, but also within the church the critical judgment of biblical scholars and theologians. The New Testament's distinction between different forms and functions of speech is a fact, and the conscientious preacher must come to grips with it.

PROCLAMATION

We must begin with proclamation, which in the New Testament is the only form of speech that is called preaching. Preaching is

always proclamation, *kērugma* being the substance of the proclamation, and *kērussein* being the act of proclaiming it, or publishing it, or crying it aloud as the herald, the *kērux,* announces whatever the king gives him to proclaim. These terms are so restricted
and so exact in their meaning as to be technical terms in the New
Testament.

Preaching in its technical New Testament sense includes the
substance communicated. A man does not merely "preach." He
preaches the King's message. Preaching has no existence apart
from the thing preached.

In the New Testament's own phrases, a man preaches "the
gospel," the good news. He preaches "the gospel of God," or
"the gospel of the kingdom," or simply "the kingdom." He
preaches "the gospel of Christ." He preaches "Christ crucified,"
or "Christ raised from the dead," or "Christ as the one ordained
of God to be judge of the living and the dead," or "Christ in you
the hope of glory," or he preaches simply "Christ." He preaches
"the acceptable year of the Lord," preaches "release to the
captives," preaches "repentance and forgiveness of sins." He
preaches "this gospel."

So all important is the content of preaching, and so specifically
is it identified as "this gospel," that a second technical term com-
bines both content and act of speaking it in one Greek word,
euaggelizein, to "preach-the-gospel," to proclaim the good news as
a messenger announces the king's proclamation. The word is used
more than seventy times in the New Testament and always with
this exact meaning.

About the content of this gospel there was no uncertainty or
difference of opinion. The New Testament reflects differences
about the life and practice of believers, about theological and
religious questions, but not about the substantial content of the
gospel. The phrases quoted above are not meant to describe the
full content of the *kerygma.* That is a task for biblical and
systematic theology. A book on preaching cannot describe it
adequately.

The gospel is the news of God's redemptive action in Jesus Christ our Lord, revealing God's love toward men and his purpose in history, manifesting at once his judgment and his mercy, furnishing a new basis for the relation between men and God—compassion, forgiveness, unmerited favor and help—and calling into being a reconstituted humanity joined with Christ and living no longer by its biological possibilities but by participation in Christ's life.

Stated thus—and its import cannot be stated in lesser terms than these—this gospel is obviously the whole of the Christian faith. When Christians teach, they will not teach some other thing than this gospel. When they exhort, the exhortation will not rest on lower grounds than this. For a Christian, nothing in heaven or earth can be greater than this, and nothing in heaven or earth can be understood apart from this. Christian theology will deal with this gospel, not with some greater or different subjects. Christian duty, ethics, can properly be related to nothing but this gospel. The common day-to-day existence can have no meaning except the meaning it has in the light of this gospel.

This is to say that the New Testament recognizes no difference between preaching and teaching, so far as content is concerned. The difference is only in the form this message takes in proclamation. Preaching in the New Testament sense takes a characteristic form, the form of official announcement, proclamation of God's action and offer, by the mouth of a chosen human messenger.

The word for *messenger* and that for *angel* is the same, *aggelos*. The delivery of God's message makes both an angel and a preacher. It makes a prophet too. Thus the apostolic church saw the gospel, the good news, the *eu-aggelion,* as a fulfilment of prophecy, and saw its preaching as a continuation of the prophet's work. The man-who-preaches-the-gospel, the *euaggelistes,* is a messenger (angel) of good news from God to the people God is addressing.

In this form of communication, the Sender of the message comes first in importance, and after him the substance of the message. Next in importance are the people to whom the message is addressed. The preacher comes fourth in importance. Rather, the preacher has no importance other than as an instrument, but he has a great importance as an instrument.

The form of proclamation is a form following function. The gospel message takes the form of proclamation because it is sent for a definite purpose to people in a definite condition. The gospel is not broadcast on the impersonal air, but is personally addressed to persons. In the New Testament's own phrases, the gospel is the "good news of great joy" from God to "the poor, the captives, the blind, the oppressed," to "those who are far off and to those who are near," to "those who sit in darkness and the shadow of death," to "those who are dead in trespasses and in sins," to "every creature," to "you," to "you and to your children and to all that are far off, every one whom the Lord our God calls to him."

Equally important is the purpose for which the gospel is sent. It is sent to those who have not heard of God's redemptive action in Christ. That is why the proclamation to them must take the form of announcement, first of all, for if it were not announced, it could never be known. The good news is sent to those who are alienated from God and are wandering each in his own way. That is why its proclamation to them must take the form of a call—not the messenger's call to God, but the call of God to the wanderer to return and believe the gospel. If the gospel does not take the form of God's own call by the mouth of his messenger, the wanderer will not understand that it is God who calls him and to whom he must answer.

The good news is sent to those who are, as the apostle puts it, "dead in trespasses and sins." That is why its proclamation to them must take the form of an offer of life—not merely the messenger's offer in God's name, but God's offer made directly and personally to the hearer, an offer of life from the Source of life. If the proclamation does not take the form of an offer which God seriously means, the hearer will not have the courage to embrace it wholeheartedly.

The good news is sent to those who are without God and without hope in the world, who are either in despair of themselves or betrayed by trust in themselves. That is why its proclamation to them must take the form of promise—not a promise concerning God, but a promise made by God, a promise of forgiveness and help, of liberation and joy, of hope and of glory. If the gospel does not take the form of God's own promise and pledge, the hearer will not be won to trust that promise and act upon it with the full, confident commitment which is faith.

Thus the proclamation of the gospel is a form of speech which results from the nature of the gospel as God's own Word and from the purpose of the gospel to reach and reclaim the lost. It takes the form of an announcement that waits to be heard and believed, a direct call from God to be answered, a personal offer to be embraced, a personal promise to be trusted and acted upon. It takes this form the better to serve as the channel of a personal transaction between God and the soul of the hearer, a transaction that creates a new life in Christ on a new basis furnished by God's redemptive action in Christ.

Because the gospel is this personal word of God to men, the apostolic church recognized it as the power of God and the wisdom of God, "the power of God for salvation to every one who has faith." Paul could remind the Corinthian Christians that he was their only human father because, when he preached the gospel to them, he had begotten them in Christ. It was through the proclamation of this gospel, by its power and by no other means, that the church came into being, that men were converted, were "turned to God," were "born again of the Spirit," "put on Christ" in baptism, became "a new creation" in Christ, died and were buried with Christ and rose with him "in the power of his resurrection," were "delivered from the dominion of darkness and transferred into the kingdom of his beloved Son."

According to the evidence, the church began with only a command to preach and witness to this gospel, without any clear theory of its power, and with no thought of using the gospel as a technique for success. When the account of Jesus' command reaches us, it is already a command to preach the gospel to all men everywhere, without distinction of race or background. But apparently Christians had to learn what the gospel could do by seeing what it did. They evidently did not expect the results it accomplished, had not planned for the conversions it effected, and had to learn how to handle its converts, especially its Gentile converts, after they had them.

What happened when Peter preached on the day of Pentecost (Acts 2) ought to have prepared them, it seems. But that account can mislead a modern reader. In spite of the melodious wonder in this catalog of nations, all these people were Jews or proselytes or devout sympathizers. Besides, these people were present by accident or by their own choice. They were not invited, and the Christians had not gone to them.

A sense of wonder and unexpectedness is in all the narratives, as if something is happening which the Christians never planned, which gave them joy but also created perplexing situations. There is a sort of breathless surprise in the account of Philip's being sent by immediate divine intervention to preach in the Ethiopian eunuch's chariot, followed by the eunuch's conversion and baptism (Acts 8).

When Philip proclaimed the Christ to the people of Samaria (Acts 8), the result was a spilling over, a break in church order, including some apparent irregularity in Philip's baptism, which it took a delegation of apostles from Jerusalem to repair. Everywhere, the gospel worked too fast for the church. The Gentile church at Antioch (Acts 11:19-30), and afterwards in Asia Minor and Europe, was a fact accomplished by the preached gospel long before a theological basis could be shown for it even by Paul. The problem of coexistence was never really solved; it only subsided in the disappearance of the Jewish church.

Peter's experience at the house of Cornelius the Gentile (Acts 10) is the most vivid demonstration that when the gospel is proclaimed it does its own work far beyond the expectation and for that matter beyond the intention of the preacher. Deliberately to go to

Cornelius' house, even on invitation, was a thing so irregular, so contrary to good ecclesiastical order, that it took two visions, two angels, and the voice of God's Spirit himself to get Christ's all-too-human angel into Cornelius' house at all.

When Peter, finally there, begins to speak, his introduction, saying that he now sees God is not partial, sounds like a belated if not a somewhat reluctant admission. His sermon is strictly functional, its function being to announce what God has done, to issue God's call, tender his offer, convey his promise. All this it does with the greatest economy of means.

After the introduction in verses 34-35, all the rest except the last verse (43) is simple announcement. He says God sent the word of peace to Israel by Jesus Christ who is Lord of all; that God anointed Jesus with the Holy Spirit and power; that Jesus went about doing good and healing those oppressed by the devil because God was with him; that Peter and the others witnessed this; that, when men crucified Jesus, God raised him up; that God showed Jesus to chosen witnesses who ate and drank with him after he rose; that God commanded these witnesses to preach Christ as the one ordained to be Judge of the living and the dead. All this Peter simply announces as something God has done without consulting anybody, without human sanction or approval.

The call, offer, and promise begin in the last verse: "To him all the prophets bear witness [further announcement] that every one who believes in him receives forgiveness of sins through his name." But the sermon was never finished. It was interrupted when the Holy Spirit fell on all who heard the Word, to Peter's surprise, and to the amazement of the Jewish Christians who had come with Peter. Back in Jerusalem, it required a full and meticulous report to square Peter with his colleagues, and every one of the visions and angels was needed.

By no modern standard could this sermon of Peter's, judging by this brief account of it, be called a great speech or even a skilful speech. It employs no oratorical techniques whatever. It advances no arguments. It furnishes no illustrations. It uses no psychology.

It describes no need of the listeners, defines no problem, makes no appeal to motives or emotions. It has no sort of salesmanship in it. It uses no devices to secure or hold interest, to impress, or to charm. It does, however, proclaim the basic points of the *kerygma*. It is functional; it preaches the gospel.

If the young preacher wants to see what the proclamation of the gospel is in its basic essentials, if he wants to see the difference between preaching the gospel and much of the pulpit talk to which he is accustomed, he can see it here. This is the kind of preaching, done by apostles and by private Christians, that brought the church into existence and spread it over the Roman Empire. It was not the act of speaking that did it. It was God at work in the gospel.

This is not saying that our proclamation of the gospel should be as bare as the accounts of the sermons in Acts. We cannot suppose that these accounts give more than the basic assertions of the preacher. Nevertheless, there is always danger that a form of speech which goes beyond function will cloud the Source and confuse the view of the gospel's power.

This, too, the apostles knew quite well. Paul had it in mind when he told the Corinthians why he had not come proclaiming the testimony of God to them in lofty words or wisdom, why his speech and message were not in plausible words, why he decided to know nothing but Christ crucified, namely, in order that the result of his message might be a "demonstration of the Spirit and power, that your faith might not rest in the wisdom of men but in the power of God" (I Corinthians 2:1-5). There is always danger that human speech may get in God's way and become itself the object of attention.

Looked at thus from the point of view of historical Christianity, there is a compelling reason why the church's minister must know the difference between the proclamation of the gospel and all other forms of religious discourse. As the power of God working in the gospel alone could bring the church into existence, so the gospel alone can keep it in existence. The church is created person by person, and it takes a miracle of grace, an act of God, to transform and to recreate every single one of those persons, and to graft him as a member into the body of Christ. And nothing but the gospel has power to do this.

If the church were only a human institution, its leaders could recruit it by human teaching, persuasion, sales promotion, and propaganda. When these means are employed, they do produce just that: a human institution. And the prosperous condition of such an institution often makes us forget how dismally it fails to exemplify the one holy catholic and apostolic church. But if the church is a reconstituted humanity, a newly created community of Christ's love, then its continuance on earth depends on a constant miracle of grace, a person-by-person recreation by the power of God at work in the gospel. The church is where the gospel is preached; that is the first sign of its presence. Where the gospel is not preached, there may still be a flourishing institution. Only one thing cannot possibly be where the gospel is not preached; the church cannot be there.

I have dealt at some length with this first of the functional forms, proclamation, because it is for obvious reasons the only form of discourse known as true preaching in the apostolic church. I cannot leave it without one further word.

Throughout its history, Christian preaching at its best has had this proclamation of the gospel as its dominant note. It has been regarded functionally too, though that word was not used. I mean that the best preaching has tried to announce what God has done, to issue the call, tender the offer, convey the promise, with the confident hope that the preaching would be used by the Holy Spirit and that the results would follow. In an older day the terms used to describe those results were repentance, confession, conversion, regeneration, faith, justification, sanctification, and so on. The preacher preached with an eye to these results.

It may perhaps shock the reader, when he examines the preaching of our day, to see how little of it calls for such a radical transformation of people, or reflects the possibility or expectation that

such a change may take place. Yet until recently the preaching of
the gospel was expected to result in changed people, and the popular notion that they did not need to be changed, as common then
as it is now, was no deterrent.

Reaction against a mistaken emphasis on sudden emotional conversion is understandable, but it passes comprehension that the
servant of God's Word should no longer expect it to accomplish
that purpose for which God sends it forth, should despair of it
and turn to other things.

The condition of human beings in our day in no way warrants
the assumption that they need no revolutionary change but only
a visit to the religious beauty parlor. A vitalized and realistic
theology sanctions no hope for people short of a total transformation by which a rebellious and self-centered person becomes God-
centered. Psychology, with its dark picture of human brokenness,
neurosis, inner conflict, divided and disintegrated selves, its call
for a complete reorientation and reintegration of personality, is no
less radical. Theology prefers a new vocabulary: despair, encounter, decision, commitment, and so on. The words do not matter, neither the old nor the new, if the thing is understood. The
words have changed; the human condition is the same.

Thus if historical Christianity is right, then people in whom no
act of God is taking place are not Christians; a person does not
recreate himself by taking up religion as a hobby. Nothing and
no one but God working in the gospel can make Christians. If
the gospel is not preached, it cannot be heard. If the gospel is not
heard, we need not expect our so-called churches to be more than
human institutions, clubs of religious-minded people; we cannot
hope that they will contain a reconstituted humanity, the community of Christ's love.

Finally, however—and this is the crux of our frustration—we
cannot adopt and employ the gospel as a success measure. The
gospel will not submit to becoming the preacher's new hobby, his
secret magic formula for effectiveness. We cannot copy the form
of gospel proclamation as a mere means of making our churches

thrive. We cannot proclaim the good news from God unless we believe it for its own sake alone.

A PROCLAMATION OF THE GOSPEL
Acts 2:14-39
"This is [the fulfilment of] what was spoken."

(It is seen in the outpoured Spirit which Joel prophesied.)

"And in the last days it shall be, God declares, that I will pour out my Spirit upon all flesh, and your sons and your daughters shall prophesy, and your young men shall see visions, and your old men shall dream dreams; yea, and on my menservants and my maidservants in those days I will pour out my Spirit; and they shall prophesy. And I will show wonders in the heaven above and signs on the earth beneath, blood, and fire, and vapor of smoke; the sun shall be turned into darkness and the moon into blood, before the day of the Lord comes, the great and manifest day. And it shall be that whoever calls on the name of the Lord shall be saved."

(It is seen in the life and death of Jesus according to God's plan.)

"Men of Israel, hear these words: Jesus of Nazareth, a man attested to you by God with mighty works and wonders and signs which God did through him in your midst, as you yourselves know—this Jesus, delivered up according to the definite plan and foreknowledge of God, you crucified and killed by the hands of lawless men."

(It is seen in Jesus' resurrection, prophesied by David, accomplished by God.)

"But God raised him up, having loosed the pangs of death, because it was not possible for him to be held by it. For David says concerning him, 'I saw the Lord always before me, for he is at my right hand that I may not be shaken; therefore my heart was glad, and my tongue rejoiced; moreover my flesh will dwell in hope. For thou wilt not abandon my soul to Hades, nor let thy Holy One see corruption. Thou hast made known to me the ways of life; thou wilt make me full of gladness with thy presence.'

"Brethren, I may say to you confidently of the patriarch David that he both died and was buried, and his tomb is with us to this day. Being therefore a prophet, and knowing that God had sworn with an oath to him that he would set one of his descendants upon his throne, he foresaw and spoke of the resurrection of the Christ, that he was not abandoned to Hades, nor did his flesh see corruption. This Jesus God raised up, and of that we all are witnesses."

(It is seen in Jesus' exaltation to lordship, in his pouring out the Spirit.)

"Being therefore exalted at the right hand of God, and having received from the Father the promise of the Holy Spirit, he has poured out this which you see and hear. For David did not ascend into the heavens, but he himself says, 'The Lord said to my Lord, Sit at my right hand, till I make thy enemies a stool for thy feet.'

"Let all the house of Israel therefore know assuredly that God has made him both Lord and Christ, this Jesus whom you crucified."

(It is God's call to you to repent and believe.)

"Repent, and be baptized every one of you in the name of Jesus Christ for the forgiveness of your sins; and you shall receive the gift of the Holy Spirit. For the promise is to you and to your children and to all that are far off, every one whom the Lord our God calls to him."

SUGGESTIONS

If you were born after 1930, it will not be easy for you to realize the change in theological climate since the 1920's. You cannot adjust to it, of course, by a little additional reading in connection with this chapter. Dodd's words, quoted on page 106 and written before the churches' ordeal in the last war, shocked homileticians who had not studied Barth, Gogarten, Brunner, Niebuhr, Kierkegaard, Forsyth, or other important theological writers.

If you have not yet found your way, study theological rather than homiletical books. If you have done this, I advise you to read Dodd's two books (36 and 37) and go on to trace *kerygma* through the best New Testament studies you know. Kantonen's (40) first chapter, "The Contemporary Theological Scene," is a useful survey, and the whole of his book should be read now. Add to it Farmer (22), a book that has had great and wholesome influence. If you have not read Nygren (46), read it now. The same suggestion applies to Thompson (49).

In any case it seems to me that a preacher in these times ought very calmly to contemplate the tragic possibility that in his lifetime the last day may come for that fashion of existence we think of as civilized life—to think of it without either hysteria or fear, and to ask what, if God shall permit that to happen, he wants his ministers to be saying in these last days.

But now I must try to take you further than it was Dodd's purpose to go. From the fact that nothing but proclamation of the *kerygma* was called preaching, you may infer that nothing else is legitimate in the pulpit. That is not correct. I hope you will see that proclamation is that one of the functional forms of gospel communication whose definite purpose was and is to reach unbelievers. In the assembly of believers other functional forms of gospel communication, though not called preaching, were nevertheless used and were, and are, not only legitimate but necessary. In the next chapter we must see what those other forms are.

CHAPTER 8

Functional Forms: Teaching and Therapy

> Unless spiritual knowledge and the Spirit himself speak through the preachers . . . the final result will be that everyone preaches his own whims, and instead of the gospel and its exposition we shall again have sermons on blue ducks.
>
> Martin Luther in *Deutsche Messe*, 1526.

> This is the way it has gone with preaching. . . . After the text of the Gospels is read, they take us to fairyland. One preaches from Aristotle and the heathen books, another from the papal decretals. One brings questions about his holy Order, another about blue ducks, another about hen's milk. . . . In short, this is the art in which nobody sticks to the text, from which people might have had the gospel.
>
> Luther in *Winkelmesse und Pfaffenweihe*, 1533.

The second functional form of communication recognized in the New Testament is teaching. The act is called *didaskein,* which means to instruct by means of discourse with others. It is a technical term used nearly a hundred times in the same sense, but it is restricted to no definite content.

Two nouns are used to designate the content, the first being *didachē,* simply that which is taught, or one person's teaching, whoever he may be and whatever he may teach. The second word, *didaskalia,* can also mean anything that is taught, but it seems more strongly to indicate consistent teaching according to some standard.

At different places in the New Testament, and especially in the Pastoral Epistles, both these nouns tend to become technical terms for Christian doctrine, theology, and ethics. Faith, the act of believing, sometimes becomes "the faith," the substance of things believed. We read of "good doctrine," "sound words," "sound teaching," "knowledge," "wisdom."

Teaching is not held in lower esteem than preaching in the New Testament church. According to the record, Jesus both preached the kingdom of God and taught concerning it, and we should not doubt that the evangelist means both when he says both. So Peter and Paul and all the rest both preached and taught. Teaching is included in every important listing of a minister's duties in the New Testament.

Teaching, like preaching, is done at God's command and in his name, with the full assurance that he works through it. The teacher, like the preacher, is qualified for his task by direct endowment of the Holy Spirit: teaching is by charismatic gift, like every other function in the body of Christ. Teaching no less than preaching has God for its author and supporter.

The fact is that in the New Testament's references to the Christian assembly the characteristic forms of speech are called teaching and prophecy rather than preaching. It is said that after Pentecost the believers "devoted themselves to the apostles' teaching (*didachē*) and fellowship, to the breaking of bread and the prayers," but nothing is said about preaching (Acts 2:42). Writing to the Roman church, which was not Pauline, the apostle mentions prophecy, service, teaching, exhortation, along with some nonverbal functions performed in the body of Christ, but does not include preaching (Romans 12:6-8). Paul gives a long list of charismatic functions in the Corinthian church (I Corinthians 12:8-10, 28-30). Prophets and teachers are there, and so are administrators and helpers, but again preachers and preaching are not mentioned. Only one such list, that in Ephesians (4:11), includes the evangelist.

As his title indicates, the first work of an apostle was to preach the gospel. Preaching was done at Pentecost when unbelievers came to see what was going on in the Christian assembly (Acts 2). Preaching was done in Solomon's Porch at the temple (Acts 3), before the Sanhedrin (Acts 4:5-12; 5:29-32; Acts 7), and in the eunuch's chariot (Acts 8:26-40). Preaching was consistently done in the synagogues where Christians, Jews, proselytes, and other interested persons worshiped together.

However, in the epistles of the New Testament, which were written to be read aloud in the assemblies of believers, the preach-

ing of the gospel is commonly mentioned as something they had
heard in time past. Thus Paul calls the Galatian Christians back
to the gospel which he had preached to them in the beginning,
which they had already received, and from which they are turning
to a different gospel (Galatians 1:6-9). Likewise he reminds the
Corinthians of the content of the gospel he had first preached to
them, which they had received, in which they already stood and
by which they are saved (I Corinthians 15:1-11). He draws his
teaching and his arguments from that gospel, but speaks of its
preaching to them as a fact accomplished in time past.

The epistles also refer frequently to the preaching of the gospel
as something being done in the present outside the Christian assembly, among the Gentiles, to Jews and Greeks. There, of course,
the Christian message takes the form of proclamation, announcement to those persons who either have not heard it or have not
received it as true, takes the form of call to those who have not
heeded nor answered, takes the form of offer to those who have
not embraced God's offer or moved to take up the option by
confessing Christ as Lord, takes the form of promise to those who
have not trusted or thrown themselves upon the promise of God.
Preaching takes this form because in this situation its function is
to make Christians of people who are not Christians.

Paul's sermon at Athens illustrates the distinctive forms we are
considering. More than any other reported sermon, perhaps, it
makes use of theological and philosophical discussion—teaching.
As a "new teaching" it was heard with true Athenian curiosity and
interest. But Paul did not stop with teaching. "What you worship
as unknown," he said, "this I proclaim to you." The thing which
produced mockery in most but belief in a few was his message
when it took the characteristic form of proclamation, of announcement and call and offer:

"The times of ignorance God overlooked, but now he commands all
men everywhere to repent, because he has fixed a day on which he
will judge the world in righteousness by a man whom he has appointed,
and of this he has given assurance to all men by raising him from the
dead" (Acts 17:16-31).

Christians did not preach one message and teach another. In the New Testament the *kerygma* is the content of both. Both deal with the action and Word of God, the call and promise of God in Christ. Both center in Christ, Christian ethics and theology no less than the Christian proclamation. The minister teaches the Christian tradition, "What you have received of me," and "what I have received" (Paul), "the word of God," "the way of God," "the way of Christ," "the things of the Lord," "the things concerning Jesus," "the truth as it is in Christ Jesus."

There is nevertheless a difference when this gospel is spoken of to an assembly of Christians. The New Testament epistles are letters to be read aloud in such groups. They are addressed to the understanding of those who are in Christ, and not to people in general. Here the characteristic discourse no longer centers in the proclamation of the gospel as good news waiting to be received. It is assumed that the listeners have already heard and believed the gospel. The apostle does not turn from the facts of the *kerygma* to other matters. He moves on into the implications of the gospel for believers, to building on the foundation of the gospel, to a *didachē* that has relevance only to believers.

It is hard for a modern person to feel the revolutionary character of the gospel as the early church felt it. The early Christians knew themselves to be living—jointly with one another and with Christ, in God—as a completely changed and reconstituted humanity, in an existence on an entirely new basis, in a new age which was at the same time a fulfilment of God's ancient purpose and promise. It was not that Christians simply thought of themselves as morally reformed; it was that they were newly created persons in a newly created world.

This new creation and new life took recognizable form in certain visible experiences. One was baptism, the cleansing of new generation, new begetting, new parentage, death and resurrection with Christ. In baptism they received the Holy Spirit, and must manifest his presence, every one of them (Acts 8:14-17). Another form was the communion loaf and cup, the given and risen body and the blood, the life, of Christ. In the communion they partook of Christ's life and immortality.

To the early Christians these and like experiences were not mere symbols of what God was doing to them. Nor were they magic means to bring God's action about, to get him to act. Such interpretations could arise only among later Christians who no longer felt themselves to be a reconstituted humanity, sharing a new existence on a new basis in a new age—all by the intervention, the direct action of God. The sacraments were not in themselves miraculous to the apostolic church. They were the visible manifestations of the new existence, itself the tremendous mystery.

The entrance on this new existence took place when one heard and believed the gospel. It was the action of God, a birth by water and the Spirit, and they did not have to understand it to make it happen. One does not have to understand his own birth, or consent to it, in order to be born.

Being in this new existence, however, the Christian needed to understand it as far as he was able. Teaching is needed in order to understand the meaning and the basis of his new existence, to explicate the content of the faith, to make his life conform to his faith. Far from thinking he is a morally reformed person, the new Christian will have to learn the pattern of a life that comports with the new existence. He will have to discipline himself, go into training and fight for that manner of life. The teaching belongs to the training in the new life.

A letter of Paul to one of the churches he has founded is an interesting example of this teaching. The *kerygma* is presupposed in everything he says, and nothing he says would make sense without it. The letter is roughly in two parts. The first part is teaching about the character of the new existence, its basis in God's action, its relation to his eternal purpose, its constitution in Christ, the new status it gives to those who are in it. The second part of the letter is ethical but never mere ethics. Rather it is teaching about a kind of life that conforms with the new existence.

There can be no doubt that in the ongoing life of the church, and in its public ministry in our day, teaching not only has a legitimate place, but also performs an indispensable function. The great Christian preachers have always been both heralds of the gospel and teachers. Indeed, while proclamation and teaching can easily be distinguished as types of discourse, in practice it is by no means easy to tell where one leaves off and the other begins.

The valid criticism of contemporary preaching by theologians and biblical scholars is not on the score of its form as teaching. The criticism is rather of the content of the teaching, that it is something far less than the full biblical message and often incompatible with that message. It seems to me that the case can be summed up in two points of danger which the conscientious preacher cannot afford to overlook.

First, there is danger that we may neglect the radical biblical message of Christianity and teach a moral and religious idealism alone as a religion, a way of life sufficient in itself, possible for all men and profitable for all. Secondly, there is danger that we may teach and commend ethical and religious conduct in such a way as to suggest that nothing more is needed, no radical change, no new existence such as the gospel promises.

The meaning and ethic of a new kind of existence can be relevant only to that existence. Without the new life, its meaning will seem nonsensical and its ethic impossible. Much worse, without the new life, one who hears teaching about the character and ethic of the new existence may suppose that he can recreate himself by mental gymnastic with the teaching about its character and by moral gymnastic with its ethic. There need be no surprise when he fails.

This is what has happened in Christian history. The congregation did not long continue to be composed exclusively of people who felt themselves already to be sharing a new existence with Christ, already to be inhabitants of a new city whose builder and maker is God. In the modern congregation, perhaps there are only a very few persons who believe that any miracle of God's grace has taken place in them, only a few who walk by faith, only a few in whose lives Christ is Lord indeed. In these, however few or many, the apostolic church is present in our modern congregation. For them, teaching is indispensable. Because of them, the pastoral discourse which takes the form of true Christian teaching is not only legitimate, but required.

But by far the greater number in our churches stand where the onlookers at Pentecost stood—and feel no wind, see no tongues of flame, and hear in no language "the mighty works of God." They hear the mighty works of man instead. They wait, that is, for the proclamation of the gospel, and are not ripe for Christian teaching. And outside the church doors, where the millions breed and die, the Lord's announcement is not made.

A great deal of preaching in our day continues to be not so much a proclamation of the gospel as a mental gymnastic with teaching about a new life that ought to be but is not, and a moral gymnastic with its ethic. The upshot is that preachers have become accomplices in men's attempt to do without God's offered new creation, and no longer expect or even wish for it.

The often-repeated injunction to preach for a verdict, a decision, shows that we know our conventional pulpit discussion of moral and religious questions is less than true preaching. The verdict and the decision we ought to preach for is itself that radical transformation of which we have been speaking: not a change of opinion but a change of purpose, not a new fashion of life but a new foundation for existence. If we call for nothing better than moral improvement, we shall get nothing better. If we wish for nothing better, if we believe in nothing better, we shall not even get that.

AN EXAMPLE OF TEACHING

And I will show you a still more excellent way.

If I speak in the tongues of men and of angels, but have not love, I am a noisy gong or a clanging cymbal. And if I have prophetic powers, and understand all mysteries and all knowledge, and if I have all faith, so as to remove mountains, but have not love, I am nothing. If I give away all I have, and if I deliver my body to be burned, but have not love, I gain nothing.

Love is patient and kind; love is not jealous or boastful; it is not arrogant or rude. Love does not insist on its own way; it is not irritable or resentful; it does not rejoice at wrong, but rejoices in the right. Love bears all things, believes all things, hopes all things, endures all things.

Love never ends; as for prophecy, it will pass away; as for tongues, they will cease; as for knowledge, it will pass away. For our knowledge is imperfect and our prophecy is imperfect; but when the perfect comes, the imperfect will pass away. When I was a child, I spoke like a child, I thought like a child, I reasoned like a child; when I became a man, I gave up childish ways. For now we see in a mirror dimly, but then face to face. Now I know in part; then I shall understand fully, even as I have been fully understood. So faith, hope, love abide, these three; but the greatest of these is love. (1 Corinthians 13)

THERAPY

A third functional form of discourse recognizable in the New Testament is speech for the purpose of effecting some improvement in the hearer, some change in his state or condition, mental, emotional, or religious.

Let us call it therapeutic speech. *Therapeuein* is a good New Testament word, meaning to serve or do service, to cure or restore to health. It is not used there to describe a function of speech. In homiletical literature the word oftenest used in this general sense is *exhortation,* but that word has to be reserved for one especially significant form of therapeutic speech.

In all forms of speech for improvement, the attention centers on the human listener as it does not to the same degree in preaching the gospel or in teaching the content of the faith. In both of these the first emphasis is on the Object of faith. The immediate concern of preaching is to broadcast the announcement. The immediate concern of teaching is to impart the truth of Christ. But the immediate concern of therapeutic speech is to remedy or improve the existing condition of the hearer.

There is no one word in the New Testament that covers all kinds of such speech. The word *paraklēsis* which includes its most important forms has no such exact technical meaning as the words for preaching and teaching have. It is used in different ways and has to be variously translated.

To perform the action is *parakalein,* whose native meaning is to summon, to call to one's side, as a friend or helper or advocate is called to the side of one in trouble or danger. The noun *paraklēsis* is also in its native meaning the act of summoning a helper. This meaning is not conveyed by our Latin word exhortation, and I know no English word that conveys it.

The helper summoned is a *paraklētos.* This is the Holy Spirit's title in the Gospel of John. He is the Paraclete, the Counselor, the Helper, the Advocate, not simply the Comforter. The meaning goes back to the Greek court of law, where one who had a case pending might, instead of pleading his own cause, call to his aid some honorable person who would stand behind him and compose the speech in his behalf. The Christian before the authorities is not to be anxious what he shall say, for it is not he who speaks but the Holy Spirit at his side as his Paraclete (Mark 13:11).

Thus Christian exhortation has its roots deep in the native meaning of these words. Their primary meaning suggests that exhortation is far more deeply rooted in the realities of the Christian gospel and teaching than we are accustomed to think. Exhortation is more than the practice of psychology, more than the exercise of the preacher's influence and powers of persuasion.

The New Testament does not always use these words in their original sense. The verb *parakalein* is often translated as *I exhort* or *beseech* or *appeal* in places where these deeper meanings must be understood. But the word sometimes means to beg or urge, appeal or entreat, encourage or strengthen, console or comfort.

In like manner, the meaning of the noun *paraklēsis* varies. In its highest sense exhortation can hardly mean less than calling the Lord to the believer's side for his counsel and help. It is unfortunate that the deeper meaning is dimmed if not lost in all translations: I exhort, I beseech, I appeal. It is worse that all these translations throw the weight of emphasis on the exhorter's urgency rather than on the Lord at one's side.

In other places *paraklēsis* means less exalted forms of incitation: simply appeal or persuasion, encouragement or consolation, or nothing more definite than a hortatory address.

Exhortation in all these forms is considered useful for all Christians. The apostles exhorted believers thus, and encouraged believers to exhort one another. It is a function needed in the Christian life. It does not imply that those exhorted are remiss or faulty. We get the feel of Christian exhortation in Paul's letters:

And indeed you do love all the brethren throughout Macedonia. But we *exhort* you, brethren, to do so more and more.
(I Thessalonians 4:10)

I *appeal* to you therefore, brethren, by the mercies of God, to present your bodies a living sacrifice. (Romans 12:1)

I thought it necessary to *urge* the brethren to go on to you before me.
(II Corinthians 9:5)

There are forms of speech other than exhortation which also have a necessary place in the ministry to believers. One is *paramutheomai,* speaking to encourage or console:

He who prophesies speaks to men for their upbuilding and encouragement and consolation [*oikodomēn kai paraklēsin kai paramuthian*].
(I Corinthians 14:3)

Another such word is *nouthetein,* to put in mind, to admonish. It ranges in meaning from instruction, its dominant significance, to something like warning:

Let the word of Christ dwell in you richly, as you teach and *admonish* one another in all wisdom, and as you sing psalms and hymns and spiritual songs with thankfulness in your hearts to God.
(Colossians 3:16)

But we beseech you, brethren, to respect those who labor among you and are over you in the Lord and *admonish* [instruct] you. . . .
(I Thessalonians 5:12)

Therefore be alert, remembering that for three years I did not cease night or day to *admonish* every one with tears. (Acts 20:31)

Him we proclaim, warning [training] every man and teaching every man in all wisdom, that we may present every man mature in Christ.
(Colossians 1:28)

In some passages the Revised Standard Version translates this word *nouthetein* as *to instruct,* its dominant sense. We may be sure that such instruction is more than imparting information. It is putting Christians in mind of the tremendous realities of the faith, the truths of the gospel:

> I myself am satisfied about you, my brethren, that you yourselves are full of goodness, filled with all knowledge, and able to *instruct* one another.   (Romans 15:14)
>
> Now these things happened to them as a warning, but they were written down for our *instruction,* upon whom the end of the ages has come.
>   (I Corinthians 10:11)
>
> Fathers, do not provoke your children to anger, but bring them up in the discipline and *instruction* of the Lord.   (Ephesians 6:4)

Two words are used in the New Testament to describe the good accomplished in the lives of Christians by these forms of therapeutic speech. One is *epistērizein,* to strengthen or confirm. The other is *oikodomein,* to build up or edify as an edifice is built.

The word *epistērizein* lets us see an important therapeutic function of speech in the church of the New Testament. In the Acts of the Apostles it is part of a formula describing visitations of the churches:

> And he [Paul] went through Syria and Cilicia strengthening [*epistēri-zōn*] the churches.   (Acts 15:41)
>
> They [Paul and Barnabas] returned to Lystra and to Iconium and to Antioch, strengthening [*epistērizontes*] the souls of the disciples, exhorting [*parakalountes*] them to continue in the faith, and saying. . . .
>   (Acts 14:21-22)
>
> And Judas and Silas, who were themselves prophets, exhorted [*parekalesan*] the brethren with many words and strengthened [*epestērixan*] them.   (Acts 15:32)

The second word, *oikodomeō,* is even more illuminating. In the Septuagint it is used to designate creative acts of God, and in the New Testament it is used to describe God's act in building the eternal city Christians seek, and in building the church on earth:

> We are fellow workmen for God; you are God's field, God's building [*oikodomē*].   (I Corinthians 3:9)

The word is used also of speech for improvement in the horizontal relation between believers:

Therefore encourage [*parakaleite*] one another and build one another up [*oikodomeite*], just as you are doing. (I Thessalonians 5:11)

He who speaks in a tongue edifies [*oikodomei*] himself, but he who prophesies edifies the church. . . . He who prophesies is greater than he who speaks in tongues, unless someone interprets, so that the church may be edified. (I Corinthians 14:4-5)

Let no evil talk come out of your mouths, but only such as is good for edifying [*pros oikodomēn*], as fits the occasion, that it may impart grace to those who hear. (Ephesians 4:29)

His gifts were that some should be apostles, some prophets, some evangelists, some pastors and teachers, for the equipment of the saints, for the work of the ministry, for building up [*eis oikodomēn*] the body of Christ. (Ephesians 4:11-12)

This form of Christian therapy might be called integration, not integration of personality within the individual, but integration of believers with one another into the one body, the one perfect life in Christ:

Christ Jesus himself being the chief cornerstone, in whom the whole structure [*oikodomé*] is joined together and grows up into a holy temple in the Lord; in whom you also are built into it for a dwelling place of God in the Spirit. (Ephesians 2:20-22)

Therapy, then, is clearly recognized as one function of discourse within the church. The best Christians needed it. There are also forms of speech used for curative or corrective purposes within the church. Christians believe themselves forgiven, but know they are imperfect and sinful. Exhortation and admonition must both become corrective wherever there is fault or remissness.

And we exhort you, brethren, *admonish* the idle, *encourage* the fainthearted, help the weak, be patient with them all. (I Thessalonians 5:14)

For we hear that some of you are living in idleness, mere busybodies, not doing any work. Now such persons we command and *exhort* in the Lord Jesus Christ to do their work in quietness and to earn their own living. (II Thessalonians 3:11-12)

If any one refuses to obey what we say in this letter . . . Do not look on him as an enemy, but warn him [*noutheteite*: instruct] as a brother. (II Thessalonians 3:14-15)

Moreover, there are forms of speech confined entirely to the function of correction. The most common is *elegchein,* to rebuke, reprove, expose, convict, confute. *Epitiman* and *epiplēssein* also mean to rebuke.

According to the evidence, rebuke has little place within the church in New Testament times. Rebuke of believers is not mentioned outside the Pastoral Epistles, and there it seems to be reserved for flagrant and intransigent wickedness.

Dialectic also makes a poor showing in the records of the church of the Apostles. The principal terms are the verb *dialegomai* and the noun *dialogismos,* whose meanings range from mere thinking and talking, through discussion, to argument, disputing, and quarreling.

Thus Paul did not preach till midnight at Troas (Acts 20:7-10), but talked (*dielegeto*) until the young Eutychus fell asleep and out of the window. Mankind, when they turned from God, became futile in their thinking (*dialogismois*) and their senseless minds were darkened (Romans 1:21). The disciples of Jesus discussed (*dielechthēsan*) with one another who was the greatest (Mark 9:34). Paul, at Corinth and Athens and everywhere he went, argued (*dielegeto*) from the Scriptures about Christ and the kingdom of God, but only in the synagogue or the hall of Tyranus, not in the Christian assembly.

In the Christian assembly, the weak in faith are to be welcomed, but not for *"disputes* over opinions" (Romans 14:1). In the Christian assembly, men are to lift up holy hands without anger or quarreling (*dialogismou,* I Timothy 2:8); everything is to be done without grumbling or questioning (*dialogismōn,* Philippians 2:14)—which does not mean without wanting to know why, but means without debating about it.

In the light of this all-too-brief report on the sources, it is evident that in the apostolic church this third functional form of speech (whatever it is called: therapy, exhortation, persuasion) has not only a legitimate but a necessary place in the public ministry. As early as the fifties of the first century, the function called exhortation, called healing and helping, was known in the Christian assembly at Corinth and at Rome. It was provided for by personal endowment of the same Spirit who endowed prophecy, teaching, speaking in tongues, interpretation—and love, the greatest of all the Spirit's gifts. Like all other functions, therapy was performed through persons "God has appointed in the church" for that purpose. Like preaching and teaching and the rest, it was an act of God performed through his servants.

There can be no doubt that in the ministry of the historical church, where "preaching" has come to include all functional forms of discourse, there is a place for therapeutic, hortatory, or persuasive speech. There is no question about that.

But there are other serious questions about it. The first is a question about where it stands in the experience of redemption, in relation to the gospel and teaching. Is it first, second, or third in sequence? Is it first, second, or third in power?

The second is a question of the extent to which it should be used in preaching. In relation to the gospel and teaching, what proportion of preaching should be exhortation and persuasion? Should it be first, second, or third in extent?

With respect to these two questions, the preacher faces serious dangers in our day. There is danger that the proclamation of the gospel may be displaced—danger that we shall not preach at all, but only teach, exhort, and persuade. In its benign form, this error may be nothing more than our faulty sense of proportion, or our overanxiousness to do good. In its malignant form it may be the blasphemy of thinking God is mistaken about men: that it does not require the gospel to save men, but only the right kind of teaching and persuasion.

Hardly less serious is the danger of a premature attempt at therapy. Nothing is more futile than an exhortation to persons who are not ready to act on it, nothing more hopeless than the attempt to reassure persons in a situation that does not justify reassurance. People in a condition of felt guilt and lostness cannot be comforted until the condition is changed. That is to say, the mere instruction, exhortation, admonition, persuasion, which form so large a portion of contemporary pulpit speaking, is largely fruitless because it is premature. The people to whom it is addressed are not ready to profit by it. A person who has not taken and will not take any of the basic steps toward becoming a Christian is not ripe for true Christian exhortation or any form of Christian therapy. Something much more radical is called for.

There is a third question: What motives should be appealed to in exhortation and persuasion? What kind of exhortation or appeal is proper to the Christian message?

It should be worth while to remind ourselves what motives the apostles appealed to in their exhortation. They are clear enough, and they are certainly illuminating. They reveal the motivation of that special kind of person called a Christian.

1. The apostles appealed to God, to motives centering in him:

> Be imitators of God, as beloved children.   (Ephesians 5:1)
> I appeal to you . . . by the mercies of God.   (Romans 12:1)
> If God so loved us, we also ought to love one another.
> (1 John 4:11)
> Do all to the glory of God.   (I Corinthians 10:31)
> We beseech and exhort you . . . that as you have learned from us how you ought to live and to please God . . . you do so more and more.   (I Thessalonians 4:1)
> We exhorted each one of you and encouraged you and charged you to lead a life worthy of God, who calls you into his own kingdom and glory.   (I Thessalonians 2:11-12)

2. The apostles appealed to motives centering in Christ:

> I appeal . . . by our Lord Jesus Christ, and by the love of the Spirit.   (Romans 15:30)
> I appeal . . . by the name of our Lord Jesus Christ.
> (I Corinthians 1:10)
> I entreat . . . by the meekness and gentleness of Christ.
> (II Corinthians 10:1)
> And walk in love, as Christ loved us and gave himself up for us, a fragrant offering and sacrifice to God.   (Ephesians 5:2)
> So if there is any encouragement in Christ, any incentive of love, any participation in the Spirit, any affection and sympathy, com-

plete my joy by being of the same mind, having the same love, being in full accord and of one mind.　　　(Philippians 2:1-2)

3. They appealed to motives centering in the Christian hope for eternity:

Rejoice in your hope.　　　　　　　　　　(Romans 12:12)

We rejoice in our hope of sharing the glory of God.

(Romans 5:2)

Those who by patience in well-doing seek for glory and honor and immortality.　　　　　　　　　　　　　(Romans 2:7)

So that . . . we who have fled for refuge might have strong encouragement to seize the hope set before us.　　(Hebrews 6:18)

Since we have such a hope, we are very bold.

(II Corinthians 3:12)

I beseech you as aliens and exiles.　　　　(1 Peter 2:11)

Mark those who live. . . . For many . . . live as enemies of the cross of Christ. . . . But our commonwealth is in heaven, and from it we await a Savior, the Lord Jesus Christ.

(Philippians 3:17-20)

It must be evident to the reader that if ministers began to confine their appeal to such motives as these, it would produce a revolution in the character of preaching. Should it be done? Could it be done?

As a preacher, can I assume that the goodness and glory of God, the mercy and love of Christ, the hope of sharing a life redeemed and eternal—can I count on these as motives operating in the people to whom I speak? Can I call to these things in my people with any confidence of being heard?

The answer is that I must think so if I believe that the one holy catholic and apostolic church is there among my people. Christians, the Lord's own people, are there. I do not know who they are, but he does. Every Christian under the sound of my voice will feel the Christian motive if I speak to it. If I cannot believe that the glory of God is as powerful a motive as self-interest in some of my people, my doubt does not prove that it is not. My doubt proves only my cynical presumption in judging Another's servants.

And how about the others, the unbelievers and the half-

believers? What motives can I appeal to in them? Can I count
on their feeling and responding to Christian motives? Who knows
the hearts of men? They too are God's children, even if ungrateful
and rebellious children. Not they alone, but Christians as well,
know how strong are the other motives: self-interest, defense,
aggression, domination, mastery, love-hunger, and the like. The
Christian motives must always win, if at all, in competition with
these.

But that is not the point. The point is that if I cannot count
on the Christian motives, I dare not appeal to sub-Christian
motives. Any successful appeal to selfish motives, however "religious" the form it takes, leads my victim farther away from the
lordship of Christ. I cannot sell Christ, I cannot sell the mysteries
of Christ, by a skilful appeal to motives of self-interest. I can only
sell him short.

We are much too hasty in supposing that our sophisticated
modern listeners are a brand new type of human being, that people
in past ages were less bent on getting their own way even with God.
Beside our contemporary bargainers, seekers of escape, seekers
for peace and security through religion, seekers of success, I set
the conclusion of the homily we call II Clement—which makes the
second century seem familiar, theological, psychological, modern,
and gives me a new respect for that old anonymous preacher of
the gospel.

No righteous man has reaped his reward quickly, but he waits for it.
For if God paid the reward of the good man speedily, we would at once
be training ourselves in commerce, not in godliness; for we would appear
to be righteous when we were seeking not godliness but gain.[1]

A CHRISTIAN EXHORTATION

I appeal to you therefore, brethren, by the mercies of God, to present
your bodies as a living sacrifice, holy and acceptable to God, which is
your spiritual worship. Do not be conformed to this world but be
transformed by the renewal of your mind, that you may prove what is
the will of God, what is good and acceptable and perfect.

For by the grace given to me I bid every one among you not to think
of himself more highly than he ought to think, but to think with sober

[1] See any edition of *The Apostolic Fathers*. Translation composite.

judgment, each according to the measure of faith which God has assigned him. For as in one body we have many members, and all the members do not have the same function, so we, though many, are one body in Christ, and individually members one of another. Having gifts that differ according to the grace given to us, let us use them: if prophecy, in proportion to our faith; if service, in our serving; he who teaches, in his teaching; he who exhorts, in his exhortation; he who contributes, in liberality; he who gives aid, with zeal; he who does acts of mercy, with cheerfulness.

Let love be genuine; hate what is evil, hold fast to what is good; love one another with brotherly affection; outdo one another in showing honor. Never flag in zeal, be aglow with the Spirit, serve the Lord. Rejoice in your hope, be patient in tribulation, be constant in prayer. Contribute to the needs of the saints, practice hospitality.

Bless those who persecute you; bless and do not curse them. Rejoice with those who rejoice, weep with those who weep. Live in harmony with one another; do not be haughty, but associate with the lowly; never be conceited. Repay no one evil for evil, but take thought for what is noble in the sight of all. If possible, so far as it depends upon you, live peaceably with all. Beloved, never avenge yourselves, but leave it to the wrath of God; for it is written, "Vengeance is mine, I will repay, says the Lord." No, "if your enemy is hungry, feed him; if he is thirsty, give him drink; for by so doing you will heap burning coals upon his head." Do not be overcome by evil, but overcome evil with good. Romans 12.

SUGGESTIONS

You can avoid confusion about this whole matter of "preaching the gospel," if you recognize clearly that the difference between proclamation and teaching-therapy is a difference of form, primarily, not a difference of substance.

There are, to be sure, "other gospels," false gospels, "other Christs" —there have been since Paul's day, and always will be—religious ideologies in the name of Christianity but lacking the substance of the gospel. But these are just as illegitimate for teaching and therapy as for proclamation. Whatever its functional form, Christian preaching deals with the substance of the gospel.

I suggest that your further reading go in two directions. The first is to follow "Didache" or "Teaching" through the best New Testament studies you can get your hands on. You should rely on the biblical disciplines, not on essays by homileticians. In the light of such studies, read Scherer (28), Chapter 6, pages 176-206. Kennedy's two books (41 and 42) both view the Christian message mainly as teaching.

The second direction is psychology—a tentative and uncertain field from which the substance of the gospel is often missing. I have used the word *therapy* with some misgivings, for you will see that in this book it does not mean the much-talked-of and popular fashions in psychotherapy. You will certainly use in preaching whatever insights have come to you from your studies in this field, and important insights are furnished by these studies. But I hope you will see that the empirical approach of the therapist often lacks any theological basis, or, indeed, any adequate theoretical foundation of any kind. And I hope you will remain a preacher, not become a psychological manipulator of people. In this connection I suggest the two books below, not in the bibliography, but deserving of careful study.

OUTLER, ALBERT C. *Psychotherapy and the Christian Message.* New York: Harper & Brothers, 1954.

ROBERTS, DAVID E. *Psychotherapy and a Christian View of Man.* New York: Charles Scribner's Sons, 1950.

CHAPTER 9

Organic Forms

A Subject Discussed
A Thesis Supported
A Message Illumined
A Question Propounded
A Story Told

A sermon should show nothing but its own unfolding parts:
Branches that thrust out by the force of its inner life
Sentences like leaves native to this very spray
True to the species
Not taken from alien growths.

By organic form I mean the structure a sermon assumes as a result of the state in which the germinal thought exists in the preacher's mind. Sermon ideas do not all take the same form. The form of the original thought in large measure determines the structure of the sermon.

Look again, for example, at Chalmers' sermon on page 31. The generative thought is complete with subject and predicate: "Only a new love for God can expel the love of the world and the things in it." What the sermon as a whole must say is in fact already said in that sentence. The structure of the sermon is largely determined beforehand. The sermon must develop a completed thought whose important element is that predicate: *only this can expel.* The contributory thoughts, the points of the sermon, must be generalizations that support or illuminate that all-inclusive statement. The trunk of the tree consists of both subject and predicate, and the branches thrust out from a complete thought as follows:

Only a new love for God can expel the love of the world:
Only a new love can expel an old love.
Only the love of God can expel the love of the world.
Only by preaching the gospel of redeeming love can we present a God who inspires such love.

Only by believing the gospel and its promises can a man experience this new love.

If Jowett's procedure, described on page 37, were strictly followed in the making of every sermon, if a man never proceeded with the development of any sermon till he had first expressed its whole theme in one clear complete sentence like Chalmers', then the structure of all sermons would be basically the same; every sermon would be a series of points in support or illumination of the same predicate, the predicate of the theme sentence. This is one excellent way to make a sermon, but it is not the only way. As a simple matter of honest reporting, good preachers do not invariably follow this procedure. As trees are not all of like organic structure, so sermons are not all of like structure.

Take Fosdick's sermon discussed on page 60. He offers only a subject, forgiveness of sins, a noun subject with no predicate. It is not a complete thought. One could predicate many things about the forgiveness of sins: that it is unjust, that it is impossible, that it is a belief born of wishful thinking. In his sermon Dr. Fosdick says not one but two things about forgiveness of sins: forgiveness is difficult, and forgiveness is necessary. There is no single all-inclusive predicate as there is in Chalmers' theme. There are two independent predicates. The sermon is like a tree that has no single trunk, but twin stems dividing near the ground.

Coming without a predicate, this subject determines what the organic structure of the sermon will be. It must be a series of two or more predicates, of two or more things said about the subject. The contributory thoughts (structural assertions, points, divisions, heads—call them what you will; the words all mean the same thing) must be a series of things said about the forgiveness of sins.

There must be a series because there is no one thing to be said. The points must be statements made about the subject, the forgiveness of sins, because there is no predicate they can develop. The branches must grow out of the bare subject, because the tree has no central trunk. They divide as follows:

> Forgiveness of sins:
> Every one of us needs forgiveness.
> Forgiveness is very difficult and costly.
> Yet forgiveness is our deepest necessity.

Evidently, these two sermons represent different types of organic form and of sermonic design. There are still other types of structure resulting from different forms of the sermon idea. Each one has its advantages in the right spot, and each has its own problems that grow out of its very nature. We shall now proceed to examine some of the most important types of structure.

We must clearly distinguish between content and form. The form does not produce the substance, what the sermon actually says. Rather, the substance takes on the form. If the thought content of the following sermons interests us, we must not let it divert our attention from the form. As quickly as possible we must get through with our admiration of the substance or our quarrel with it, and get back to a craftsman's interest in the forms.

Let me repeat that in selecting the following examples my interest is not in the preacher, nor in the quality of the content. The examples are not chosen for their excellence as preaching, but only because they illustrate those details of sermonic design which we are studying. The use of a sermon does not mean that I approve of its content or agree with it. Any attempt to appraise the quality of the content would wholly confuse our task.[1]

A SUBJECT DISCUSSED

As Fosdick's sermon demonstrates, a germinal idea may take the form of a subject to be discussed. It may be an incomplete thought which the sermon must complete.

As distinguished from all other structural forms, this subject of which I speak is a noun subject without any hint of a predicate; it carries no suggestion at all of what is to be said. If it suggested a predicate, it would no longer be simply a subject to be discussed; it would then suggest a complete thought.

This difference is extremely important to the man who is design-

[1] See "Note on the Use of Examples," p. 30.

ing a sermon. "The Character of Christ" is this kind of subject, for it does not commit me to any particular assertion about the character of Jesus. When I am working with a noun subject of this kind, I must remember also that having the subject does not guarantee that I have anything in particular to say about it. This is the first fact that the designer must keep in mind: not that a noun subject is not proper, but that a noun subject is not yet a complete thought.

"Grateful Living" is another such subject. I can announce the subject without having anything to say about it. But "The Joy of Grateful Living" is not an incomplete thought. By reason of its strongly suggesting a predicate, it commits my sermon to develop an assertion: there is joy in grateful living. If I do not develop that assertion, my subject has given a false lead. If I do develop it, I am no longer simply discussing a subject.

Thus the completeness or incompleteness of the original thought determines the task my whole sermon must accomplish and provides its organic form. The noun subject requires that the sermon take the form of distributed predication, a number of things said about the subject. The germinal idea expands by adding predicates to the subject.

Clow's sermon, discussed on page 71, is another in this form. The subject, the cross and the memory of sin, mildly suggests a predicate: that the cross makes some difference in the memory of sin. But that does not really change its aspect. "Difference" is also a noun. The thing to be talked about is still simply a noun subject: the difference the cross makes in the memory of sin. Nothing the preacher means to say is expressed or even hinted at as yet. There is simply a subject to be discussed, and the structure of the sermon is predetermined; it must introduce a series of things said about this difference. It turns out as follows:

> The difference the cross makes in the memory of sin:
> The cross takes the sting out of the memory of sin.
> The cross makes the memory of sin a means of grace:
> The memory becomes a barrier against future sin.

> It may become an equipment for service.
> It becomes a source of love to Christ.
> The cross shall finally obliterate the memory of sin.

Again there is no central trunk to this tree. Three large stems rise from the ground or near it, and one of them divides into three secondary branches. That is to say, no one of these predicates completes the thought; it takes all three of them to constitute the full idea as it was in Clow's mind. Since there is no all-inclusive predicate, no effective one-sentence theme could be devised.

Now that the predicates are added, the significant content also appears, the generalized content whose development will be simply the particularizing of these six contributory assertions.

Like all other forms discussed in this chapter, this is an organic form, not a functional form. In other words, a sermon in this form can be preached for any purpose: the proclamation of the gospel, teaching, exhortation, denouncing, praising, or merely entertaining. This is the form of countless lectures, essays, and articles. The structural form has no necessary relation to function.

Clow's predicates reveal that the purpose of his sermon is kerygmatic, proclamation of the beneficent power of the cross in the life of a believer. If the function had been exhortation, the predicates would have been different in statement if not different in substance. And so, structurally, this sermon is a subject discussed; functionally, it is proclamation.

OUR REFORMATION INHERITANCE. by Angus Dun[2]

Angus Dun, Episcopalian bishop of Washington, D. C., preached this Reformation sermon before the Chicago Sunday Evening Club in 1951. Its form is that of a subject discussed. A useful example, it shows how flexible this form is and how it can be adapted.

His points were not lined out as they are below, but they emerged very clearly when he was heard, and a comparison with the printed sermon shows them to be the substance of what was said.

[2] A. M. Motter, *Sunday Evening Sermons* (New York: Harper, 1952), p. 31. Used by permission.

"Our Reformation Inheritance"
We are Christ's people, first, then Protestant witnesses.
We hold this as the catholic faith, not as partisan belief.
There is a Protestant heritage and witness:
    That God and Christ stand forever above the church.
    That the Bible is a sure record of God's self-disclosure.
    That men are to be confronted with Christ and summoned to make
    each his own answer to him.
    That the gospel and the Bible must be available to everyone.
    That the Christian is in bondage to no man, hierarchy, or priesthood.
    That God's blessing is only received through a response of penitence,
    obedience, and trust.
    That a man's standing with God is the gift of God's love.
We deny what is opposed to this, but must not judge others.
We confess our own Protestant sins.
We believe there is security only in God, his kingdom, his Word.
We rejoice and stand fast in this faith.

Here too the points, being complete sentences, bring through the thought content of the sermon. They do it because they are completed assertions. Noun elements alone cannot express it.

However, the discussion of a subject may be outlined with nouns, subtopics which in themselves contain no predication. In other words, the verbal design may consist only of a subject divided into component subjects, asserting nothing, containing no predication at all. For example:

SINS AND SORROWS OF THE CITY, by Thomas Guthrie[3]

Guthrie was a great preacher of Edinburgh, Scotland, in the nineteenth century. The above title is not his true subject. He is talking about the intemperance for which Edinburgh was notorious.

        Intemperance in Edinburgh
        1. Its Extent.
        2. Its Effects.
        3. Its Cure:
          a. Legislation.
          b. Example of Abstaining.

This outline merely proposes things to talk about. In contrast with previous sketches, it says nothing, brings through no completed thought. In this outline one can see no hint of the powerful, compassionate plea this sermon actually is. The substance of the sermon, its thought as well as its feeling, is simply absent. These five topics are like rootstocks in the ground, from which plants can grow but which show no life as yet.

Many a great sermon has been preached, and many will yet be preached, on this kind of outline. At least it exhibits an organic structure of parts within a subject. It has some utility. It can guide the preacher in distributing his materials and in preaching the sermon. It can help the listener to follow the sermon's movement. It is clear, simple, and easy to remember—all great virtues.

But the beginner should understand that this sort of outline, any noun outline however elaborate or simple, is incomplete and may be misleading. It is incomplete in that it brings to expression nothing of the sermon's most important elements: its predication, what it will say. It may mislead the preacher, lull him into a false security, make him think his pattern of subjects conveys thought, when it really conveys nothing at all definite. It may thus cause him to stop work on his design when he is only now ready to begin it.

Once in my classroom a student put on the blackboard the following outline:

> The Ten Virgins
> 1. Preparation
> 2. Anticipation
> 3. Coming
> 4. Consummation

As usual, there were some lewd interpreters present. Only when the snicker swelled into a roar did the victim realize he had said nothing but suggested what he never dreamed of. Because it was no idea, it could become any that one might read into it.

A THESIS SUPPORTED

A sermon idea may take the form of a proposition to be proved, a thesis to be supported.

This differs from the preceding form in that the proposition from which the sermon expands is a completed idea, having both subject and predicate. A proposition or thesis is itself an assertion.

It differs from the forms that are still to come in that it is an assertion one undertakes to prove or support by evidence, or by reasoning, or by both. It is dialectical in its attitude. Its methods are argument and demonstration.

The propositional form of this idea requires that the sermon be designed to support it. The form of the idea thus determines the structural form of the sermon. The structural assertions will be generalizations of evidence and logic calculated to convince the listener that the proposition is true. Whatever the sermon's ultimate purpose, its immediate aim must be to win belief in the truth of the proposition. Everything else depends on it.

What happens in this form of sermon is that attention centers in the second functional question: "Is this true? Why, or why not?" This question is the chief thing at issue in the propositional sermon, and the issue must be resolved before we can go on to anything else. Evidently, this form of preaching will be especially congenial in an approach to religion that is chiefly intellectual. Some older textbooks in homiletics use the word *proposition* as a synonym for *theme*. Some indeed speak as if it were a rule that every sermon ought to state a proposition and then speak in support of it. But this is only one way of structuring a sermon, and a theme is not the same thing as a proposition to be supported.

Nothing said above should be construed as a suggestion that the propositional is an antiquated form. It has today all the merits it ever had. It can still be used, and used for any purpose, to proclaim the gospel as well as to teach. It may indeed be especially useful in preparing the way for the gospel, meeting intellectual objections. Paul was doing that when he argued in the synagogues.

THE SECOND CHANCE, by Horace Bushnell[4]

This title refers to another chance, or more than one, after this life, which some people believe will be given to bad people, and

4 Macartney, *op. cit.*, p. 415.

continue to be given until all people have become righteous. Bushnell takes as his text Hebrews 9:27,

"And it is appointed unto men once to die, but after that the judgment."

In his introduction he states that many hold this opinion, cites
the text as unfavorable to it, repeats arguments made in favor of
it, and then draws his thesis: that *"no benefit would come of such
a second chance; it would not be for our real advantage as respects
the training of our character.* That it would not, I am firmly convinced, for reasons that I now undertake to set forth."

Argument:
1. If we really regretted our present failure, we would not need another
   chance.
2. If we had another trial, we would be slack in this one.
3. The second chance would have to begin where the first leaves off;
   we would begin worse than we did the first time.
4. The new chance would therefore be very unpromising, less promising
   than the first.
5. Youth is more favorable to improvement than age; we are past the
   opportunity for a new beginning.

Notice how the proposition is limited. The argument is not
about the justice of a second chance, not about its reasonableness,
but about its advantage. Advantage is narrowed to advantage for
training, and training is narrowed to training in character—not, for
example, training in a view of reality or in the appreciation of
ideals. The argument is about the advantage of a second chance
for such training.

Above all, the proposition is limited to the negative. It results
in a negative argument and a negative sermon throughout, a negative that shapes and colors every sentence in the sermon until the
very end.

The method of supporting the proposition is chiefly logical
argument from evidence furnished by our development in this life.

The ultimate purpose of the sermon is to convince that there
will be no second chance and thus to strengthen the final admonitory question: How are we doing in this one critical chance? But

to do that, he must first win belief in the thesis: There would be no advantage in a second chance, for Bushnell concedes that if it were advantageous God would grant a second chance.

The sermon is propositional in structure, dialectic in method, and hortatory in function.

THE CRUCIFORM CHARACTER OF HUMAN EXISTENCE, by Joseph Sittler, Jr.[5]

This proposition uses a figure of speech: *cruciform* means broken, ambiguous, contradictory.

In the second short paragraph it is stated as follows: *"It is the proposition of this address that the cross of Christ has an inexhaustible fascination because it is a form descriptive of the innermost character of human existence.* It addresses life profoundly and redemptively because it addresses life truly."

The proposition centers in experience; it is human experience, its ambiguity, that becomes the true subject and branches out to form the structural elements of the sermon.

The experience of *time:* Time brings many promises, but it passes with a sense of loss.

The experience of *moral reflection:* Man knows he ought not to be the center of his existence, but he cannot get himself out of the center:

In *love* self seems to be transcended, but is actually enhanced.

In *prayer* one fluctuates between condemning and commending oneself.

The experience of *self-realization:* A man can achieve self-realization only by destroying most of his possibilities unfulfilled.

Only a cross is relevant to our cruciform existence.

The word of forgiveness is the only adequate or redemptive word that God can speak to us.

Clearly, this sermon differs sharply from Bushnell's in its method of supporting the proposition. Its method is not logical argument, but rather such a presentation of commonly ignored facts as makes us experience them as the facts of our own existence.

[5] The Chicago Lutheran Seminary *Record,* Vol. 54, No. 4, October, 1949, p. 18. Used by permission.

This difference in method is highly significant. Sittler uses description rather than argument. When he is describing the sense of loss in our experience of time, Shakespeare's "Bare ruined choirs where late the sweet birds sang," and Walter de la Mare's "But beauty vanishes, beauty passes," become integral parts of the total human experience of loss.

Notice that while this sermon is propositional in structure and descriptive in method, it is kerygmatic in function. It is for the purpose of proclaiming the gospel, or rather of clearing the way for the gospel. There is not a syllable of admonition in it. The purpose colors every sentence.

Proclamation of the gospel is not its immediate aim, however, but is its ultimate purpose. Its immediate aim is to establish the broken character of human existence, not in this sermon by winning intellectual belief, but by sharing the experience of its brokenness.

A MESSAGE ILLUMINED

A sermon idea may take the form of a message to be illuminated.

Here again, as in the propositional form, the sermon expands from a single complete idea, a sentence with subject and predicate. In this respect the two forms are like each other and unlike any of the other organic forms.

This form differs from the thesis or proposition in that it simply says what it has to say and does not pose it as an issue. The idea is an assertion, an affirmation; the preacher merely asserts it and waives the question, "Is it true?" The attention centers rather in the other functional questions, "What does it mean?" and "What difference does it make? What are its consequences?" The presence of an issue that must first be resolved gives a different feeling to the whole undertaking.

Take, for example, Channing's sermon, discussed on page 68. It is an expansion of the idea: *The character of Christ is a strong confirmation of the truth of his religion.* That idea might be posed as an issue. If so, its form as an issue determines that the sermon shall be a support, by logic or evidence, of its truth.

But Channing does not pose his idea as an issue. He states it as a fact that is not at issue, as a message that needs only to be delivered and elaborated. Thus its form as a message calls for a different treatment. The sermon will then be structured to announce the message, to throw light on its meaning, and to show its consequences to the people who hear the sermon. Its structural assertions will be generalizations of its meaning and consequences.

A sermon idea in this form is a theme in the traditional sense of the term. If Jowett's procedure were followed, every sermon would be in either this structural form or in the form of a proposition.

The message form is particularly well suited to a simple proclamation of the gospel, where the preacher's task is to announce the good news, which has to be believed without intellectual demonstration or indubitable proof.

Nevertheless, this is a structural, not a functional, form. It can be used for any purpose, as careful examination of a good collection of sermons will show.

THE LORD GOD OMNIPOTENT REIGNETH, by James Stewart[6]
This title is merely a quotation of the text, Revelation 19:6:

"Alleluia: for the Lord God omnipotent reigneth."
The biggest fact, the central fact is: "The Lord God omnipotent reigneth."
It means the liberation of life.
It means the doom of sin, the defeat of evil.
It means comfort in sorrow.
To believe it is the victory of faith. This God comes today and knocks. What will your answer be?

There is no argument in this sermon, no attempt to prove anything. From beginning to end the sermon is a song of triumphant affirmation. Every sentence is shaped and colored by that mood.

[6] *The Gates of New Life* (New York: Scribner's, 1940). Used by permission. It is No. 38 in Blackwood, *op. cit.*, p. 288.

Here this message, "The Lord God omnipotent reigneth," could fairly be called a theme, for, like a principal subject in music, it is brought in again and again at every stage of the development. He announces and celebrates the reign of God.

The body of the sermon is a three-branched answer to the question, "What does the reign of God mean?" The meaning, however, is understood in terms of its consequences. Thus the sermon really answers the question, "What difference does the reign of God make?"

The organic form is that of a message illuminated. The function is kerygmatic. The method is affirmation.

THE PERILS OF THE CHRISTIAN LIFE, by Paul Scherer[7]

This is a sermon preached before the Chicago Sunday Evening Club.

Text: Genesis 28:13, 15-17. I am the Lord God of thy father Abraham, the God of Isaac. . . . Behold, I will be with thee and will not leave thee until I have done that which I have spoken to thee of. And Jacob awakened out of his sleep, and he said, Surely the Lord is in this place, and I knew it not. And he was afraid, and said, How dreadful is this place.

> The perils of the Christian life:
> The peril of the lost aim.
> The peril of the complacent self.
> The peril of the far horizon.

Grammatically this is a noun subject and the subtopics too are nouns. But the predicate is so strongly suggested that the idea is complete and unmistakable: The Christian life has perils.

This is another sermon, like Guthrie's on page 144, whose apparently simple structure is deceptive. No one could guess from the above outline, apart from the text, that the sermon is based on facts in the life of Jacob, tracing the analogy of Jacob's dealing with God to our own attitudes before God. The sermon's content lies, not in these subtopics, but in a predication so rich and varied

[7] A. M. Motter, *Great Preaching Today* (New York: Harper, 1955), p. 189. Used by permission.

that it is impossible to do more than hint at it here. The sermon
resembles a story with a double plot, the main plot being our
peril as Christians, and the minor plot being Jacob's experience
with God.

The lost aim. We are in peril of seeing only our own purposes, knowledge, and ideas, as Jacob did. But the aim is nothing less than to meet
God and face up to him.
The complacent self. We, like Jacob, are in peril of complacency, self-
assurance. But when God is around and his eye on us, nobody is
merely comfortable or has a right to an easy conscience.
The far horizon. Our peril is that at last we have to meet God and
wrestle with him, as Jacob did. God has to oppose us in order to bless
us, to wound in order to heal. God saves by the wounds he gives.

Thus the sermon is an expansion of the perils, what they are and
what they mean. Structurally it is a message. Functionally it is
proclamation of the godhood of God.

OUR VIRGIN BIRTH, by a student

An undergraduate in one of my classes preached this sermon a
few years ago. It is based on the Gospel for the Festival of the
Holy Trinity, the conversation of Jesus with Nicodemus in John
3:1-15.

Subject: Our birth to life in the kingdom—born again from
above, *anothen*—by water and the Spirit—by that Spirit whose
sound, like the wind's, can be heard, but whose movement cannot
be marked.

The man got his idea expressed, but not in one sentence "as
clear and lucid as a cloudless moon." (The reader can undertake
that.) He got it spaciously structured, though his lines have not the
subtle perfection of Le Corbusier's.

What he says is: The new birth by the Spirit is as much a miracle
as the conception of Jesus in Mary's womb, and it deserves to be
called a virgin birth.

This is the idea, a message to be proclaimed and illuminated.
His statement of the general idea did not go beyond this strongly

predicating subject: "Our Virgin Birth." He structured it as follows:

> The life-creating Spirit comes strangely from on high.
> He comes to my world of flesh and blood.
> A struggle ensues between flesh as flesh and the Spirit.
> We must come into that struggle alone.
> The victory will be won: Alleluia!

WE DARE NOT FAIL IN OUR CHRISTIAN WITNESS, by a student

This is by another undergraduate student, preached on a September 29, the Festival of St. Michael and All Angels, from parts of the Epistle and Gospel, as follows:

And they have conquered him by the blood of the Lamb and by the word of their testimony, for they loved not their lives even unto death.
(Revelation 12:7-12, verse 11)
Whoever receives one such child in my name receives me; but whoever causes one of these little ones who believe in me to sin, it would be better for him to have a great millstone fastened round his neck and to be drowned in the depth of the sea.
(Matthew 18:1-11, verses 5 and 6)

The design of this sermon came through so clearly that not much comment is needed. The above heading is not a title and not merely a subject. It is the complete idea. It is what the sermon said, and it includes everything the sermon said.

> We dare not fail in our Christian witness.
> Not every failure is a disaster:
> God has patience with our weakness and forgives.
> Life can go on in spite of failures.
> But to fail in our witness is a disaster to
> Christ's little weak ones:
> It is to make them stumble.
> It is to deny them an indispensable service.
> And it is to fail Christ in the purpose he has for us:
> The purpose which alone gives meaning to our existence.
> His purpose to conquer evil by the word of our testimony.
> We dare not fail in our Christian witness.

The structural form is that of a message delivered and illuminated. The functional form is exhortation.

A QUESTION PROPOUNDED

A sermon idea may take the form of a question to be investigated.

This form is distinguished from all others in that its essence is not assertion but inquiry. Its method is to ask, not to tell.

The question as a sermonic form must be clearly distinguished from the question used as a mere device in communication. The rhetorical question, to which the answer is obvious, may be the strongest form of assertion, as in Paul's "Who shall separate us from the love of Christ?"

A question may be a mere device for gaining a more active attention. Clow, at the end of his introduction, uses the question form to state his subject: "How does the cross affect the memory of sin?"—and proceeds to tell how. So a preacher may use a question as the title of his sermon: "What is Heaven?"—and try to tell what heaven is. These uses of questions are not genuine inquiries.

A question may be used to demand a response from the other person. It is asked and left waiting for that response. This is an extremely important use of the question in preaching, often made at the end of a sermon. The conclusion may include such a question, or may consist entirely of the question.

The question as a sermonic form, however, is more than these. In it inquiry is the main feature, inquiry by the preacher on behalf of both his people and himself, concerning a question for which no pat answer is forthcoming from them or from him. If the question is just an excuse for telling the answer, the idea's form is assertion, not question.

The preacher is, of course, seeking an answer to the question he propounds. If he cannot answer it in full, he may answer in part. He may point to where the answer lies. He may answer it for himself alone and leave his listeners to do the same. Sometimes it may be a question he cannot answer at all, but only ask.

There are such questions. The naked bodies of three murdered boys were recently found in a ditch. The father of one, with a second sight commonly denied us all, asked, "What kind of a country do we live in?" It is a thought so terrifying that any verbal answer seems puny, and few have the courage even to ask it.

When the idea takes the form of a genuine question propounded, it determines the structural form of the sermon. It requires the sermon to discuss the question as a question, not as a ready-made answer. The sermon should expand and illuminate the question, show clearly what is at issue, show in what direction the answer lies, if it can, and move toward the answer as far as possible.

In a purely dogmatic or didactic theory of preaching, a preacher ought never to ask a question he cannot answer, and ought never to leave unanswered a question that he raises. Some teachers of homiletics lay this down as a rule.

The plain fact is that if a man confines his preaching to assertion, to telling, he will make two mistakes. He will claim to have answered many a question he has not answered, and he will leave unasked many a question he ought to ask.

The rarity of good sermons in this form is evidence that we preachers consider ourselves the world's original answer-men. Why is there not more preaching in this form? Surely the most profound question is one whose answer no man can give to another.

BUT WHEN LIFE TUMBLES IN, WHAT THEN? by Arthur Gossip[8]

This is the first sermon Arthur Gossip, of Glasgow, preached after the sudden death of his wife. It is based on the two questions in Jeremiah 12:5.

> If thou hast run with the footmen, and they have wearied thee, then how canst thou contend with horses? And if in the land of peace, wherein thou trustedst, they wearied thee, then how wilt thou do in the swelling of Jordan?

Throughout the first half of this sermon, Gossip does nothing but press the above question, describe the tumbling in of life that makes it a critical question, and say that now, for the first time in

---

[8] *The Hero in Thy Soul* (New York: Scribner's, 1929). Used by permission. It is No. 24 in Blackwood, *op. cit.,* p. 198.

his life, he has a right to speak to this question. He proceeds as follows:

What will happen when we, peevish at little ills, have to face some event that crashes life in completely? What if you had to face what Job faced? Or Jesus?

Such disasters come. What then?

Religion is meant for such a time. But how will it be with you and me? I've had a happy life. People had a right to ask me, "Would you be so sure if you had to face real trouble?"

I have a right to speak now.

I do not understand life. But if we turn from faith in trouble, what shall we turn to? Have we not lost enough without losing that too?

When life crashes in, we have nothing else.

Would it not be a pity if we received life's discipline in vain?

I've found that faith's most audacious promises are true. The Comforter *is* with us. I've become sure of God's tenderness, that he does not willingly afflict us.

One becomes certain about immortality. I am past doubt of that.

We are wrong to brood over our own loss. What does such brooding mean? Would it not be better to think of what it must mean to those who go? Do we dare compare what our love can give them with the glory Christ gives them? I love to think of that.

Must our dearest be taken from us by force? Will we not give them willingly and proudly to God? I learned to do that.

But our gift is not absolute. Never again will I think of them or of heaven as far away. The communion of saints has become a fact.

Now to pray is to turn home.

Now not forgetfulness but memory consoles.

What can separate us from God's love? Not death.

I have tried to give a sufficiently full summary to show how he keeps turning the material back into the question.

There is much assertion in this sermon, of course. One cannot talk about anything without making assertions. What makes this an example of the question form is that the question is so handled that it remains a question to be answered by every listener for himself.

Notice exactly what the sermon does. It asks the question with tragic force, and it gives one man's answer, his witness that the gospel has answered the question for him. Just because the witness is genuinely and personally his, it speaks to other men forcefully.

In structure this sermon is a question. In function it is proclamation.

A STORY TOLD

A sermon idea may take the form of a narrative of events, persons, actions, and words. The distinguishing feature of this form is that the idea is embodied in a structure of events and persons, rather than in a structure of verbal generalizations, whether assertions or questions.

Thomas Mann has put the difference this way: "Sometimes now I have days when I would rather state things in general terms than go on telling stories." He means that the stories state his ideas in one form, and that he sometimes wants to use the other form, verbal generalization.

The preacher's case is the opposite of the novelist's. Verbal generalization is the usual way with him. But we preachers forget that the gospel itself is for the most part a simple narrative of persons, places, happenings, and conversation. It is not a verbal exposition of general ideas. Nine-tenths of our preaching is verbal exposition and argument, but not one tenth of the gospel is exposition. Its ideas are mainly in the form of a story told.

Within the gospel, the parable is simply a narrative which expressed its idea to Jesus' contemporaries, usually without verbal explanation. Scholars believe that most of the interpretative general remarks which now accompany Jesus' parables were added to them in the preaching of the church, that Jesus usually did not add general comment to the stories. Jesus' contemporaries got the idea without comment, and killed him for it.

The story of the passion was most perfectly crystallized of all, and remained most purely a narrative without interpretative comment. Unfortunately, its power as a narrative is little used in modern preaching. Sermons of Lent and Holy Week consist almost entirely of verbal exposition and comment.

The different treatment may be illustrated by musical settings of the passion history. Bach and Schuetz both preach the passion according to St. Matthew and St. John. Bach's setting has much general and devotional comment, chorales and other verses, added to the Scripture text. Outside the tenor and bass recitatives, Bach's incomparable music is like modern preaching—general discussion of the story. Seldom do we hear the passion preached as it was at first, as it is preached by Schuetz, where the text of the story stands without additional comment and the music simply illumines the text.

Christmas and Easter sermons are for many the hardest to preach, for the good reason that there the bare narrative is so overwhelming that our best comment seems shoddy and presumptuous in comparison. Yet how few preachers on these festivals trust that a really good telling of the story will be preaching! There are not many. Peter Marshall's "The Grave in the Garden"[9] comes nearer than most. But the telling of this story had power to spread the church throughout the Roman Empire in the first century of Christian history.

We overestimate the power of assertion, and we underestimate the power of a narrative to communicate meaning and influence the lives of our people. We do it in spite of the obvious power of the myths, legends, and epics of mankind, and the tremendous influence which the novel and the drama—on stage, screen, radio, and television—have in shaping the opinions, the ethical ideas, and the behavior of the very people to whom we preach. No assertion about life has as much power as life itself has when shown to people.

This is not a suggestion that we construct fictional narratives or fictionalize the narratives in the Gospels. Peter Marshall did that once with some success,[10] but this is not for most men. I mean that we should recognize and use the narrative element in the gospel, the persons and events, more than we do. In many a

[9] *Mr. Jones, Meet the Master* (New York: Revell, 1949), p. 101.
[10] *Ibid.*, "By Invitation of Jesus," p. 117.

sermon drawn from the parable of the talents, for instance, one would never know there were real and very human persons in this story—and in many a sermon on the crucifixion. There often is nothing in the sermon but exposition of general ideas.

By contrast, look at Stephen's discourse which fills the long seventh chapter of the Acts of the Apostles. It contains so much historical incident and so little exposition of thought that one who has not studied it may dismiss it as a tedious harangue and wonder how this kind of talking could have got Stephen killed. However, the sharp point, which comes out in the end, is embedded in every particle of the story, and his hearers did not fail to feel its sharpness.

Because of the nature of the story form, it is nearly impossible to illustrate it briefly. The whole narrative is the structure of the idea. The detailed actions and words are the means of communicating the thought. Any mere sketch tends to be a digest in general terms, and tends to leave out the particulars which constitute the story.

Not wishing to do violence to some other man's work, I will take one more imperfect sermon of my own for this demonstration.

A MAN WHO HAD TOO LITTLE AT STAKE

This is the narrative of the supper in the house of Simon the Pharisee, Luke 7:36-50. The idea expressed in the title is an interpretation of Simon's character based on details in the narrative itself. Simon's character makes a secondary theme, why meeting Jesus did him no good, a foil for the principal theme, Christ's forgiveness of the penitent woman. The story itself carries the principal theme, which is not verbally developed in the sermon.

The sermon is at least five times as long as the following abridgment, and what is omitted is narrative detail, so that the sketch contains a greater proportion of generalization than the complete sermon. The structure of the story is as follows:

This man Simon was a man not deeply involved in anything.

He was a Pharisee but not a very good one. He had so little partisan prejudice as to invite Jesus to dinner. He could stand Jesus' strong talk about widows' houses and long prayers, perhaps admitted some truth in it.

He was broadminded, and Jesus was influential. It would do Simon no harm, he thought, to be decent to this brilliant young teacher. It takes all kinds of men to make a world.

This invitation need not commit Simon to anything. It didn't mean he agreed with everything Jesus said. He needn't fall on Jesus' neck and kiss him, give water for his feet or oil for his head, or make an honored guest of him—just a casual meal, perhaps.

Simon was urbane, polished, adaptable, no fanatic. He had the smoothness if not the slipperiness of a man of the world. He would have done well in Rome or New York or Chicago.

So it was. Jesus Christ talked to him across his table, and Simon never batted an eye.

While they talked, this woman of the town came in past the servants, apparently without an objection, and found her way to Jesus' feet.

Simon knew her well—or thought he did. For a man like Simon could never know her in this act. The plain truth about her was the last thing Simon could imagine or believe. That some new erotic twist might bring her here—that he could believe. But the genuineness of a harlot's tears—that he couldn't believe. He knew too much.

Simon is logical. He looks with sharp and practiced eyes: If this rabbi is a prophet, he will know what this woman is and will have nothing to do with her. Simon has them both figured out, the woman and Jesus. He cuts them down to his own little scheme of things, and there is no room in it for what is happening before his eyes.

The plain truth about Jesus also is the last thing Simon would dream of: that he could be true, good, and a prophet, could know exactly what the woman is, and receive her just the same. There is no room in Simon's little scheme of things for that either.

Simon looks at what is happening and doesn't even see it. The tears fall. The hands clutch hair and mop them up. The alabaster tinkles in fingers that tremble. The lips seek unwashed feet.

Simon reasons: "He ought to know she is a sinner." But while he is thinking this, Love changes the tenses on Simon. "No, Simon. She *was* a sinner."

Simon never suspects. There is much which no man with so little at stake will ever see.

Jesus tries to open Simon's eyes, speaks of large debts and small debts, of great love and little love, and of people on whom love is wasted because they do not care enough.

Jesus asks Simon about that. But all a safe man like Simon can say on the subject of love is "I suppose"! "I suppose that in a theoretical case like that, the one forgiven most will love most."

And so Simon, who had not love at stake, meets the Christ, and it does him no good. For others, not for him, the words: "Thy sins are forgiven. Go in peace."

It is necessary to keep in mind the inherent limitations of the narrative as a sermonic form, as well as its inherent strength. The story conveys meaning indirectly, through its characters, their conversation, and their interaction. It speaks by suggestion rather than in direct and explicit statement. Consequently, it cannot rely on direct and definite assertion. A little too much "preaching" quickly destroys the inherent force of the narrative.

Furthermore, if the hearer is to catch the deeper meanings of the story, there must be a more active listening than that required to follow the thought of an assertive sermon. The hearer will not get the important message unless he identifies himself with the characters in the story, lives through the incidents with them, understands their motives, and renders his own verdict on their opinions, character, and actions. Every hearer does this intuitively to some extent. But there is always the chance that he will hear nothing but the more superficial action of the story. Yet the teller of the story must trust the story to convey its meaning. If he over-interprets it or loads it down with explanations, he will destroy the inherent force of the narrative.

And yet again, a story is inevitably in the past tense and is about other persons than the listener. The teller of the story can apply it to his hearers only by hints and suggestive touches here and there. If he does more than this, if he steps outside the story to make pointed reference to his hearers, he must do it with great skill or he will spoil the effect of the whole. The listener must draw his own conclusions and make his own application to him-self, or he will miss the point of the story. If a preacher cannot trust his hearers to do this, he should not use the story form.

For all these and for still other reasons, the preacher, especially the beginner, is warned that the story is not for everyday use as

the form of the entire sermon. It is not suitable for every kind
of text or theme. Its successful use requires a high degree of
literary skill. It is not a natural form for most preachers, and
overuse or incautious use of it will make a man's work seem artificial, posed, and therefore insincere.

After all this is said, however, it remains a fact that too little
use is made of narrative in contemporary preaching, and that on
rare occasions a good telling of the biblical story would be more
effective than the best exposition of general ideas of which the
preacher is capable.

SUGGESTIONS

I fear you will not find much help in the literature of preaching on
the problems of this chapter. I hope the chapter itself gives you sufficiently definite suggestions to enable you to attempt these forms in
your own work.

You will do well to study the different ways of organizing speeches
in Monroe (59) and in Sarett and Foster (65). The problem of adapt-
ing speech forms to the work of preaching should not be insurmountable.

If you feel yourself inadequately prepared for this work, do not
waste your time and effort, but begin properly by a careful study of the
kinds of discourse—Exposition, Argument, Description, and Narration
—in Brooks and Warren (52), pages 40-315.

The *homily* is not a definite sermonic form. In its early phase, it
was an informal, discursive talk, in which digression, passing from
one subject to another, was rather the rule than the exception. The
early homily used no text and developed no particular theme. Later in
the history of preaching, the term came to mean almost the opposite:
an ordered exposition of a passage of Scripture. The hundreds of sermons by Chrysostom, Augustine, and the other fathers, have come
down to us as "homilies" in this latter sense. The term is not useful
for our purposes. You may be interested in what is said about the
homily in Garvie (8), pages 57-58 and on page 348.

CHAPTER 10

Continuity: Nature and Types

The figure a poem makes. It begins in delight and ends in wisdom. . . .
It begins in delight, it inclines to the impulse, it assumes direction with
the first line laid down, it runs a course of lucky events, and ends in a
clarification of life—not necessarily a great clarification, such as sects
and cults are founded on, but in a momentary stay against confusion.
It has denouement. It has an outcome that though unforeseen was
predestined from the first image of the original mood—and indeed from
the very mood. . . .

A poem may be worked over once it is in being, but may not be
worried into being. Its most precious quality will remain its having
run itself and carried away the poet with it.—Robert Frost.[1]

The proper design of a sermon is a movement in time. It begins
at a given moment, it ends at a given moment, and it moves
through the intervening moments one after another.

In order to design a sermon well, we must think of it in this
way. A sermon is not a manuscript, not a paper outline simple or
elaborate, not a sketch like one of those in this book. A sermon
is a continuity of sounds, looks, gestures, which follow one another
in time.

A sermon is not static like a painting. A painting shows itself
as a whole in a single instant. Not only its entire composition, all
its subjects and their arrangement, but all its minutest details stand
there together, fixed in their intended relation to one another and
to the whole. It is a visible design, complete and static. The eye
takes it all in at once. A sermon is never like that, never has the
objective completeness of a picture or a building.

A sermon is like music, not music in the score but in the live
performance, where bar is heard after bar, theme after theme,
and never all at once. A sermon is like a play, not the printed
book but the action on a stage, which moves from a first act
through a second to a third, and the drama is never seen all at

---

[1] "The Figure a Poem Makes," in *Collected Poems* (New York: Holt,
1939). Quoted by permission.

once. A sermon is like a story told aloud, where each sentence has gone forever into the past before the next is spoken. If we wish to learn from other arts, we must learn from these arts based on a time sequence.

If nobody but the preacher were involved, this difference would not be of great importance. Once I have worked my idea through in its structure and its development, in its generals and its particulars, I can see it all at once in my mind. It is then like a picture to me.

But preaching is communicating with other people. My listener cannot see the total picture as it is in my mind. I can never transfer my picture as a whole from my mind to his. I cannot even attempt to transfer it as a whole. I have to take it apart as if it were a jigsaw puzzle and hand it to him one piece at a time. If there is ever to be a complete picture in his mind, he has to see where each piece fits and put the picture together for himself.

This is what Quiller-Couch means by his remark, "We can only produce our effect by a series of successive small impressions, dripping our meaning into the reader's mind." [2] Good writing does this too, of course. But the necessity of it in oral communication is absolute.

The whole problem of design, of perspective, foreground and background, high light and low light, emphasis on what is structural and subordination of details—the whole problem becomes different when this time factor is taken into account. It becomes a problem of continuity, the order in which the pieces are to be presented. Moreover, it becomes a problem which must be solved for the listener, from his point of view, not from the point of view of the preacher.

THE HEARING SITUATION

In oral communication language reverts to its original character: sound, audible meaning. Writing, printing is not language, strictly speaking, only an arrangement of arbitrary visual symbols to indicate the sounds of speech. Speech is a medium of communication

[2] Quiller-Couch, *op. cit.*, p. 292f.

through the ear; writing is a medium of communication through the eye. One is the language of pure sound, like music. The othei is the language of shapes, color, space, and light, like painting and architecture. As media of communication, speech and writing differ as radically as these arts differ.

We cannot see the problems we face until we realize the radical difference between the hearing and the reading situations.

The first difference is that the listener has nothing to go by but the sounds he hears, the expressions on the preacher's face, and the postures and movements of his body—nothing else whatever. The visible marks of sentence structure, the capitals, commas, periods, and such, he does not hear. He cannot hear the paragraph indentations, nor any grouping of sentences except such grouping as the voice and the thought itself can make. He cannot hear the wide spaces or the captions like "The Hearing Situation" above, unless the caption is spoken. He cannot hear the Roman II in the margin, which reminds the preacher that he is passing from one thing to another. The number gives the hearer no help unless it is spoken.

The point is that the forms necessary in organizing a manuscript, the visible design, may betray the preacher, may make him think his design is clear when to the listener it is thoroughly jumbled. The only design useful to the listener is a design he can grasp through his ears, an audible movement of the thought.

The outline of the sermon, if it is to be of any use to the listener, must be clear and simple. It must have only a few structural divisions or points. Each of these divisions must begin perceptibly in time, run its course, and come to an end in time. One division must follow another like the movements of a symphony or the acts of a play. If the outline becomes elaborate or complicated, with many divisions, subdivisions, and sub-subdivisions, it may look attractive and orderly on paper, but it will be worse than useless to the listener.

> A - - - - - - - - - - - - - - - -
> I - - - - - - - - - - - - - -

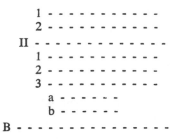

What can my listener make of this? If I do not speak the numbers, he will never know there are any numbers; my beautiful analysis of relationships between the points will be nonexistent for him. If I do speak the numbers, I will confuse him more. How can he remember that this *b* is a second constituent, along with *a,* of 3, which is of equal rank with 1 and 2 under Roman II, which itself is a second consideration, along with I, of a division A, which is the only thing yet said that is of equal rank with B which will be spoken in a few minutes? As if it were not already complicated enough, it is not at all impossible that this *b*—under 3 under II under A—may interest the listener more than anything that has been said before it, so that he gives it a rank even higher than A.

Obviously, such an elaborate outline is not worth the labor it takes to build it. Worse, it is a fraud and a delusion to the preacher, a misdirected effort, a substitute for the clear audible continuity that would have helped the listener.

The second difference between hearing and reading is an inevitable consequence of the movement in time. The listener has only one chance to understand any particular thing I may say, and that is in the instant I say it. Ten seconds later is for ever too late. What he does not grasp instantly he loses for good.

If a sentence does not at once convey its meaning, he cannot read it three times, figure it out, reconstruct it. If there is a word whose purport in that sentence is not immediately clear to him, he cannot look it up and then come back to see what it signifies in this place. If the bearing of an anecdote, an argument, or a quotation is not plain at once, he cannot stop listening and search out its connection, then pick up at the same spot and go on. A reader can do these things; a listener cannot.

These are mere details—granted. A hearer might understand me without that unfamiliar word, unclear sentence, or pointless story. But, unfortunately, he has not only lost what these might have contributed; they have interrupted and diverted his attention from the continuity of thought. The listener has only one chance to follow the continuous progress of my thought, and that is to go along with every step I take in moving toward my goal. That is his only chance to get where I hope to lead him.

A third difference between hearing and reading is that the listener has nothing but his memory to depend on as he tries to put the successive pieces of my thought together into a whole idea. He cannot go back and see again the thing I said earlier which now assumes a new importance. If he did not understand it at the time, he will not remember it now. If he understood it at the time, he still may not remember it. Yet that thing may be a very important component of the thought structure. If he does not remember it, it cannot contribute to the growing design of the thought in his mind. Thus my hope to communicate my idea to him is at the mercy of his memory.

Oral and written communication are so different, in these and other respects, that the highest excellence in one can be a fault in the other. To be sure, good writing also requires a careful continuity and a distribution of emphasis that signalizes each important element. But the highest responsibility of a writer is to create a design of thought and words that will continue to stand up after a number of readings. And the highest merit of a literary work is a quality and arrangement of thoughts that will have some new thing to give at the twentieth reading, that can no more be taken in fully with one reading than all that a fine symphony has in it can be recognized at the first hearing.

This is not the highest merit in a sermon meant to be heard once. The highest responsibility of the preacher is not to create such a permanent literary design. The test of my sermon design is not how well it stands up under re-examination and analysis. A good audible design will of course stand up under analysis. But that is not the test of its excellence. Nothing can be excellent about it which does not come through clearly the first and only time my listener will hear it.

Thus the listener depends on his memory, and his memory is at the mercy of my design. It is his task to listen; it is my task to know the difference between oral and written communication and to furnish an audible design which he can grasp, that is, to emphasize my important thoughts, subordinate the incidentals, and keep to a recognizable order.

It is my responsibility to introduce my important assertions, all the organic elements in my thought structure, in such a way as will mark them for the important elements they are. I must play them as a musician plays his principal themes. Each must be stated clearly and firmly. The developmental detail must be so related to the principal thought as to augment and not obscure it. I must give my hearer each new thought at the exact time when it will fit in with what has gone before, when its connection is obvious.

If I can do this, his memory will retain the structure of my thought as we move from point to point, and the design will grow in his mind. To revert to the figure of a jigsaw puzzle, if I hand him the pieces one at a time in the right order, if he does not have to pick the right one out of a handful of various shapes and sizes, the connection of each will be obvious, and he can put them together as we go along.

Something very like this happens in effective oral communication. As in listening to music or a play, my hearer receives a series of thoughts and impressions. There is progress. But if my idea is to take on wholeness and reality in his mind at the end of the sermon, he must get and hold in his memory these successive thoughts and impressions. He must build them up, put them together for himself, and hold them together as a unity in his own mind. I must employ his apprehension, his memory, and his constructive imagination.

AUDIBLE DESIGN

Consider an appalling fact. In the course of one sermon we are going to throw at our defenseless listener several thousands of words and two or three hundred assertions.

Among these thousands of words there will be two or three words which have within them the essence of the whole matter, as in this chapter the words *continuity, visible,* and *audible* contain the essence of what I am trying to say. Among the hundreds of assertions, there will be from one to a half dozen that contain, in distillation, the whole idea in its organic structure, as in this chapter the whole is contained in two assertions:

> The proper design of a sermon is a continuity in time.
> It is an audible, not a visible, continuity.

The important words of the sermon will be comparatively general words, as *continuity,* etc., are general. The important assertions will be generalizations like the two above, that is, they will be general as compared with the hundreds of assertions. Only in a generalization can we attempt to present a whole idea at once.

A good generalization can, in an instant of time, mark the full scope and contain the full meaning of the idea. Our difficulty is that a generalization cannot convey an experience of the idea to one who does not already experience it. An experience of the idea's meaning, a conviction of its truth, an apprehension of its consequences—these all rise out of particulars, as I hope an experience of audible continuity is evoked by mention of successive themes in music. The generalization is abstracted from many particulars, but it does not convey any of them; the word *continuity* does not convey the sequence of music, play, or story.

The sermon is an attempt to convey to the listener a view of the idea's meaning, truth, consequences, which he may not have had before. The conveying has to be done through particulars, no one of which is more than a fragment of the idea.

This may help us to understand both the nature of our task and the problems it presents. We have a problem, first, of showing our listener the relation between general assertions and the particulars we use to convey them. The second problem is that of presenting the generals and the particulars in such an order as will keep their relation clear while leading the hearer toward a full view of the idea.

With respect to relation, the problem of design is to present the three hundred particularizing sentences in compact groups clearly recognizable by the listener, each group cohering in one of the structural assertions which at once includes them all and is in turn illuminated by them.

This problem is intensified because the particulars, being concrete and more human, compete unfairly with the general assertions for the hearer's interest. The general assertion can, however, be given the advantage of a naturally strong position in a time sequence. What is said first and what is said last is emphasized by position. This gives a choice between three procedures, all used by effective speakers, the third being by no means excessive when used in thoughtful communication:

> First state the general point, then particularize it (deduction).
> Present particulars first; state the point last (induction).
> First state, then particularize, then restate at the last.

With respect to time, the problem of design is to arrange a sequence of structural parts which will also be a continuity of the listener's experience, in which each new element of the thought will be felt as a further thrust of the expanding idea.

Clearly, this continuity will include the whole sermon from the first sentence to the last. For the entire sermon, as for every one of its points, first and last are the positions of natural strength.

This is what gives the introduction and conclusion an importance out of proportion to their length. Indeed, many books on preaching in our time divide a sermon into three parts, introduction, body, and conclusion, as if they were of equal rank. The books often give no more attention to the body than to the introduction or the conclusion, as if the bodies of sermons were all alike.

However, introduction and conclusion must be parts of that continuity which is the whole design of the sermon. They are so intimately related to the idea and its development that it is impossible to treat them as if they had a separate existence apart from the whole design of the sermon. Sermons are not all of like design, and the introduction and conclusion cannot be planned until the main design is grasped.

TYPES OF CONTINUITY

The structural elements of a sermon are the elements out of which the continuity will be constructed. They are as follows, illustrated by the elements of "Design for a Sermon," page 15:

1. *A subject,* what will be talked about:
   A sermon
2. *An inclusive predicate,* one main thing the whole sermon will say about it, the central point the sermon will make:
   should be like a tree
3. *A series of structural assertions.* From two to a half dozen things that must be said to develop the idea, the different points the sermon will make. In our example as follows:
   It should be a living organism
   It should have deep roots
   It should show nothing but its own unfolding parts
   It should bear flowers and fruit at the same time
   To do all this it must grow in a warm climate

We have seen that the second of the above elements is dispensable. There may be no single predicate that includes all the structural assertions, at least not in the actual delivery of the sermon. The unity may be provided by the subject alone. The idea may not be complete without the whole series of contributing thoughts. There may be no part corresponding to 2 above.

However, in this example 1 and 2 together do make a complete idea, the central thing the address will say: a sermon should be like a tree. If a sermon has real unity, some inclusive predicate is often present in the preacher's mind though not spoken in delivering the sermon.

These are the elements out of which my continuity is to be built. I cannot begin it until, from the mass of notes I have made

in my study of the text and subject, the idea congeals and all the
main assertions are set down on paper or firmly fixed in my mind.

The first step

Since my design is to be a continuity, the first step is to fix the
goal of the sermon. I cannot plan a movement until I know in
what direction to go, and I cannot know the direction until I know
the point I wish to reach.

This means that from the series of structural assertions, whatever the order in which they may have been set down, I must
choose first the one that is to come last. My choice is influenced
by a variety of reasons. The last point should do two things at
once: it should bring the idea to its fullest stature, and it should
bring the people to the point of decision concerning the issue, the
"So what?" of the sermon.

The second step

My second step is to choose the structural assertion that is to
come first. The point of beginning and the point of ending mark
the limits of the entire movement, and determine its direction. The
beginning and the end are the two points that establish the line of
movement.

The reasons influencing this choice are even more varied. The
first point should always be one that meets my people where
they are. That is the only invariable consideration. But what it
should be in any given series of assertions depends on the
structural form of the idea and the type of continuity that is being
devised.

The third step

My next step, of course, is to arrange the order of the intervening points. That order is largely dictated by the beginning and
the end. It should be a step-by-step progress from the first point
to the last, planned for the people, each point being an enlarge-
ment of their view and a movement toward the goal.

To put the whole matter of continuity in a word, there must be
something to begin with and something to get to at the end. There

must be steps for getting from one to the other. There must be something that runs through all the points and relates them all to one another, to which they all refer.

The fourth step

When I have before me in their proper order all the points that are to be made, there remains one other highly important step: to allot to each point the exact number of minutes or even half-minutes allowed for its development. I shall have to learn how many words I customarily speak in one minute and exactly how much space they take on the page I am accustomed to write. To do this well is a discipline that will correct many faults in the design and the delivery of sermons.

If the material is to receive a balanced treatment within a given number of minutes, this step must be carried out faithfully. I cannot say too little about one contributing thought, or talk too long about another without distorting the shape and marring the effect of the sermon. If I have to introduce an idea, make six important points about it, and conclude within twenty-five minutes, I have an average of less than four minutes for each, and I cannot talk about any one of them as if I had ten minutes to give to it. If one point deserves more time than four minutes, it must be taken from the other points. If I cannot adequately develop these six points in, say, twenty-two minutes, then I have too many things to say, and I will have to prepare a simpler sketch of the sermon.

In all four of these steps, we face the fact that sermons are not all alike. The order of points is influenced by the character of the continuity. There is one order if the procedure is deductive and a different order if it is inductive. There is one order if the procedure is logically linked as in an argument, another if it is chronologically linked as in a narrative. There is still another order if the procedure is dramatic as in the acts of a play, or as in the form of the thesis-antithesis-synthesis.

Let me repeat: A proper continuity is necessary for the sake of the people who have to listen. It is not a luxury or refinement to enhance the style of the preacher. It is a means to successful oral communication. These types of continuity which we are about to examine all represent patterns in which the mind naturally moves. Worked out into a clear order, any one of them provides an audible progress of thought, and the people will follow it. They will not and cannot follow a jumbled order. If the procedure is inductive, it had better be clearly ordered induction. If the procedure is logically linked, it had better be logical. If it is a dramatic continuity, it had better adhere to the dramatic order strictly.

A Deductive Continuity

We must keep clear the distinction between induction and deduction as processes of thought. I move through a number of particulars: Men devise schemes for security, engage in cutthroat competition, are jealous and envious of one another, are driven by worries, get stomach ulcers, and so on—I move through these and reach a general conclusion that sums them up: men have a deep anxiety. That is induction.

Contrarily, I begin with the general statement: Men are deeply anxious. Then I move through the particulars that give it content: the schemes for security, the competition, the envy, the worry, the ulcers. That, so far as our present purpose is concerned, is deduction.

Strictly speaking, these are processes of thought and not types of continuity. Both may be used in the same sermon, one point being handled deductively and another approached inductively. However, since these are the major movements of thought, every sermon design itself is either deductive or inductive in method, moves either from a general assertion to particulars or from particulars to a general conclusion.

When I lead off with a complete idea, both subject and predicate, in the form of a proposition or message, then the movement is necessarily from this general idea to its particulars and is deductive. The five major assertions of "Design for a Sermon," page 15, describe particular tree-like characteristics of a sermon. The sketch is a deductive continuity.

These five assertions were not written at first in the order they now have in the design. I chose for the goal, the climax of the presentation, "To do this it must grow in a warm climate" because, while the other four points have to do with the sermon, this one deals with the climate of the preacher's very life. The issue is that if I am to preach fruitfully I must live richly.

The first assertion has to be "It should be a living organism" for two reasons. This is the assertion which immediately explains the idea, "A sermon should be like a tree." And again, this point is necessary as the foundation for the succeeding points.

The next assertion to be placed was the fourth, "It should bear flowers and fruit at the same time." This is not the last point, but is the last that deals with the character of the sermon itself. It also adds a new consideration: the high purpose served by this sermon and all preaching. Consequently, this point is climactic as regards the character of sermons. Also, its mention of continuous flowering and fruiting already hints at the warm climate.

The order of the two remaining points was determined by the naturalness of the steps. It seems natural to go from "living organism" to "deep roots." It seems natural to go from the life that depends on a deep and hidden system of roots to the life unfolding on the branches. And it seems natural to go from the "unfolding parts" the tree bears to the "flowers and fruits" it bears.

An Inductive Continuity

In preaching, induction commonly plays a secondary role though often an important one. That is, induction is commonly used as a method of development rather than a design for the whole sermon. But it is also used as an organizing principle.

Every sermon which begins with a description of persons or a narrative of events is proceeding inductively for the time being. Or, more correctly, it ought to be using induction. Sometimes it is not. It is not true induction unless it leads through the particulars to adequate generalization without undue loss of time.

Thousands of mediocre sermons achieve mediocrity by talking only of persons, places, incidents, quotations, and all sorts of details, never coming to the point, never making adequate generalizations.

Particulars have more "human interest" than generals. An inductive introduction may be effective if it does the proper work of an introduction with dispatch, if the particulars are so chosen and handled as to lead at once to a statement of the idea. That is a big *if,* always a hazard, often a deathtrap for the unskilful.

A more extended use of induction is not uncommon. Roughly the first half of the sermon may be inductive, leading to a statement of the central idea somewhere about the middle; the idea is handled deductively from that point onward.

Robert I. Gannon, S.J., has a Lenten sermon in this form[3] on John 17:9, "I pray not for the world, but for them whom thou hast given me." The subject is "The Spirit of the World."

The first half of the sermon is narrative. The scene is Herod's court in Jerusalem when the magis arrive. Annas and Caiaphas are there among the party men and scholars, and it becomes the story of Caiaphas. He chooses Herod's side, casts his lot with the spirit of the world, marries Annas' daughter, later becomes high priest and profits from the temple business.

The story is vividly told. At almost the exact middle of the sermon, the idea is first generalized: Caiaphas "was a symbol. He stood for the world that Christ refused to pray for." From that point on to the end of the sermon, this spirit of the world is handled deductively.

Although induction is more commonly used thus to lead up to the statement of the idea, it may extend to the whole continuity of the sermon. That is, the text or the general idea, or both, may be withheld until the end of the sermon. They are of course known to the preacher, and shape the sermon as definitely as if he started

---

[3] G. Paul Butler *Best Sermons* (New York: Macmillan, 1952), p. 93.

with them. They are simply withheld and made the climax and goal of the sermon rather than its starting point. The whole sermon will then be moving through particulars to reach the full idea, the theme or message, only at the end. Any general assertions used in the progress of the development will be particularizing assertions within the body of the central thought.

The story leading to a generalization is an ancient and familiar literary form. It is as old as Aesop's fables, as contemporary as the fables of James Thurber and the *Rootabaga Stories* of Carl Sandburg, as significant as the final conversation between Nina and Marsden in O'Neill's *Strange Interlude,* or the comment on life by the dead at the end of Thornton Wilder's *Our Town,* or the post-mortem on Willy Loman that closes Arthur Miller's *Death of a Salesman.*

But the structure of an inductive continuity does not have to be a story. The sermon on "God Cares," page 76, could be preached inductively. The text is I Peter 5:7, "Cast all your anxiety on him, for he cares about you." The text and message would not be announced at the beginning. The steps may be indicated by the following structural points, but each one of these would be reached by beginning with particulars and moving from them to the general assertion.

> Particulars leading to: It often seems that God does not care about us.
> Particulars: There is a traditional belief that he cares.
> Particulars: Most don't believe it, some do (anxiety, trust).
>
> Particulars: We have his words that he cares.
> The issue is either anxiety or trust.

A Logical Continuity

This is hardly a "type," rather a large and variable class which includes all continuities not marked by some special characteristic. All continuities are "logical" in some sense.

If the sermon is a piece of formal reasoning, it will necessarily follow some order of formal logic. The last point will be the one which states the conclusion, and the first will be the one which points most directly to the major premise on which the argument is based. Indeed, a sermon of this kind may be something like an extended syllogism or enthymeme, as is the following:

JUDGE NOT, by a student beginner

Text: Matthew 7:4. "Or how can you say to your brother, 'Let me take the speck out of your eye,' when there is a log in your own eye?"
To judge truthfully one must have perfect insight into what is to be judged.
But our judgment is blinded by our sin.
Therefore, we cannot presume to judge our fellows.

An argument may proceed from one conclusion to another in a longer chain. This requires the most careful selection beforehand of the final conclusion, for that will determine the whole tenor of the sermon and its chief point. The first point will be one which this particular group of listeners will accept as a premise.

In the following specimen the movement from thesis to antithesis and back again is noteworthy:

ACCEPTABLE OFFERING, by a student beginner

Text: Romans 12:1-2. I appeal to you . . . to present your bodies as a living sacrifice, holy and acceptable to God. . . . Be transformed by the renewal of your mind, that you may prove what is the will of God, what is good and acceptable and perfect.
We like to say that a man cannot save himself by his good works.
This, true as it is, tends to discredit all good works.
We fail to distinguish good works which are the result of true faith and regeneration from those "good" works which are intended to set a man right with God.
It is impossible for a man to right himself with God by works.
But it is equally impossible to have true faith that does not manifest itself in good works.
When a man is reborn through faith, he subjects his own will to the will of God.
Therefore, all that a regenerate man does expresses the will of God in some imperfect fashion.
Since the will of God is truly good, the works of a regenerate man must necessarily be good.
Such good works are acceptable in the eye of God.

There is a logic of impressions as well as of propositions. In a good continuity each new step will seem to the people like a natural consequence of what has gone before. There is a mental readiness for it which is as much a matter of feeling as of thinking. When the listener's view of one point has reached a certain fulness, the new thrust of the idea is more natural than standing still.

Something like this, a matter of intuitive feeling as much as of thought, is what often guides a preacher in arranging the continuity of his points. It is his inner sense of form and rhythmical movement coming into play. It guided us on page 171 in our arrangement of the points in "Design for a Sermon."

STEADFASTNESS IN THE LORD, by a beginner

Text: Philippians 4:1. Therefore, my brethren, whom I love and long for, my joy and crown, stand firm thus in the Lord, my beloved.

This means that we stand firm:
In our allegiance to the Lord.
In the knowledge of our dependence on him.
In our expectation of his future advent.

In this example the last point was evidently chosen because of its eschatological finality. The attitude of expecting the ultimate judgment and reign of Christ is a larger characteristic of the life of a believer than either his allegiance or his dependence.

But why begin with allegiance? Is not the fact of dependence prior to allegiance? And is not the knowledge of dependence one factor in the motivation of allegiance? These points would be better if reversed.

THE GOOD SHEPHERD, by a beginner

Text: John 10:11. I am the good shepherd. The good shepherd lays down his life for the sheep.

He owns the sheep.
He knows his sheep.
He feeds his sheep.
He leads his sheep.

In this example the problem of order is more subtle. The continuity will be produced by a mixture of logical and psychological cogency in which the psychological factor will perhaps be the more decisive.

As in the preceding example, the last point is apparently chosen for its eschatological reference: He leads through life and death. But the sound of the words must also be suspected: owns—knows —feeds—leads.

Ownership is undoubtedly the place to begin. It is basic to knowing and feeding, for it affects the quality of the knowing and feeding; he knows and feeds them as his own.

But the choice of the last point, the goal, depends on the function of the sermon. If the purpose is teaching, to convey an understanding of what the shepherd's full work is, then the continuity should be as it stands in the above sketch.

On the other hand, if the purpose is to convey an assurance of the shepherd's care, the goal of the sermon will be, *He knows his sheep;* he calls them every one by name. In that rather than in his distant provision his care becomes personal and wonderful.

This shows the importance of setting the goal first. The choice of this last point not only determines where the sermon will go, where the preacher will try to take his people and where he will leave them; it also determines the character of his development, how he will treat every point from the first one.

A Chronological Continuity

A narrative is more than a succession of events. It is a unified series in which persons and happenings interact to produce a crisis and outcome. When it has once been told, everything and every person in the narrative becomes a necessary part of the whole. Strung on a thread of time, it is more than a mere chronology.

A successful story sermon must achieve the unity of a narrative. The unity centers in the crisis, and everything in the sermon must be related to that. The outcome depends on the nature of the crisis and the forces that produce it.

Since it is not feasible to display a new story sermon for study, we look again at Simon the Pharisee.

A MAN WHO HAD TOO LITTLE AT STAKE (See page 159)

This is Simon's story. He furnishes the point of view from which the whole action is seen. The crisis comes when the woman's penitent devotion and Christ's forgiveness both pass before Simon's eyes and he fails to see either. The outcome for the woman is Christ's word of forgiveness. For Simon it is his failure to profit by Jesus' personal appeal to him.

The story leading up to the crisis and forecasting the outcome for Simon was produced by working backward from the outcome through the details supplied by Luke's account. Thus the absence of water, oil, and welcoming salutation, which comes out only in Jesus' words at the end, is put back near the beginning in the interpretation of Simon's character. The description of Simon's attitude as being uninvolved and noncommittal is no mere guess. It is indicated by every shred of the evidence.

Listening to this story, if it is well told, people will first meet a human being. The truth of existence will confront them not in mental abstractions but in the concrete form of a person so like themselves that they may compare and also identify themselves with him. They can sit with him in the presence of Jesus and go with him to the moment of supreme possibility and supreme testing. The experience is closer to seeing with their own eyes than to being told about it.

Many a sermon not in the form of a story is yet organized chronologically. Perhaps most sermons on the parables of Jesus and on biblical incidents follow a continuity of time without any deliberate intention to do so. I shall give only one example:

ADVENTURE AT EMMAUS, by a beginner

Text: Luke 24:13-35. The two disciples and Jesus on the first Easter Day.

> Two men.
> Three men.
> Two men.

This noun outline of a chronological sequence is yet so dramatic in its suggestion that it might serve as an example of the next type also.

A Dramatic Continuity

Many sermons fall into a continuity of three steps so related as to produce a dramatic action.

The dramatic quality of the action is wholly in the dynamic relation of the steps, not in the number three. Such an action is well illustrated by the modern three-act play. But the action of a one-act or five-act play is the same kind of action.

First phase: *Exposition.* Persons are introduced in such a way as to reveal a problem situation and start the action moving in a given direction.

Second phase: *Complication.* The action runs into difficulties, meets opposing forces which impede its movement, threaten it, and produce conflict.

Third phase: *Resolution.* The action reaches a climax and passes into an outcome which resolves the conflict or brings victory to one side and disposes of the other.

Evidently, this pattern is present more or less distinctly in every good story. There is something elemental about it. Our attempt to understand existence falls so constantly into this pattern that we may come to see it as the pattern of existence itself, as Hegel did.

Moreover, this is a constantly recurring pattern of thought as well as of action:

> A directional thrust of thought: *thesis.*
> A counterthrust: *antithesis*—conflict, paradox, dilemma.
> Resolution: a new *synthesis.*

As they apply to preaching, we may consider these patterns as one. Both produce the same kind of continuity which we shall call *dramatic.*

This dramatic quality is inherent in a great many sermon ideas. Sometimes the material falls into this form of itself without the preacher's deliberate intention. More often the preacher, having an underdeveloped sense of form, fails to see and use the dramatic tension of his own thought.

FALSE PROPHETS (See pages 82, 91)

This sermon took form as a dramatic continuity without my knowledge. Only when planning this chapter did I notice that it is an example of this type of continuity.

EXPOSITION: The precarious situation of the man in the pulpit.
The Lord warns his people that the man in the pulpit may be a false prophet; he makes the preacher listen to that warning.
The only certain thing about the preacher is that he does come in sheep's clothing.
He may be a good man but a false prophet; nothing but his message can vouch for him.
True prophecy differs from human speech not in quality but in kind; it is of a different species.

COMPLICATION: The preacher's unwillingness to function as a true prophet.
The man in the pulpit
   Resists the Spirit who commands him to prophesy,
   Constructs rational defenses against the Spirit,
   Claims to speak and act in the Lord's name,
   Thinks he is doing the Father's will.
In all this he is just like the many who are rejected.

RESOLUTION: The preacher's true relation to his Lord.
The true preacher trembles before
   The stern, negative warning of Christ,
   The mystery of that kingdom he may not be in,
   The absolute, uncompromising Will he risks not doing,
   The holy Love he can serve but cannot emulate.
It is well that we have to hear this warning; it leaves the issue as the Lord put it.

The final example is one of the first five sermon sketches prepared by a beginner. I am quite sure he was not trying to work out a dramatic continuity. The antithesis was in his thought itself.

Let me explain that this man had been instructed not to bother about any secondary, particularizing points except what might come of themselves as he worked. The major assertions were our only concern at that stage. I give his work in its unfinished condition, for it shows vividly how the idea was then fermenting and expanding in his mind. But the continuity is to be found in the three structural assertions.

A Sketch on RIGHTEOUSNESS, by a beginner

Text: Romans 10:3. For, being ignorant of the righteousness that comes from God, and seeking to establish their own, they did not submit to God's righteousness.

It is a part of human nature to seek to establish our own righteousness.
We desire merit.
We set our own standards.
We try to establish a "Christian ethic."

This striving contains the seed of its own destruction.
We become legalistic.
We become egocentric.
We fail to address the real moral issues.
We strain out gnats and swallow camels.
We look down on those "less pious."
We think it possible to do more than necessary.
We fail to understand our debt before God.

We can have no righteousness of our own, but it is given us to submit to God's righteousness.
True life in the form of purity is denied us.
True life in the form of repentance is ours.

We have studied these types of continuity not to learn them as self-conscious devices for artificial use, but to awaken our sense of the forms thought actually takes in communication.

Every one of these forms comes into being as a result of a man's attempt to provide for the people before him a continuous and enlarging experience of the idea that is in his own mind.

SUGGESTIONS

You should now be able to clear up, or begin to clear up, the confusion which exists with regard to the classification of sermons. Sermons must be classified in two independent ways: structurally, as regards form, and functionally, as regards purpose. These are confused in the literature.

For example, in Sangster (12), Chapters II and III, certainly one of the most significant classifications, the six categories on page 32 are only in part descriptions of subject matter. It is necessary for him to say that "biblical interpretation" is related to all kinds of preaching.

"Philosophical and apologetic" preaching is marked by purpose and method as much as by subject matter. And such categories as "social" and "evangelistic" are clearly functional rather than descriptive of distinct kinds of subject matter.

These newer descriptions of sermon types are nevertheless useful. Learn all you can about them from Sangster. Study the classification in Blackwood (3), Chapters XI and XII, pages 125-151. Read Ferris (7) with imagination, for it is written with imagination. His Chapter II is the one in which he proposes a classification, quite functional in its emphasis.

CHAPTER II

Continuity: Introduction and Conclusion

The first words of a book are not simply those which happen to stand at the top of the first page. They are the beginning of a new experience for both the author and the reader, and they point towards the end of that experience.

The first words need not be dramatic: they need not even be clear; but they must grip the mind of the reader and begin to mold his mood.
Gilbert Highet, "The First Few Words" [1]

In the previous chapter we tried to see the whole sermon as a movement in time, from the moment it begins to the moment it ends. We were particularly concerned with the major stages of that movement, represented by the succession of structural assertions, and with some distinctive patterns into which the movement most commonly falls. We now turn to the two short but decisive moments in that movement, its beginning and end.

When searching for elements of audible design, we noticed that, because the first thing and the last thing are in positions of natural emphasis, the introduction and conclusion of the sermon are more important than their brevity would suggest.

The varied types of continuity show why the introduction and conclusion cannot be planned as if they existed apart from the whole movement of the sermon. An inductive sermon is not introduced in the same way as a deductive sermon. A story does not begin as a logical argument begins.

INTRODUCTION

The often-repeated rules for the introduction of a sermon are two: it should win attention; it should gain interest. The verbs are *to attend* and *to interest*. Both are transitive verbs. People do not simply attend; they attend to something, to somebody. We do

[1] Radio talk. By permission of the Book-of-the-Month Club and the copyright owner, Oxford University Press.

not simply interest people; we interest them in something or in someone, ourselves or somebody else.

The purpose of an introduction is *to introduce,* also transitive. "Let me introduce" is not a complete thought. Introduce what? The main idea or some competing thought? Win attention to and interest in whom? The preacher? Hardly! In whom or in what then?

The preacher's peril is not that attention is hard to win. His greatest peril is that attention and interest are too easy to win from the people who come to church. These people keep coming, often in spite of repeated disappointments, ready to listen and hoping— against hope?—that today there will be something to hear. If a man has a thing worth saying and says it well, he need have no worry about people's attention.

The people want to get to the point at once, no hedging or foolishness about it; the preacher may not, but the people do. If he plays a game with their interest, if, for example, he gives them a story that is interesting but irrelevant, they will be as trusting as he is dishonest. They will take what he gives them as being to the point whether it is or not. They will be waiting for him to go on with the subject he has introduced.

If later he wants their attention to something else than the thing he started with, he will have two jobs on his hands: first he will have to win them back from the interest he has misdirected toward the wrong thing, then win a brand new interest in the right thing. The misdirected interest, far from being a gain, becomes a heavy liability. Many a sermon never recovers from a story told in the introduction. The more interesting the story the more disruptive it may be.

The introduction should introduce the central idea, whether subject, proposition, message, question, or narrative. It should do this as quickly and pertinently, with as strict economy of means as it can. It should avoid every word that does not point toward the central idea, for any extraneous thought is liable to be a false lead. No two sermons are alike, and no two should begin the same way.

If the introduction could possibly be used for any other sermon than this, it is not a good introduction to this sermon.

An idea fit for a sermon is more than a mental concept, a thought of the preacher. It is a word of truth from God to every person who will hear. It carries an issue of life and death. To confront this word is to confront the issue, and to confront the issue is to confront God in one's own life.

If the preacher's central thought meets the requirements for a sermon idea, there is nothing better or more interesting he can give the people. The surest begetter of the congregation's interest is the preacher's own interest in what he has to say. His reluctance or slowness to get down to business is his weakest bid for a listener's interest.

The introduction should be thought of as the first two minutes of a twenty- to twenty-five-minute experience by the people of the sermon's thought. It is their first encounter with the idea, the first phase of a growing experience.

The first two minutes of a twenty-minute continuity should not be like the first two minutes of a sixty-minute continuity. If anything important is to be accomplished in twenty minutes, there is no time for beating about the bush in the first critical minutes.

The introduction of a well-designed sermon fits the functional form of the sermon, whether proclamation, teaching, or therapy. It also fits the structural form, whether proposition, message, question, or narrative. It furnishes a significant encounter with the idea, the beginning of an experience shared by preacher and people.

The first two minutes may do little more than answer one or both of the structural questions: "What is he going to talk about today?" and "What in general is he going to say about it?"

Our Reformation Inheritance, by Bishop Dun (See page 143)

This sermon is a subject to be supplied with predicates: Our Reformation heritage is belief in this and this and this and this. He introduces it as follows:

Our text is a phrase from the opening verse of St. Luke's Gospel: "A declaration of those things which are most surely believed among us."

Dearly beloved in the Lord, we gather here as those who rejoice to share together the Reformation inheritance. We meet as those who bear unashamedly the name of Protestants. Our very coming together is "a declaration of those things which are most surely believed among us," even though I succeed very imperfectly in declaring what those things are.[2]

Only at great peril can the introduction do less than this: name what is to be talked about and foreshadow what is to be said. Even when the idea takes the form of a story told, it is risky to do less.

A MAN WHO HAD TOO LITTLE AT STAKE (See pages 159, 181)

This is the story of a man who was so smooth that nothing, not even meeting the Lord face to face, could do him any good. He had so little at stake in the game of life that it made no great difference to him how it was played. He meant to make his own rules anyway.

The first minute or two can, however, do more than announce the subject or introduce the thought. They can raise one or more of the functional questions as well: "Is this true? Do we believe it?" "So what? What issue does it present to me, the listener?" That is to say, the people's first experience of the idea may be an encounter with the life-issue it presents to them, their stake in it, its relevance, its challenge, its appeal to them.

By doing this, the preacher can make sure that he will meet his people where they are, that the sermon will address them personally in such a way that they know it speaks to them. Its relevance is assured in the first minute.

Dr. George Buttrick teaches this raising of the issue as one of the four requisites of every introduction, along with brevity, interestingness, and appropriateness to that particular sermon.[3]

FORGIVENESS OF SINS, by Harry Emerson Fosdick
(See pages 60, 140f)

The structural form is that of a subject discussed under three predicates, or two if *need* and *necessity* are taken as one. The movement is a logical continuity, and it is introduced as follows:

[2] A. M. Motter, *Sunday Evening Sermons.* Used by permission.
[3] In an unpublished lecture.

The only persons to whom this message is addressed are those conscious of moral wrongdoing. If there is any hearer with no uneasy stirrings of conscience about his attitude toward anything or his relationship with anybody, then this sermon is not for him. For we are going to talk about forgiveness of sins.[4]

This introduction raises the question, "What difference does it make to me? Do I need forgiveness, perhaps without knowing it?"

FALSE PROPHETS (See pages 91, 183)

This is a dramatic continuity. Strictly speaking, there is no formal introduction. The first paragraph which follows below is the beginning of the exposition; it generalizes the precarious situation of the man in the pulpit.

This text stops us preachers in our tracks and makes us listen while God talks to our people about us. Take warning, he says, Stop, look, and listen! He cautions our people: Danger ahead! Road unsafe! Travel at your own risk! "Beware of false prophets, who come to you in sheep's clothing."

Since the sermon is preached to a group of preachers, this raises the question, "Is this true of me? Is it possible that I may be a false prophet such as Christ is speaking about?"

"BLESSED ARE THE MEEK," by George A. Buttrick

We quarrel with this text in both its parts. We doubt that meekness is blessed, and we are reasonably sure that it does not inherit the earth. Is there anybody in this congregation who would like to be called "a meek little man"? The adjective little and the adjective meek somehow seem to belong together. The Hindu in India who heard this text for the first time remarked, "The Englishman may inherit the earth, but he would be insulted if you called him meek." [5]

This introduction illustrates the strategy of meeting the hearer at the point of his doubt with something better than tolerance. Instead of raising the question, "Is this true?" it begins by asserting that we all doubt it, preacher and hearers alike—which raises the question of its truth in a more portentous form.

[4] From *The Secret of Victorious Living* (New York: Harper, 1934). Blackwood, *op. cit.*, p. 191. Used by permission.
[5] In the lecture cited above. Copy confirmed by Dr. Buttrick and used by his kind permission.

Men who have studied preaching under Dr. Fosdick report a saying of his, "Tell all you know in the first sentence." Not having had the good fortune to be one of Dr. Fosdick's students, I cannot be certain what he means by that injunction. I can guess some things he might mean.

One thing he might mean is the way a first sentence willy-nilly sets the tone for those which are to follow, whether casual or purposeful, trivial or serious. The first sentence sounds a key that is not easy to change. Robert Frost means the same thing when he says that the outcome of a poem, though unforeseen, is predestined from the first line, and even from the mood that produced the first image. Gilbert Highet, in the talk quoted at the head of this chapter, discussed a number of such great first sentences, each foreshadowing the whole book, conspicuous among them being the tremendous opening of *Moby Dick:* "Call me Ishmael."

Another thing is that a good first sentence can open a view to the very heart of the matter, and we cannot get to the heart of the matter too soon. This is virtually saying that a formal introduction may not be necessary. And surely the introduction does not exist for the sake of having an introduction. Every sermon must have a beginning, certainly, but not necessarily an appendage called an introduction. If we can tell all we know in the first sentence, then speaking that sentence will put us at once in the middle of the idea and will at least make sure that we get there. For example:

THE CANDLE OF THE LORD, by Phillips Brooks

Preaching on Proverbs 20:27, "The spirit of man is the candle of the Lord," Brooks begins:

The essential connection between the life of God and the life of man is the great truth of the world; and that is the truth which Solomon sets forth in the striking words which I have chosen for my text this morning.[6]

EASTER SERMON, by Fulton J. Sheen

The sermon is not based on any particular text. The first two sentences are one thought:

[6] Macartney, *op. cit.,* p. 513.

There is not the joy this Easter that there ought to be. The enemies of God are too optimistic, and the friends of God are too pessimistic.[7]

The whole message is contained in those two sentences. The sermon is nothing else than a development of the antithesis contained in these few words. This thought makes the sermon, *is* the sermon in short. The preacher takes apart and recombines the terms of this antithesis exactly as Beethoven does with the principal subject in one of his symphonies. Easter Day and our day are alike in that the enemies and the friends of God are both wrong in their opposite attitudes: false optimism, unwarranted despair.

Thus the first two minutes of a well-designed sermon continuity gives its hearers an encounter with the central thought, a carefully chosen first phase of an enlarging experience of the idea.

THE CONCLUSION

The last minute or two of a well-designed sermon will give the people a final view of the central thought. After all that has been said, the view should now be fuller, should have a deeper significance than was possible at any time before.

The conclusion is the moment in which listeners can come nearest to seeing the idea whole and all at one time. It is the moment in which the issue can be seen at its clearest, felt at its sharpest, and carried back into life where, if anywhere, it must be resolved. The conclusion is the last chance to accomplish the sermon's purpose, whatever that may be.

Consequently, this moment is perhaps the most important single moment in the entire continuity. A sermon should conclude, not just stop; it should finish, not just dribble off.

The above remarks contain about everything that can be said concerning the conclusion in general. Nothing more specific would be true of every conclusion found in the work of good preachers. Sermons are not all alike, do not all have the same purpose, and do not all take the same form. Variety in conclusions is as great as variety in sermons themselves, or even greater.

[7] Butler, *op. cit.*, p. 128.

Perhaps the first thing to say is that not every sermon has a formal conclusion. Many a good sermon finishes with its last point. The traditional purposes of the conclusion, such as application, exhortation, appeal, etc., are accomplished in connection with the last point.

At any rate, in a twenty-five-minute continuity a master preacher will not postpone the application, the goal or purpose of the sermon, to the few minutes of the conclusion. He will have been moving steadily toward it throughout, and the carefully chosen last point will have brought him to the goal, the issue. When he has finished with this point, he may speak his closing words and stop. This is what Clow does.

THE CROSS AND THE MEMORY OF SIN (See pages 71, 142)

The true subject is the difference the cross makes in the memory of sin, and the last point is that it will finally obliterate the memory of sin. He concludes on this point without turning back to the subject as a whole. He concludes on a note of heightened affirmation. There is no application, no exhortation, no verbal plea.

Sometimes we fear that we shall remember, with the rich man, the neglected beggar at our gate, the undone duty of our life, the lost opportunities of our service, the deed that ruined another's life. No, my brethren, the lash of memory will be felt, as it is felt here and now, only in hell. It is, let me repeat, the unforgiven sin whose stain is indelible. But in heaven, when men will sing that new song of the Redeemed, "Worthy is the Lamb that was slain," when the Cross shall have become a dearer and more significant symbol than on earth, when the entrancing preoccupation of a completed salvation shall seize and hold both heart and mind, the evil words and deeds of time shall pass away like a forgotten dream. No sin can live under the felt power of the Cross.[8]

A more formal conclusion turns back after the last point to look once again at the whole idea, whether it be subject, proposition, message, question, or story. This is called for in case the last point does not represent the whole idea and its important consequences. It is necessary in a truly inductive sermon where no point is more than a part contributing to the whole. In induction, unless the

[8] Clow, *op. cit.* Used by permission. Blackwood, *op. cit.,* p. 157.

central thought is completed in the conclusion, it will never be completed. In many other sermons there is gain in looking back at the whole idea, if it is done well, swiftly, and without tiresome reiteration. For example:

WHY PEOPLE DO GO TO CHURCH, by Leslie D. Weatherhead

The points are that people go to church to worship God, to find forgiveness, to find fellowship, to find spiritual power for living. The development of the last point ends with the assertion that the power people go to find is God. That assertion is the goal of the sermon. But after that he concludes as follows:

Those who go to church and find the real God answer for themselves the question with which we started, "Why do men go to church?" They go to worship; they go to find pardon; they go to enter a fellowship; they go to get power. No! No! We need not divide it thus. They go to find all their deepest longings satisfied when they find God himself. He is the goal toward which our spirits move. He is the reality behind all men's dreams. He is the answer to all our prayers. Jesus, who was the supreme Master of the art of living, could not live without God. Can you?[9]

Here there is a looking back at the whole subject, and a recapitulation of all the points made, not for the sake of repeating them, but in order to bind them into a unity of the whole idea. There is no exhortation or verbal plea. He ends on the note of affirmation, proclamation, to which he adds a personal question.

Whatever else the conclusion of a contemporary sermon is, if well designed it is brief and to the point. It is the last two minutes of twenty-five, not of sixty or more. A devious or lingering conclusion, appropriate, say, to Spurgeon's sermon "Songs in the Night," [10] will completely destroy the balance and the effect of a sermon in our day, with a time limit of twenty to thirty minutes.

Commonly recognized purposes of the conclusion mostly come within the category I have called therapy. A conclusion may take the form of exhortation, of entreaty or appeal, of encouragement and consolation. It may take the form of warning, but seldom

[9] *The Significance of Silence* (Nashville: Abingdon-Cokesbury, 1946). Quoted by permission. It is No. 39 in Blackwood, *op. cit.*, p. 295.
[10] Blackwood, *op. cit.*, p. 127f.

is negative only; if it warns, it promises at the same time; it sets the warning over against the promise. This exhortation, entreaty, encouragement, warning, or promise is legitimately addressed to those who consider themselves believers. There need be no doubt that a conclusion may properly take any of these forms.

The conclusion may also take the form of invitation, call, or earnest plea to turn and believe, to embrace the promise and act on it, a plea addressed to persons who presumably have not yet believed. Such an appeal is made in God's name by an ambassador of Christ acting in place of Christ. It is an appeal for a decision, for a verdict. There can be no doubt that this appeal is a necessary part of the full proclamation of the gospel, in the technical sense of the term, no doubt therefore that the conclusion of a kerygmatic sermon may properly take the form of such a plea.

However, the often-repeated injunction that, since the preacher is a herald of Christ, the conclusion of every sermon should take the form of a plea—that is a different matter entirely. This rule assumes a great deal more than that the preacher is a herald of Christ. It assumes that the sermon is always addressed to unbelievers and not to believers. And it further assumes that the best way to secure a decision or verdict is for the preacher to make a verbal plea for one. The last assumption is particularly doubtful. It is neither certain that a plea is always the best way of preaching for a verdict, nor that if such a plea is made it should always be made in the conclusion of the sermon.

At any rate, there are other forms which preaching for a verdict often takes in the conclusion of a sermon. It takes the form of challenge. It takes the form of questions asked and left open for the hearer's answer. It takes the form of clearly stated alternatives between which a choice must be made. It takes the form of an issue sharply defined and left unresolved. And it sometimes takes the form of truth simply announced, affirmed by the preacher, the form of his own personal witness.

All of these aim at the hearer's decision, and a sermon may properly end on any of these notes. Every one of them will produce a different kind of conclusion. Published sermons show examples of all these forms and more than these, in a variety of combinations far too great to describe or illustrate.

Questions raised concerning the verbal plea apply equally to exhortation. Notwithstanding its legitimate place in preaching, exhortation, admonition, advice in general, have less effective power than is sometimes attributed to them. The strongest incitation to right attitudes and right action is not always a verbal exhortation. People usually dislike, and nearly always unconsciously resist, being given a ready-made answer by the preacher.

The master preachers in our day exhort and plead less than preachers formerly did. That they usually prefer other ways of preaching for a decision is no sign that they have less zeal for truth and right. A pointed conclusion of some other sort is preferred because it is a more effective means of accomplishing the very thing exhortation aims at, more effective surely than stereotypes like, "We ought . . ." "Let us then . . ." "May we all . . ." and so on. I suspect that the preacher's partiality to such forms is due not to his zeal but to the false sense of importance and power it gives him to tell other people what they ought to do.

The conclusion, more frequently than any other part of the sermon, acts on the dubious notion that every question ought to be supplied with an intellectualized answer, every problem be given a finished solution, every uncertainty be removed, every anxiety be stilled, every soul be reassured and comforted. Preaching for a decision, on the contrary, must make clear that at any moment in time the important question remains unanswered, the critical issue undecided. In the last minute of the sermon as well as in the first, a false comfort is false, a premature reassurance is premature, and an unanswered question is unanswered. The preacher's talk may have clarified the situation but has not changed it. In his conclusion he often seems to be under the delusion that the situation has been changed.

The last minute of the sermon should of course do something positive. If the sermon is a living thing, it will have brought the preacher himself to a fresh insight, a heightened vision, which he could have reached only by way of this sermon. He reaches it as he prepares the sermon, as the sermon comes alive and takes its shape in his mind.

Furthermore, the act of communicating is a mysterious, two-way experience. If the preacher is not simply reproducing a manuscript, a sudden insight not reached in his preparation may change the last two minutes he had planned. He dare not trust that insight to come and so neglect to prepare his conclusion. But he dare not, indeed he cannot disregard it if it comes.

"Clarification" Robert Frost calls this moment of heightened vision, speaking of the end of a poem. It holds for the conclusion of a sermon as well. A good sermon, too, ends in a clarification of life, not necessarily a great clarification, but "a momentary stay against confusion" at the least. If a sermon conclusion can really do that, it need do nothing more.

All forms of conclusion mentioned above are therapeutic, with the exception of affirmation, which is kerygmatic. There are other forms which conclusions take, older forms with a proud tradition in Christian history.

A conclusion may take the form of a benediction, of blessing pronounced on the people of the Lord. It may take the form of prayer and supplication to God on behalf of the people. Or it may take the form of an ascription of glory and praise to God, the form of a doxology. These are three different forms: benediction, prayer, doxology. Each alone may produce a conclusion, or they may be combined.

The epistles of the New Testament are written to be read aloud in the Christian congregation, that is, in the very situation where pastoral preaching is done, and we may safely assume that in form they resemble the discourses delivered in the assembly of the church. That nearly all of them conclude with some such form of benediction or doxology indicates an accepted practice of Christian discourse.

The grace of the Lord Jesus Christ and the love of God and the communion of the Holy Ghost be with you all.

This has become the common New Testament benediction at the close of Christian services of worship. But originally it is the conclusion of Paul's Second Letter to the Corinthians, and it was first heard as the end of an apostolic communication to a congregation assembled for worship. Some such benediction occurs so frequently in the epistles that we may be sure it was a common form of conclusion for pastoral discourses.

Now unto him that is able to do exceeding abundantly above all that we ask or think, according to the power that worketh in us; unto him be glory in the church by Christ Jesus, throughout all ages, world without end. Amen.

The liturgy of the Presbyterian *Book of Common Worship* directs that this ascription of glory to God may follow or conclude the sermon. It is of course the doxology concluding the first section of the Letter to the Ephesians, the last two verses of Chapter 3.

The peace of God, which passeth all understanding, (shall) keep your hearts and minds through Christ Jesus.

This benediction is the liturgically prescribed conclusion of the sermon period in the Lutheran liturgy for the Service. It is the benediction that concludes the main body of the Letter to the Philippians at 4:7.

The homily known to us as II Clement, dating from the second century, immediately following the passage quoted on page 136, concludes with the following doxology, which seems in its first phrase to echo I Timothy 1:17. However, it is not a stereotype slavishly quoted, but apparently a free composition of the preacher in the spirit and form of the doxologies that may have concluded all sermons.

To the only invisible God, Father of the truth, who sent forth to us the Savior and Prince of immortality, through whom he also made manifest to us the truth and the life of heaven, to him be the glory for ever and ever.[11]

[11] See any edition of *The Apostolic Fathers*. Translation composite.

Should a benediction or doxology, such as these I have quoted, seem incongruous with the modern sermon, that fact throws graver doubt on the propriety of the sermon than on the propriety of the conclusion. If the sermon has led to a confrontation with God in Christ, why should the glory of God not be as appropriate a note to end on as preoccupation with our own personal concerns?

In any case, the example of the ancient fathers supports the preacher of today who occasionally concludes with a prayer, a benediction, or an ascription of praise. John Chrysostom, while typical, is the supreme master of this form of conclusion. Every one of his hundreds of homilies ends with a combination of prayer and doxology. He does not tack these on to the sermon but leads his thought, usually an exhortation, straight into the prayer and on to the doxology. His last homily on the Epistle to the Romans uses his closing formula at about its fullest:

Let us then, laying all this to heart, stand nobly; for Paul was a man, partaking of the same nature with us, and having everything else in common with us. But because he showed such great love toward Christ, he went up above the Heavens, and stood with the Angels. And so if we too would rouse ourselves up some little, and kindle in ourselves that fire, we shall be able to emulate that holy man. For were this impossible, he would never have cried aloud, and said, "Be ye imitators of me, as I am of Christ." Let us not then admire him only, or be struck with him only, but imitate him, that we too may, when we depart hence, be counted worthy to see him, and to share the glory unutterable, which God grant that we may all attain to by the grace and love toward man of our Lord Jesus Christ, through Whom, and with Whom, be glory (power and honor) to the Father, with the Holy Ghost, now and evermore. Amen.[12]

Spurgeon's sermon, "Songs in the Night," after a long concluding paragraph, ends with a prayer of benediction:

May God give you his blessing! I cannot preach as earnestly as I could wish; but, nevertheless, may God accept these words, and send them home to some hearts this night! and may you, my dear brethren and sisters, have songs in the night![13]

[12] *Nicene and Post Nicene Fathers*, First Series, edited by Philip Schaff Vol. XI, p. 564.
[13] Blackwood, *op. cit.*, p. 128.

Paul Scherer's sermon, "The Perils of the Christian Life," ends with a prayer of supplication:

God has saved (Paul) by the wounds he gave. And the deepest of all is this: there was One who bore it for our redemption. "Not my will, but thine, be done."

"As he passed over Penuel, the sun rose upon him, and he halted upon his thigh."

O God, thou who art untamed and perilous, who dost deal in every form of danger, and many modes of death, strip us of our pretensions and our vanities, expose to the strong his weakness, and to the wise his folly, but set in our hearts an unconquerable hope, and in thine own way fulfil it, through Jesus Christ, our Lord. Amen.[14]

James Stewart's sermon, "The Lord God Omnipotent Reigneth," ends with affirmation, challenge, question, and finally with words which, though not a true doxology, are an address to God in Christ:

This is the Lord God who has come again to the gate of your life and mine today. This is the Lord God who claims the right to reign, and from whose patient, haunting pursuit we can never in this world get free. Behold, he stands at the door, and knocks. While the sands of time are running out, and the hurrying days mould our destiny, he stands at the door and knocks. Tenderer than the kiss of a little child, mightier than the flashing lightnings of Heaven, he stands at the door and knocks. What will your answer be? "You, out there at the door, you who have been haunting and troubling me all these years—begone, and leave me in peace!" Is that it? Or is it not rather this? "Blessed and glorious Lord Almighty, dear loving Christ of God—come! Come now. My life is yours. See, here is the throne. Oh Christ, take your power—and reign!" [15]

A word of warning must be added. The form of prayer should not be used for psychological effect. When the form of prayer is used, the substance should really be prayer addressed sincerely to God. That is, it should never be merely a more subtle form of preaching addressed to the ears of the people. There is something both unscrupulous and blasphemous in the attempt to impress and manipulate people by pretending to pray. When that is the purpose, the form of prayer defeats its own purpose by

[14] A. M. Motter, *Great Preaching Today*, p. 198.
[15] Stewart, *op. cit.* Blackwood, *op. cit.*, p. 294.

ringing false, by sounding like a pious but empty noise—which it is. These remarks apply equally to benediction and doxology, and also to a prayer or an apostolic salutation at the beginning of a sermon.

SUGGESTIONS

You may wish there were more studies of organic forms and types of continuity. But you will have all you need on the introduction and the conclusion of the sermon. Almost nobody who talks about sermonic craftsmanship fails to discuss the beginning and the end of the sermon.

As usual, everything Sangster (12), in Chapters V and VI, has to say about the introduction and conclusion is worth your careful attention, particularly because he keeps close to the purpose and the type of the sermon in his discussion.

Read also Davis (6), Chapters V and VI in Part II, pages 210-220; Stewart (31), pages 122-140; Garvie (8), Part III, Chapter IV, pages 421-442; and Baxter (2), index under "Introduction" and "Conclusion.'

CHAPTER 12

Tense and Mode

It should bear flowers and fruit at the same time like the orange:
> Having something for food
>> For immediate nourishment
>
> Having something for delight
>> For present beauty and fragrance
>> For the joy of hope
>> For the harvest of a distant day.

Distinctions of tense and mode in preaching can furnish useful criteria for testing our own work and that of other men. It is all the more important to examine them, owing to the fact that the tense and mode reflect points of view of which the preacher himself is largely or wholly unconscious. In the narrow sense, tense and mode are grammatical forms of the English verb. In the larger sense, they are basic attitudes which condition all that the preacher will say.

Language at its simplest is the instrument of shared meaning, and it is seldom at its simplest. Language suggests more than it says. Its suggestions, its hints are by all odds more powerful than its explicit statements. To be the medium of communication between persons language has to undulate with every current of feeling, reflect every subtle shade of impression, conform to every fluctuation of consciousness whose very nature is fluctuation. Our language therefore constantly betrays more than we think. It could not be an effective means of sharing experience without being as treacherous as experience itself.

On the road to Emmaus the disciples said to Jesus, "We had hoped that he was the one to redeem Israel." This "we had hoped" is simply the past perfect tense, but it flashes a light into the innermost hearts of the disciples. It betrays a whole world of misunderstanding and despair. It says, "We had hoped, but we no longer hope." In this tense of the verb speaks the ghost of a dream, "the sound of a voice that is still."

"If this man were a prophet," thought Simon the Pharisee, "he would have known who and what sort of woman this is who is touching him." This "if he were" is simply the conditional mode, but it tells us all we need to know about Simon's attitude. It reveals the kind of logic that blinded him to the presence of Christ.

So it comes about that even the grammatical form of the verb has a significance far beyond grammar. A great deal more is involved in these distinctions than the mere tense and mode of the verbs used. In fact the grammatical use, while it furnishes useful clues, is not the decisive thing.

Especially is it important that we do not stop with the tense and mode of passing sentences. We must look at the central thought of the sermon and ask, "What is the essential message of this sermon? What, in its briefest and most pointed form, is the all-important thing this sermon says?" When we have that message, we shall find that it too has a tense and mode. We shall find that the tense and mode of the message reflect a definite point of view on the part of the preacher, whether he is aware of it or not.

And the point of view determines the whole view. If I stand on a hill at the north and look southward across a landscape, it will not look the same as if I stood on a mountain at the south. The mode and tense of my sermon show where I stand; they determine the perspective of all that I see.

TENSE IN PREACHING

One of the most frequently heard and most urgent demands is that preaching be contemporaneous. Rightly understood, that demand is reasonable and necessary. Great preaching is always in the present tense, always speaks to the concerns of the day in the thought-forms and language of the day. It is never antiquarian, never merely esthetic or nostalgic after the past, never neutral or detached in its attitude. Great preaching occurs when a man of compassionate discernment, with the love of the Lord and of mankind in his soul, himself fully involved in the battle of existence, stands up on his feet and lets his heart and head speak to his fellows.

On the other hand, the demand for timeliness can be mistaken. When we ask the preacher to forget the past and deal with the problems and interest of the day on their own merits alone, as if they were unrelated to history, to Bible times, to the continuous stream of philosophical and theological thought, then the demand is surely mistaken and unrealistic. The faithful herald of the Lord will adjure that kind of timeliness and the popularity it might win.

The tense of the sermon is thus a serious and many-sided problem. To begin with, the gospel, by its very nature, is the account of God's action in time, past time. The incarnation led to a birthday on a date as fixed as my own. Every word and act in Christ's life on earth, from his first nursing at Mary's breast to his death and resurrection, is equally fixed in a moment of past time. Its once-for-all character requires that it first be once upon a time. Christian faith for ever centers in One we see as we look backward. There can be no preaching of the gospel apart from the memory of Jesus.

We who preach and those who hear us are far removed from Bible times and from the Bible's world of thought. The texts and incidents of the Gospels frequently have to be explained by means of historical and textual studies before their real meaning can be understood. Our task is not to extract "permanent values" from outdated material, but rather to discover what the Bible's message meant to its contemporaries. There is no escaping the necessity to interpret the ancient records, and to employ the results of biblical and historical research in the pulpit.

The difficulty is that instead of using its results in the pulpit we may engage in it as a game there. We may spend too much time at this game. Bible scenes and incidents may hold us too long in the past. The historical and textual introduction necessary in the study may have too large a place in the content of the sermon. Instead of a finished statue, we may offer our people the chips we made in carving it. The preacher may be so interested in the antique world or in the methods of research that he never gets beyond them, never gets down to the here and now. Mistakes such as these may keep him speaking in the past tense until finally the backward look becomes his habitual attitude.

The comparative brevity of the contemporary sermon is another difficulty, and the history of preaching furnishes precedents that exaggerate it. The old masters who preached sixty or even ninety minutes knew what they were doing. A ninety-minute continuity had room for a leisurely introduction of the subject and theme, for historical development, for theological and philosophical discussion. After seventy minutes of such treatment, there was still time for twenty minutes of "application." Ninety minutes of unbroken exhortation, appeal, challenge, of sheer proclamation, or of pointed personal reference, would destroy the force of the whole. When the preaching service was the chief entertainment and the chief intellectual adventure of the week, when people expected to stay in the church a long time anyway, this leisurely kind of treatment was called for.

But a good short sermon is not a twenty-minute slice out of a good ninety-minute sermon, as a beautiful minature is not four square inches cut out of a large picture. The whole design, the whole scale is different. There is no time in the precious twenty minutes to treat any text or message as a curiosity out of the past, as if it had no bearing on our present lives. Our study of the introduction showed how a master preacher of our day can get the sermon in the present tense in the first minute. Jesus did the same thing in his sermon at Nazareth, as we observed on page 34. We cannot afford to talk fifteen minutes about what the text meant to the people in Bible times, and have only five minutes left to talk about what it has to say to us today.

Indeed, too much is. often made of the difference between our times and the old time. Do what we will, Bible history all too easily assumes the color of a dream, a fairy tale, a "sweet story of old." Its characters seem like Santa Claus, like Cinderella, like

Hamlet, like Captain Ahab—unreal, legendary persons inhabiting a world of the imagination, with whom we may feel no real affinity. Impersonal preaching in the past tense, a disproportionate emphasis on thoughts and values abstracted from the gospel narratives, can only increase the danger.

For all these reasons, the tense of the sermon is a real problem. Its solution depends not so much on the grammatical tense we use as on discovering our real links with the past and incorporating them in our point of view.

The concept of permanent, changeless moral and spiritual values is perhaps the least reliable of such links with Bible times. Time has worked its greatest changes precisely in the sphere of thoughts and ideals. To describe an incident or quote words as from a distant past, and then only afterwards inquire what meaning and value they may still have for us today—that is to exaggerate the difference, is to make a distinction where none may in fact exist. I suspect that we preachers are far more deeply worried about the Bible's oldness than our listeners are.

Our first link with the past is that we are not unlike the people of the ancient world but are like them. Only in our superficial thoughts, rational beliefs, and mental moods are we different; in all the heart's realities we are the same. The prophet Jeremiah, the shepherd psalmist, Simon the Pharisee, the publican, Mary Magdalene, doubting Thomas or bragging Peter—one of these needs only to come alive in the sermon, and the men and women in a sophisticated city congregation immediately identify themselves with this person of ancient times, as they do with characters in novels or on the screen. The human reality is all the preacher needs to achieve. The tense of his verbs will take care of itself, and so will the present reference of his sermon.

The same can be said of the application to present conditions. The application need not be labored. The people to whom we speak are not wood and stone, and they are not helpless babes for whom we must think every thought. If what I am talking about has life and reality in it, my hearer will apply it to his own situation for himself. He knows himself better than I know him, and he can often apply it to himself better than I can. The conclusion he draws for himself will likely have more relevance, and will certainly meet less resistance, than any I could give him.

The heart of the human being of the past is thus the first link between us and the people of the Bible. The second link is that as persons we stand before God exactly as all people of all ages have stood. If secular history emphasizes the difference wrought by "chance and change," a Christian theologian and a preacher of the gospel must recognize the identical condition in which all men exist. The contemporary suburbanite no less than King Saul or Pontius Pilate has his being in the will and in the image of his Creator, is in peril by estrangement from that will, is dependent upon the mercy and grace of God. In this fact lies the real unity and solidarity of the human race. It is unreal to speak of the people of Bible times as if they lived in a spiritual world different from our own. Were we not there when they crucified the Lord? Are not the despisers and rejecters here?

The risen and ever present Lord is the final and unbreakable link between us and the people and events of Bible times. The One we meet in the Gospels, along the roads and in the houses of Palestine, is not a mysterious, legendary figure of antiquity. He is the Christ who stands today among us, who lives and works unseen in his people. What they did and what we do alike is done to him. What he did and what he said is done and said to us as to them. His eternity transcends all the mutations of time, cancels all tenses except the *now* of God.

A preacher of the gospel should learn to approach his text from a point of view in keeping with the universality of the human heart, with the identity of the human condition before God, and with the presence and lordship of Christ. These should constitute his point of view. For the sermon inevitably reflects the preacher's point of view. Of this or that sermon it is possible to say that here a man is speaking in the past tense, talking about his text as if its content were something finished and done with long ago, as if all that remains is what we may think and do about it. Of another sermon it is possible to say that here and now we face not ancient truths but the God who is truth, not history but the living Lord.

If, in the synagogue at Nazareth, Jesus had preached as many of his followers do, he would have talked first about Isaiah or about his book, about the situation at the time when Isaiah spoke, about the office of prophecy. After that he would have argued about the faithfulness of God's covenant with Israel, about the unchangeable truth of God's Word. Then he would have asked what meaning Isaiah's words had for the people in the synagogue that day, their permanent or contemporary value. Thus he might at last have reached the gospel God anointed him to preach, and to the announcement that the gospel is now fulfilled. He would have been speaking in the past tense.

Jesus, however, began very differently. He began in the present tense. The first word he spoke was *today*. "Today this scripture is fulfilled in your hearing." Perhaps this too, as well as the authority in his manner and words, was a difference noticed between Jesus' teaching and that of the scribes. Perhaps the scribes taught as too many preach today, in the past tense.

For I have before me a published sermon on Judas Iscariot. Of its six and a half pages, four and a half are given to a discussion of different motives scholars have attributed to Judas for betraying Jesus. The rest of the sermon is devoted to other historical examples of betrayal. Not until the last paragraph is there a word in the present tense, and that is too late to rehabilitate the sermon no matter what is said. But this man has evidently finished what he wanted to do. He has not kept back some penetrating word to say to his listeners in the last two minutes. The sermon dwindles out in a perfunctory reminder that we too may betray the principles by which we profess to live. That is all—too little to keep the sermon from being in the past tense.

In contrast, here is a sermon on the temptation of Jesus. It says that in the desert Jesus faced for himself the enemy of God and men who lurks in all of us and fights God with lying words: with the word of practical necessity, "You must eat. Our needs must be met first"; with the word of cynical denial, "You must deal with the world on the world's terms"; with the word of pride and special favor, "You are somebody special. God's care of you is a sign from heaven which you should use and take pride in." The sermon sets these tempters over against God, as Jesus did. The sermon is in the present tense.

MODES IN PREACHING

We can distinguish three modes in preaching, corresponding to the three modes of the English verb, the indicative, the conditional (subjunctive), and the imperative.

The *indicative* is that mode "which asserts or questions directly," or, as Webster defines it, "that mood of the verb which represents the denoted act or state as an objective fact, as distinguished from a mood representing an act or state merely entertained in thought." The indicative is the mode which says, "It is, it was, it will be," which says, "he does, he did, he will do," or which asks, "do we? did we? shall we?"

The indicative is the mode we use when we say, *it is thus and so.* This is the mode characteristic of announcement, proclamation, the mode in which the gospel is preached. Peter used it on the day of Pentecost: "This Jesus . . . you crucified and killed by the hands of lawless men. But God raised him up, having loosed the pangs of death, because it was not possible for him to be held by it."

Note the distinction between the indicative and both other modes. The indicative is the mode of objective fact; the others are modes of thought merely entertained. It follows that any preaching which represents an act or state as objective fact is in the indicative mode, and preaching in any other mode represents actions and conditions as "a matter of supposal, wish, possibility, etc." (Webster).

The *imperative* is that mode "which expresses command, entreaty, or exhortation." At its bluntest, the imperative is a positive command, authoritative, peremptory. It says, "Do this." But because in this bald form it is so unwelcome as to be ineffective, this mode of speaking commonly masks itself under polite disguises. It often says only, "Let us do this," or "we ought to do this." These are merely milder ways of expressing a wish or command, and they are used instead of direct command in a situation where the speaker knows a verbal command is inadvisable.

The imperative then is the mode which says: *"do this, let us, we ought."* The Bible makes full use of it. Jesus' teaching was distinguished from that of the scribes by the authority of his commands: "Love your enemies," "Do not be anxious about your life." The masked imperative speaks in the First Epistle of John: "Beloved, let us love one another," "If God so loved us, we also ought to love one another." Here, however, the imperative is backed by the indicative: "Love is of God, and he who loves is born of God and knows God," "We love, because he first loved us." The entire twelfth chapter of Romans, printed on page 136, is in the imperative, but the "therefore" in the first verse connects it inseparably with the eleven preceding chapters in the indicative.

The *conditional* mode is only loosely defined in grammar, is in fact seldom called a mode. For the purposes of this book it answers to Webster's definition of the conditional in grammar and logic, "expressing, containing, or implying, a supposition or condition: as a *conditional* mode or proposition." Often using subjunctive forms of the verb, it expresses "doubtful or conditional assertion." It represents an act or state "not as fact but as contingent, possible, doubtful, desirable, etc."

The conditional mode is the mode that says: *if . . . then.* But it too is masked at times. "If we do this, then a result follows." Let it be a desirable result, and we get this: The result I want is possible but contingent; it depends on fulfilling the condition, the *if.* To fulfil the *if* is the way to accomplish the desirable *then.* I fulfil the condition *in order to* get the result. Consequently, it is greatly to my interest to fulfil the condition; *it will pay me.* "It is

to my advantage that I do thus and so *in order to* . . ."—behind
all such reasoning there is a conditional proposition, an *if* . . .
then. The argument, *it will pay,* is one of the commonest disguises
of the conditional mode.

Here I must confess some trepidation as I begin to apply this
distinction of modes in preaching. The results are so far-reaching
as to bring in question the basic design of many, perhaps most, of
the sermons of our contemporaries, including the most popular
styles of preaching. But there the distinction is, for what it is
worth, and an honest workman cannot afford to ignore it. I can
console myself only in the thought that standards of real excellence
in any kind of creative work will always lead to rejection of the
mass product.

Without doubt all modes are proper and necessary to a full-
bodied preaching of the gospel. As concerns the imperative, for
example, both the preacher and his hearers stand under a divine
"do this." There can be no faith without acknowledgment of the
obligation, not to be shunned or shirked or diminished, laid on
us by the will of God. There can be no faithful preaching of the
Word which does not take his command as seriously as it takes
his promise. The essence of the gospel is the undeserved, unearned
favor of God through faith in Christ. But any preaching of faith
that induces a relaxation of moral earnestness, a complacency in
the state of justified sinners, has hidden error at the heart of it.

Which means that the faithful preacher is going to say "we must,"
"we ought," "let us." He should keep it in the first person plural;
he should say *"we* must," "let *us* do this." That is to say, he dare
not speak God's *do this* as if it came from himself and went from
him to his hearers. The very form of words can reveal a falsely
authoritarian attitude, or wrongly suggest a pompous attitude of
which the preacher is not guilty. And he should not say "let us"
for mere politeness' or strategy's sake, when he means "you do
this." He should feel himself involved exactly as his people are,
under the same requirements as they. But he is going to use the

imperative mode at times. He ought to know what he is doing and do it boldly.

Likewise, he is going to say *"If . . . then"* at times. How can he help it? "If Christ has not been raised, your faith is futile and you are still in your sins." "If you confess with your lips that Jesus is Lord and believe in your heart that God raised him from the dead, you will be saved." "If we confess our sins, he is faithful and just, and will forgive our sins and cleanse us from all unrighteousness." How can a true image of human existence be drawn without its glorious and perilous contingency, its unfulfilled possibilities, its unresolved questions? In what mode but the conditional can life be spoken of truly?

The preacher is going to speak of the desirable results that follow faith and obedience: "Bless the Lord, O my soul, and forget not all his benefits." To confer benefits is the fatherly prerogative of God, and to acknowledge them is one form of worship— but not to gloat over their possession. According to the Epistle to the Hebrews, even Moses suffered for Christ because "he had respect unto the recompense of the reward," and our Lord endured the cross and despised the shame "for the joy that was set before him." It is due to the goodness of God alone that his will is at the same time our reward, but the reward must be sought for his glory, not for our personal gain.

Thus the preacher must say in effect, "Your Father who sees in secret will reward you," but must avoid saying, "Pray in secret *in order to be rewarded.*" He dare not say "it will pay us," either so crudely as this, or subtly by implication. When the time comes to speak in the conditional mode, the preacher ought to know what he is doing and then use the mode without hesitation or uncertainty.

A certain occasion or text may even justify an entire sermon in the imperative or the conditional mode, though this raises more serious questions. By an entire sermon in the imperative I mean a sermon whose whole message, argument, pervasive implication, when summed up in a word says only that we must or ought to do thus and so. By a sermon in the conditional mode I mean one which merely says that it is to our advantage to do thus and so *"in order to. . . ."*

The point is that when a sermon's central and inclusive predicate is in the imperative or the conditional mode, that mode constitutes a limitation of the outlook, the point of view. The proclamation of the gospel calls for the indicative mode; the gospel says "It is so." "We ought" and "It is for our good" belong to didactic and therapeutic preaching. When the sermon says only "we ought" or "it is for our good," its point of view is limited, and the gospel's *it is so* is lacking. But since there is a place in the pulpit for didactic and therapeutic preaching, I repeat that the occasion or text may justify an entire sermon in the imperative or the conditional mode.

In the face of excellent sermons in these modes, a blanket rule against them would be pedantic. To give only one example, the sermon on "We dare not fail in our Christian witness," whose sketch is printed on page 153, says only "We dare not fail." Its message was in the imperative, and it was nevertheless a good sermon, even a powerful sermon.

Yet constructive criticism of our work and that of other men must recognize the limitations of all such preaching. Much more is involved than individual sermons. The preacher's whole point of view is involved, and with it the character of his entire argument and the motives to which he appeals. Not only occasional sermons of his but the whole of his preaching is stamped by its dominant mode. The mode becomes his habitual outlook and predetermines his approach to every text and theme.

The Imperative Mode

The *we ought* sermon is extremely common. The imperative is the mode of the dogmatic moralist, and of the exhorter. Its stock in trade is admonition. Its danger is legalism, for it is law only. Its weakness lies in the comparative futility of telling someone what he ought to do—which he usually knows already.

We do well to recall that secondary meaning of the word *sermon:* an annoying harangue on one's conduct or duty. That meaning was put in the dictionary because of what preachers did, because of constant and ill-considered use of the imperative mode by many of them. It reflects both the commonness of the imperative and its doubtful effect.

The temptation to speak in the imperative is very strong, and it is reinforced by the sense of power and authority such speaking gives to a mere man. How else could one so safely command others as in God's name? For the word *ought* is an old form of the verb *to owe,* signifying obligation. We *ought* means we owe it to ourselves, to one another, to conscience, to reason, to justice, in the end to God. The temptation is to confuse that authority with the authority of one's own words.

Even when successful, *we ought* is not without its dangers. If you tell me I ought to do a thing and tell me nothing else, my inference will be that by doing that thing I can make myself more secure. If my preacher's whole message takes the form of moralism, and if I believe him, I shall conclude that religion means doing this and not doing that. And the preacher should not blame me if I draw such a conclusion.

Worst of all, preaching of this kind leaves me without help and without hope. My trouble is not my ignorance of what God requires of me. Knowledge of that lies at the deepest root of my grief and anxiety. The law of God I know I ought to keep and the "Christian principles" I know I ought to live by—these alike convict me of being what I know only too well that I am. No man can help me if he has no more than these to talk about.

So long as a man preaches in the imperative mode, this is all he has to talk about. The moment he begins to proclaim the gospel he speaks in the indicative. Here, for example, is Peter's announcement on the day of Pentecost, which began the public preaching of the church: "Let all the house of Israel therefore know assuredly that God has made him both Lord and Christ, this

Jesus whom you crucified." That is in the indicative; it says *it is so,* "God has made him" Lord and Christ.

Now the exhorter and the dogmatic moralist will not preach even on this text in the indicative mode. Instead he will preach a sermon whose whole implication is in the imperative. He will say, "We ought to believe with our whole hearts that Jesus Christ is Lord, and we ought to accept and confess him as our Lord." Then the issue will not seem to rest on the fact of his lordship but on our reaction, on whether we believe, accept, confess. Such preaching shifts the action from God to us, and gives the impression that Christ is not really our Lord until we believe he is, until we ourselves "Bring forth the royal diadem and crown him Lord of all." When this text is preached on in the imperative mode, the sermon will not be an affirmation of Christ's lordship. It will be an argument why we ought to believe in him as if he were Lord, or it will be an admonition: "Let us make him Lord." Sermonic literature is full of sermons to that effect. The student will not have to go far to find them.

The Conditional Mode

The *in order to* sermon, and even the *it will pay us* sermon, is more common still. The conditional is the mode of the instrumentalist, the pragmatist, and the moral idealist. Its stock in trade is expediency, profit, gain, either temporal or "spiritual." (It somehow assumes that selfishness becomes sanctified when its object is "spiritual.") Its danger is work-righteousness, an attempt to bargain with God. The conditional mode misleads people into supposing that they secure God's favor by what they are and what they do. Its weakness lies in the fact that what we will not do because we owe it to God we will not do because it is to our advantage to do it. People dislike nothing more than being told a thing "for their own good."

When an instrumentalist takes a text like Peter's announcement of Christ's lordship above, he will not be so naive as simply to say "we ought to believe this." He will preach a sermon whose whole implication is in the conditional mode. He will say: "If we believe with all our hearts that Jesus Christ is Lord, it will be greatly to our advantage." For the instrumentalist is a more subtle man. He knows how to win an argument and influence people and make a sale by appealing to their basically selfish motives.

This man may even announce a popular title for his sermon: "The Difference Faith Makes." But if he speaks in the conditional mode, the argument of his sermon will be that it will pay us in health, happiness, and spiritual well-being to take Christ for our Lord. In this sermon it will be faith, not God, that makes the difference, that girds the soul, that sustains the strength, concentrates the effort, renders invincible, transforms the life, achieves the goal.

The Lord Jesus Christ will at best be the static object of this faith, and God will be reduced to the role of an assistant in forwarding one's chosen purpose. Some quality of human nature or some combination of qualities, called faith, will be credited with the power of victorious living. Faith will seem to be a force that would conquer even if there were no Lord, so long as a man firmly believed there is. Indeed, in many of these sermons the object of faith is not the Lord. As often as not they call it faith in mankind, in the future, in the moral consistency of the universe.

By the shortest of steps *in order to* becomes *how to*. It is true that preachers too often fail to show how the goal is to be reached. But it is equally true that the *how to* sermon is the spoiled darling of the instrumentalist. "How to Overcome Fear," "How to Face Trouble," "How to Enjoy Life and Be Useful," "How to Have a Peaceful Mind"—these are sermons actually preached. "How to Make Sauerkraut" rated a feature article in a metropolitan newspaper. It was preached by a man quoted as crediting the revival of his church, not to the Lord, but to the friendly spirit of its members, yet the sermon was by no means as bad as it sounds. "How to Make Your Future What You Want" is far worse for many reasons, the chief one being that it implies the promise that my will, not the Lord's, is going to be done.

No wonder such preaching is popular. Its good is created by its hearer's desire. Its values are measured by his profit. Its only truth is expediency. It appeals to every person's wish to make God a sort of magical servant to his wishes, and to make religion a formula for getting what he wants. Such a formula, assuming that the preacher knows it, might work—if there were no God with a mind of his own which is not my mind and a purpose which is not the projection of my purpose, and if I had no human competitor as determined to have his way as I am determined to have mine!

The Indicative Mode

We have seen what the imperative and conditional modes can do with the text, "God has made him both Lord and Christ, this Jesus." Let us see what happens when we keep it in the indicative.

To begin with, this is the announcement of an accomplished fact: God has made him Lord. God did it alone and unassisted, without consulting any man. Pilate, Herod, the Roman emperor did not make Jesus Lord. The Jewish Sanhedrin and people did not make him Lord. Peter and the disciples and the church did not make him Lord. The universal regard of mankind did not make Jesus Lord. "God has made him Lord."

This is God's arbitrary, unilateral, undemocratic action. God had no allies or confederates in this, no pacts with anybody. God did not call a world conference to discuss the proposal that Jesus be made Lord. He established no commission, appointed no fact-finding committee to report on the advisability of making Jesus Lord, or to devise ways and means to make Jesus Lord and Christ. He did not consult the Congress in Washington, the Parliament in London, or the Kremlin in Moscow. He did not wait till the Bureau of Scientific Research approved his plan as feasible. He did not stop to ask what all the professors in universities and theological schools would think if he made Jesus Lord. He just made him Lord, and then sent his messenger to announce what he had done.

The difference is between a Jesus God made Lord and a Jesus we try to make Lord. It is very hard for people like us to stay in the indicative mode. Much of our religiosity is in the imperative and subjunctive: "We should believe he is Lord," or "Let us proceed as we imagine we would if he were Lord. Let us act as if he were." We are like children playing "Let's pretend," and Christ often has no more reality to us than the fairy godmother of the child's game.

We imagine that after all God may be a good democrat like us. Maybe he did not make Jesus Lord, but only nominated him as Lord, and waits to see whether we will vote him in as Lord or not. He isn't really Lord as yet, we suppose, and cannot be Lord unless we take him as Lord. We are free Americans, are we not, and entitled to our own opinion in all such matters? Christ is not Lord without our say-so. Let us talk over the proposal that Christ be Lord; let us take it under advisement.

Then, after insisting on our right to judge Jesus instead of being judged by him, we give our verdict. "Sure enough," we say, "Jesus is good. How gentle he was, how understanding, how self-forgetful, how noble, tolerant, and kind! He has my vote; he deserves to be Lord. I will be glad to acknowledge a Master like him, if only he will let me set him up in the lordship business. Let us all get together and make him Lord."

Or we look at the beautiful and comfortable playhouse of civilization that we have built and think how dreadful it would be to lose it. And we say, "Christ or somebody like him had better be made Lord, if we want to keep what we have. Let us do something about it, organize a campaign of education, get some effective publicity, propagandize to get everybody to make him Lord. Let us so convincingly pretend that he is our Lord that people will take him as their Lord too. That is how to keep what we have." It is shocking to see how much of our teaching and preaching is just such propaganda.

This figurehead Christ that we propose to set up is not the Jesus whom God made Lord. If we were able to set him up as Lord, that would not make him Lord. If he is Lord, then he is Lord even if not a single man, woman, or child on earth believes in him or confesses him. If he is not Lord by God's own *it is so,* then he would not be Lord though every soul on earth "accepted" him as Lord. If his being Lord depends on anybody's confession, then he is not Lord at all, but only a puppet lordling created by human decision and subject to human opinion.

If there is anything certain about us, it is that we would never of ourselves choose a Lord who is Lord without our consent and in opposition to our will. We would not mind so much to have a lord we ourselves could make or unmake, who owed his lordship to our election, for that would leave us our feeling of power and control. But to have a Lord I did not help to make, who is not responsible to me but to whom I am responsible—that offends my pride, cancels my right to judge and decide, and denies my ability, my competence to know and choose my way and control my destiny. It cuts me down to my proper size, and I do not like it at first. Yet I am so diminished if he is thus exalted. No lesser Christ can be the Lord of Christian faith. Only on these terms can I deal with a Christ whom God has made Lord.

SUGGESTIONS

Do these distinctions interest you? You will find them useful but perhaps not as easy as you might think to apply to someone else's sermon, until you get a little practice at it. You can get lost in the forest of language and thoughts, where any tense and mode may be used without becoming decisive for the entire sermon. You will need to stand off from the sermon and look at its elemental form, its subject and principal assertions, its assumptions and implications, and its general tone and direction.

My hope is of course that this will become a habit with you and carry over into your own work without much time and effort on your part. If you conclude from this chapter and the next that I am trying to make a critic of you, you are right. I would like to make you particularly critical of your own work. I do not wish, however, to make you snobbish toward the work of others, only discriminating. And even about your own work I do not wish to make you meticulous, that is, timidly or excessively cautious.

Beyond the usual call for timeliness, not much is made of tense and mode in homiletical writings.   But you will find an interesting treatment of these and other possibilities in the first chapters of Ferris' little book (7), though you may not think his sermon in Chapter IV keeps to the indicative as faithfully as it might.

CHAPTER 13

Processes in Interpretation

1. Diagnosis	Description	What have we?
2. Etiology	Causation	How come?
3. Prescription	Recommendation	What to do?

A man who mounts a pulpit and speaks to his fellows cannot choose whether or not to be an interpreter of life. He will not speak more than a few words on any subject before there begins to emerge a picture of the material universe and of mankind as they look to him. The only question is what kind of a picture he will draw.

This question concerning a man's work is often overlooked, and its importance is underestimated. Once again we are dealing with a matter of attitude and point of view, largely unconscious, but none the less decisive. We can no more assess the value of a sermon or a year's output of sermons without attention to the preacher's outlook than we can ignore the broad picture of life in a novel or play.

As an interpreter of the human scene, the average preacher may feel that he holds an obscure and insignificant place. Just the same there is a group of people for whom his view of the world is of the greatest importance. The people who respect and love him and hear him every week, particularly the immature persons who hear him, are influenced more than anyone could measure by looking at existence through his eyes. And that is only one side of the question. The clarity, breadth, justice, sympathy of his view, as much as anything else, will give weight to everything he says, while a narrow, warped, or unrealistic view will lead to rejection of both himself and his message.

It is no idle or academic matter, then, to look at a sermon and ask what broad picture of the world it draws, how it judges human beings, what vision of good and evil it reflects, what life and society would be like if the preacher had his way. This is not too much to ask of a single sermon, for tacit assumptions speak through the very texture of the thought and through the style of word and phrase used to express it.

Let me give an example. A few years ago a well-known actress, whom I shall call Miss W., left her child and husband, Dr. H., for a lover. She asked for a divorce, which Dr. H. refused. Then she bore a child by her lover.

When the talk was at its loudest, a newspaper man solicited comment on this case from a number of persons with different occupations and points of view: a popular preacher, a prominent judge, a university dean, a divorce lawyer, a housewife, and a policeman. The comments were printed together in a column of the newspaper, as they appear below.

While I was reading this column, I temporarily lost interest in the merits of the case, or, more accurately, I became far more deeply interested in the variety of opinions expressed and the intellectual, cultural, and emotional forces that produced them. Each of these short statements is a window opening on a whole view of life, and the language, even the stereotyped phrases, throws more light on the speaker than on the subjects of the gossip. The statements sound like voices from different worlds, as indeed they are.

The minister:
The whole affair is a very great tragedy. The child, of course, should not be censured. Probably, though, society will see to it that it is. This is a great moral wrong, and Miss W. should be kept from decent society.[1]

The judge:
These people are setting an example which will reflect in countless court statistics. The whole affair is disgraceful, and I can't approve any of it.

The university dean:
Apart from a moral judgment, I must say that the whole thing was in extremely bad taste. I am reminded of a critic's remark about a bad

[1] This and the following quotations are printed by permission of the Chicago *Sun-Times* from its issue of February 4, 1950.

performance of "Romeo and Juliet"—instead of love at first sight, it was lust at first sight.

The divorce lawyer:
Dr. H. was morally right. He was, however, wrong in the practical sense. It is obviously useless to continue a marriage when the partners are incompatible. His agreement to a divorce last year would have saved a child much future anguish and embarrassment.

The housewife:
He should have granted her a divorce when she first asked for it. After all, they are two adults in an adult world, and if she fell in love with another man, it made their marriage invalid.

The policeman:
Look, they came over from Sweden, they had a child, they spent many years in what seemed to be a happy marriage. They'd gone too far to break it off for any reason.

In the study of interpretation we need to distinguish the three steps which stand at the head of this chapter. They are closely related to one another, but are separate processes. The first words used to designate these steps are drawn from the vocabulary of medicine. My use of them is not intended to suggest that the interpretation of human existence is or can be an exact science. A look at the terms in the second column, and especially at the questions in the third column, will make it evident that all three of these processes are constantly at work in preaching.

Diagnosis is the observation and description of facts as symptoms of a condition, leading to a judgment or opinion in answer to the question, "What have we here?" Etiology is a search for causes, leading to a judgment or opinion in answer to the question, "How did this condition get to be as it is? What caused it?" Prescription is the recommendation of treatment, antidote for disease and program for health, answering the question, "What should be done about it?"

Many and many a sermon is given its main direction and even its outline by these questions, without the preacher's noticing it at all; as some discerning but unliterary person put it: "The fix we're in—How we got this way—What we can do about it."

Diagnosis is all-important. Correct etiology and prescription depend on a correct diagnosis. But it does not work the other way around. The diagnosis may be correct but the etiology and the treatment wrong. The diagnosis and etiology may both be correct and the treatment still be wrong. The validity of a man's prescription for mankind depends on the correctness of his account of both the human condition and its causes. And yet many a man is able to make a brilliant diagnosis of the human condition, who fails dismally in his attempt to assign causes and prescribe remedies.

Henry D. Thoreau is diagnosing in *Walden* when he says, "The mass of men lead lives of quiet desperation." In that sentence he has generalized the result of his examination of the life of ordinary people. He was trying "to drive life into a corner, and reduce it to its lowest terms" in order to "confront only the essential facts of life." For, he said, "I did not wish to live what was not life," and it seemed to him that was what most of the people about him were doing. This is his diagnosis, and a large part of his famous book consists of his keen observation of the symptoms in detail. The diagnosis is desperation, the desperation of slavery to life's machinery and its senseless routines. After a hundred years it seems more startlingly true than when first written.

But it seems to me that Thoreau is not anywhere nearly as clear about the causes of this desperation and slavery. Can we say that people are desperate simply because they have too many things, tools, and possessions? That is surely an oversimplification. And when he comes to recommendations, he seems no more convincing. Is plain living and high thinking the way out, to strip life of its machinery, to live in harmony with nature, and to be rich in the things we can do without? His etiology and his prescription lack the sure touch of his diagnosis.

Friedrich Nietzsche is impressive in his diagnosis of Western civilization. When he points out that classes and individuals have increasingly been reduced to the level of the common man, whose chief virtues are those of docility and conformity, many, perhaps most of us, must agree, even if we resent his terms of herd morality, the virtues of slaves. Surely Hogarth and Goya agree with regard to vices as well as virtues. So does Georges Rouault when he paints "The Three Judges" or "Mr. X." So do the novelists of our century.

The point is that while Nietzsche has many to support his judgment that the truth about us is not pleasant, his attempt to state the causes and prescribe the cure seems quite fantastic. For etiology, he can only say that "all society makes one somehow, somewhere, or sometime commonplace," [2] and that the slave morality is a result of the religion of Jesus the Jew. As for treatment, he can recommend nothing better than that we aspire to be supermen and develop the will to power.

T. S. Eliot is perhaps the most influential contemporary poet and critic in the English-speaking world. He won his commanding position largely through a diagnosis of the human condition: modern men are "Hollow Men," living in "The Waste Land," without faith, without any certain sense of purpose, unhappy, and pathetically dull. His great early work consists of little more than a description of the symptoms of this condition. His account of how men came to be in this condition, though he evidently works in the light of Christian theology, seems less clear. And his prescription for its cure seems still less explicit. What is it? Is it only a private and traditional sainthood compounded of such tenuous virtues as renunciation, sympathy, discipline, sacrifice, martyrdom? If it is more than this, what is it precisely? My purpose is not to disparage Eliot's work, but to show that the power of his diagnosis is not matched with an equal power in his etiology and prescription.

These examples point to a significant fact. A great deal of the best literature does not go beyond diagnosis. There is a great deal more which we read and value for its diagnosis, although we do not agree with its etiology or its prescription. It is enough if it "shows us life" in one or more of its manifestations.

What do we want in a book or play or poem? We want to see ourselves there, do we not? We want to discover ourselves there.

---

[2] F. W. Nietzsche, *Beyond Good and Evil* (Regnery Edition, 1949), p. 218.

We want to see ourselves more clearly and more truly than we have done before. We want what is hidden in us to come out and be recognized. In order to show us ourselves, the picture does not have to be pleasant, but it does have to be true. Indeed, we can see ourselves only in a character who has weakness as well as strength, faults as well as virtues. We want a diagnosis that makes us say, "Yes, that is myself. I understand this character because I am like him." This diagnostic quality alone is enough to make us value a piece of writing.

Hamlet is one of the most complex and mysterious characters in literature. Nobody can fully understand him, and that is part of his universal fascination, for none of us can fully understand himself. If a character is too good, too normal and reasonable, we know at once that he is a puppet, not a real person. No one has been able to explain Hamlet, and the guesses are often fantastic, diagnosing the diagnoser more successfully than the patient.

For all that, none of us fails to respond to Hamlet's diagnosis of life and of himself. This:

> How weary, stale, flat, and unprofitable
> Seem to me all the uses of this world!
> Fie on 't! O fie! 'tis an unweeded garden,
> That grows to seed; things rank and gross in nature
> Possess it merely.

Or this:

This goodly frame, the earth, seems to me a sterile promontory; this most excellent canopy, the air, look you, this brave o'erhanging firmament, this majestical roof fretted with golden fire, why, it appears no other thing to me but a foul and pestilent congregation of vapors. What a piece of work is man! How noble in reason! how infinite in faculty! in form, in moving, how express and admirable! in action, how like an angel! in apprehension how like a god! the beauty of the world! the paragon of animals! And yet, to me, what is this quintessence of dust? man delights not me; no, nor woman neither, though by your smiling, you seem to say so.

Or this, in anguish to Ophelia:

I am myself indifferent honest; but yet I could accuse me of such things, that it were better my mother had not borne me. I am very

proud, revengeful, ambitious; with more offences at my beck, than
I have thoughts to put them in, imagination to give them shape, or time
to act them in. What should such fellows as I do crawling between
heaven and earth?

There is power to purge in such diagnosis, even by a man who
allegedly could not make up his own mind. It renders cheap and
false all the words of Polonius and Laertes and the king, who had
no trouble at all making up their minds. It puts us on Hamlet's
side, not on theirs. And we do our souls good by taking Hamlet's
part.

Hamlet is immortal for the very reason that it has no etiology,
just because no reason is assigned or assignable for the hero's
condition. And would he be more admirable if he had killed the
king at once and, as the new king of Denmark, announced that he
had done it because his father's ghost had revealed a crime?

Or here is a diagnosis, a judgment of humankind by Miranda,
that young girl in *The Tempest* who had grown up without seeing
a man except her father and the misshapen Caliban, when she
looks first with unpolluted eyes at the people who had plotted to
dispossess and murder her father and herself:

> O, wonder!
> How many goodly creatures are there here!
> How beauteous mankind is! O brave new world,
> That has such people in it!

We smile when we quote this. We smile at Miranda's naivete.
We think how much ignorance of the world as well as innocence is
required to say that. We marvel at the profound knowledge of the
heart Shakespeare had, to be able to look at the world and the
race and see it fresh and unspoiled, as if it had been newly created
the moment before. Do we not also perhaps remember the unclouded vision our own eyes saw as children? And thus before
we know it we are inside Miranda's skin too, and she is speaking
for the selves we used to be. And we may have the grace to wonder
if our adult cynicism is the mark of intelligence or of something
else, if the truth we know about these treacherous people is worth
calling the truth at all, if wisdom may not lie rather in the eyes of

Miranda than in ours. At any rate her diagnosis of mankind has
served a useful purpose for us too. It may even have served as a
sort of confessional.

Even music is diagnostic. An experienced and sensitive listener
in my household says, not wholly as a joke, that for her the history
of music might just as well have ended when Mozart died. She
does not like the Valkyrie version of existence or any of the heart's
symptoms as described at Bayreuth. She can see herself in Vienna
in all its moods, cheerful or tragic, lighthearted or sublime. She
responds to Beethoven's Ninth even more than to the Pastoral.
She would feel poorer without Schubert. For all their shattering
of complacent patterns, the symphonies of Sibelius still speak to
her, but her ultimate limit is his "Voces intimae" and Schoenberg's
"Verklaerte Nacht." Beyond that, let Freudian neuroses and life's
disagreeable frenzies get into music if they will; the music they
get into is not for her.

DIAGNOSIS IN PREACHING

Thus the preacher is going to be an interpreter of life, as much
as is a novelist, playwright, sculptor, painter, columnist or
musician, whether he wants to or not, whether he knows it or not.
He cannot speak more than a few words about anything without
expressing or implying some judgment of mankind and the universe,
some reason for people being as they are, some recommendation
as to what should and what should not be done.

The divine source of his message does not make him an infallible
interpreter. It does not give him eyes to see human trouble, its
cause and its cure, more clearly than other men, though it ought
to furnish him a light in which to see. There is grave doubt that
if preachers ran the world it would be run better than it is, that
people would be better off if their pastors could make all their
decisions for them. God's authority is not the preacher's authority,
and God's wisdom is not more accessible to preachers than to
other people.

Consequently, the preacher's function of interpreter should give him serious concern. He should not preach for six months or a year without looking back upon his work and asking what kind of an account it gives of human beings and what would happen if people followed his suggestions. It would be well for him to scrutinize every sermon he preaches, particularly while he is young in his calling, and discipline himself to a view of man that is at once just and merciful.

The work of interpretation begins with diagnosis. And just because he is a servant of the gospel, a preacher is obligated to an honest realism. He can afford no romantic illusions about mankind. The closer he is to his people, the more will he be aware of their failings as well as their virtues, of their conflicts and anxieties, their doubts and betrayals, as well as their courage and endurance. The honest preacher cannot be simply an apologist for mankind; he cannot take man's side in the mutiny against the holy Will.

Even today, the pulpit too often renders a favorable report on the condition of man, a diagnosis of health and not sickness. Here, for example, is a sermon of 1954, preached by a man just back from a tour of the Near East. He apparently saw no restive discontent, strife, hate, or dangerous antagonism, such as others report. The sermon is a psalm in praise of people. He preaches that all people are fundamentally good, kind and loving—so much for diagnosis. Since there is no disease, no etiology is called for. As for prescription, this sermon says that all we need to do is to trust people, believe in them, love them, and be kind to them, and we shall solve the world's problems.

Unfortunately, this sermon is not a rare or exceptional specimen. Renewed interest in religion has just this danger; many people go from believing too little to believing too much and believing it too easily, in which case people always believe what they want to believe, and believe it because it seems expedient, for their own gain. It is a form of wishful credulity, not faith in God.

Such a favorable diagnosis of the human condition is based on a partial report. Its argument is like a collection of testimonials to the virtues of a patent medicine. Among human beings with infinitely variable fortunes, one can always find a certain number of people who have been in trouble, who have readjusted by adopting a more positive mental attitude, and afterwards gone on to achieve success, happiness, and some degree of prominence. It does not follow that everyone who takes a notion can do the same. There are enough such cases to seem impressive, when the method consists of stringing together a few anecdotes of this kind and passing over the millions who try as hard but fail.

One can support any conclusion by this kind of minority report. But such a report is always a false diagnosis of humanity. Its falseness is betrayed by the emphasis it puts on noteworthy success and prominence. The success story is its stock in trade. But to be notably successful and prominent is to be one in thousands. We all can no more do it at once than we can all be perfectly strong and healthy. In this strange world the healthiest are not those who live hygienically, and a meticulous fussing over the state of health is itself a form of sickness.

Deadly danger lurks in the superficial diagnosis of human ills and in the nostrums dispensed for their alleviation across the counters of popular religion and psychology. If there is nothing deeply and incorrigibly wrong with people, redemption by the cross and resurrection is dramatic nonsense. But if desperate sickness and cancerous self-consumption is the truth about us, if nothing short of God's own surgery can save us, the necessity of that radical treatment can be shown only by a true diagnosis. Otherwise we shall be covering malignant sores on the fair body of man with a sugary ointment. From prophet to priest, we shall be dealing falsely, in a style older than Jeremiah; we shall be healing the wounds of God's people lightly, saying "Peace [of mind], peace, when there is no peace."

A report of health may be the most dangerous false diagnosis, but it is not the only one current among us. At the middle of the twentieth century, we are liable to distort our preaching by a morbid fascination with the ugly condition of mankind. This too can result from a faulty method of preaching, a stringing together of quotations. Some of the most eloquent writing of our time is found in bitter descriptions of human depravity, lust, greed, thirst for power, hate, and selfish egotism. Somehow the preacher loves these descriptions, never tires of quoting them, and becomes more eloquent himself when he speaks of such things. If many a sermon is rendered false by a string of success stories or of optimistic quotations, many another is rendered equally false by quotations from the dark prophets who see men as they truly are but without the gospel.

For the preacher of the gospel, however he sees the dark state of man, must see no less clearly man's possibilities under the grace of God. That side of the picture is as real as the other. Human delinquency is tragic only because the human being is a child of God even in his delinquency. Without that, man is not tragic, only contemptible. He can be worse than a beast only because he can be infinitely more than a beast. Any diagnosis of the human condition which leaves that out is false diagnosis. This error, too, mars much of the preaching of our time. Unfortunately, men with some theological depth seem especially susceptible to it.

Here is another sermon, this one on "Apart from me you can do nothing." The preacher's whole emphasis is that of ourselves we can neither gain God's consideration, deserve it, nor believe in it. We can do absolutely nothing about it; God must do it all without us. The sermon's falseness is not that it points out our helplessness to help ourselves but that it stops with saying this, as if it were the whole truth about our situation, or even the important truth.

Management of the diagnostic material within a given sermon is a matter of both design and strategy, not to say art. There is no ideal order, but a man ought to know what he is doing. A logical procedure usually starts with "the fix we're in," but that order is considerably shopworn. Its uncritical use tends strongly to instrumentalism, to make religion seem a form of expediency. A dramatic continuity may quite well start with something else and bring the diagnosis in as complication. Once he knows what diagnosis is, the preacher can discover for himself ways to use it.

But more than strategy and more than art is involved. Diagnosis must be honest and realistic, I have said. It must also be patient, factual, descriptive. A preacher has no right to hurl an ugly abstraction like the name of "sin" at people who neither understand the word nor see their faults, unless, when he looks at them and at himself, he can see and describe the thing called sin in the particularity of people's deeds and words and thoughts. The Bible declares God's judgment, but it does not put the preacher in Christ's place as judge of the living and the dead. The preacher must be patient and factual in this description. He must not use the abstract word to save time, for he is not sent to save time but to seek and save the lost.

Moreover, diagnosis must be made in love and compassion, by a man who knows himself a sharer in all the folly and evil that afflict mankind. He can discern no sin to which he is not subject himself, can announce no judgment which does not begin with him and under which he does not stand convicted. A man who does not diagnose himself with the same honesty, who does not feel his own share in all the guilt and shame of the world, forfeits his right to scrutinize his fellow-men, and disqualifies himself to preach the gospel.

ETIOLOGY IN PREACHING

We have seen that literature, even great literature, often is little more than diagnosis, observation, and description of the multifarious aspects of human existence. Perhaps it is not too much to say that the permanent value of literature lies mostly here in its diagnostic quality. Certainly much great literature lives for us by reason of its diagnosis after its etiology and prescription have ceased to be acceptable or meaningful. Reading the Greek tragedies, we feel our kinship with Oedipus, Antigone, or Orestes, we recognize the face life turned to them as the face of the life we know, even if we do not believe they suffered at the hands of a fate older and stronger than any deity, as the Greeks believed.

Yet no serious writing or speaking can avoid the later steps in interpretation entirely. Any adequate description of the human being must deal not only with his nature but also with his relationship to his fellows and to the universe of matter and spirit. When thought goes beyond observation and description, when it passes from diagnosis to etiology, it moves into metaphysics or theology. The search for causes is a search after ultimate relations.

The simplest word one person speaks to another is framed by the profoundest questions of the human mind. Why are we as we are? Where do our troubles come from? Where, indeed, do we ourselves come from? What does our existence mean, if anything? What purpose are we meant to serve, which to lose is to lose ourselves, in which to fail is to perish?

Within these and like questions the simplest sermon, in the obscurest meetinghouse of the remotest countryside, ventures toward some answer, tentative or confident. The preacher speaks to such questions in some fashion, whether he will or no.

One further thing is certain. Into these questions no man will go alone, unsupported by the thought of others, an original investigator starting with no assumptions. Both meaning and speculation are enterprises of a group. If a man has thought through to a theology for himself, that theology will determine his answers to etiological questions. If he has no theology, he may hold to some more or less consistent system of metaphysical philosophy, and it will provide his answers. If he has no consistent philosophy, he may hold to an empirical scientism, consciously and frankly agnostic about all ultimate questions. If he has no consistent intellectual view of any sort, he will still not be empty-handed or original. Then he will fabricate makeshift answers out of shreds and patches from the ideological grab bag of his clan.

At this point I must insist again that a book on the craft of preaching must not be relied on to teach theology. What I am attempting here is simply to show that any evaluation of any sermon is hopelessly superficial without attention to its witness concerning the ultimate questions, that a man's theology—or lack of it—is absolutely decisive for his interpretation of life, and that no discourse deserves the name of Christian preaching unless its etiology as well as its diagnosis is consonant with Christian theology. I can undertake no more than to illustrate the point by reference to some particular problems a man must study or evade.

Today we are operating in a confusion produced by differing interpretations of man. These various views are reflected on occasion in the pulpits of all denominations; no church is immune to this confusion. Indeed, outside the few exceptional preachers who not only profess but hold a consistent position, among the many who practice the merely occupational habit of delivering speeches in church, the preaching of any one man is nearly certain to reflect conflicting views from time to time.

In order to name some of these views I have to oversimplify. There is first the biblical interpretation of man; I will call it a theological interpretation. Man is the creation of God along with all other creatures. But he is distinguished from all others by being stamped with the image of his Creator in some special way. He is not as God made him and intended him to be, not as God now wills him to be, but is estranged from God and his understanding is darkened by sin—a disobedience or rebellion for which he, not God, is responsible.

That, at about its simplest, is the biblical interpretation of man's estate. The point here is that this view provides a basic etiology, an answer at least, whether true or false, to the question as to why we are in our present fix. The answers are, of course, matters of belief, not of scientific demonstration. In this they are not unique. Answers can be scientifically demonstrated only as long as we refuse to ask ultimate questions, a fact which seems to support the thesis that man is estranged from the source of his being.

A second interpretation of man has its affiliations with the Renaissance, and through it with the Greeks, rather than with the Bible. I think it not unfair to call it a rationalistic rather than a theological interpretation. Man is the hero, by virtue of his rational soul. He is, or should be, master of nature and of himself. He is, or could be, or is ultimately going to be, triumphant.

This rationalistic view, in its attempt to assign causes for men's disorders, sets up a hierarchy among man's faculties. Man is virtuous, happy, and successful when certain of his powers keep others in subjection and rule the man. He is vicious, miserable, and futile when the wrong ones are in control. In its classical forms this view holds that reason is without a doubt the faculty which ought to rule all others. But this is not always the case within rationalism. The sovereign faculty can just as well be man's moral faculty or his esthetic faculty, or, with some nowadays, even his animal instinct!

This interpretation is also, of course, a matter of sheer belief, not of demonstration, quite as much so as the theological interpretation. It becomes metaphysical with the assumption that "the higher powers" of man, and especially his "spiritual powers," his "soul," constitute some reliable link with deity, or with ultimate objective reality, if not a virtual identification with deity. All its varieties, as reflected in our contemporary pulpits, draw from man himself the law and the secret of his misery or beatitude. Man is not only the hero; he is the autonomous hero.

Thirdly, there is the psychological interpretation of man. But because the former is also in some sense a psychological interpretation, it must be clear that this means a special type of psychology which, beginning with Freud, has dominated our time, not only the pulpit but also the stage and screen, the art gallery, and most of our literature. It is not too much to say that there has emerged from this interpretation a new image of man. He is not biblical man, the fallen creature of God. He certainly is not intellectual man, the rational hero, the conqueror.

The psychological interpretation of man is noteworthy most of all for its diagnosis, its description of the hidden depth and complexity of personality, of unlovely desires, of self-deception and treacherous disguises, of subversive and conflicting forces, above all perhaps of the servitude of reason itself to nonrational wishes. By coincidence in cultural history, this diagnosis was worked out in a climate of theological skepticism. Further, it developed with a scientific outlook whose very method was to exclude metaphysical questions in order to achieve more impartial observation and experiment.

Consequently, this interpretation of mankind can furnish from within itself no account of the ultimate causes of the human condition. More impressively than was ever possible before, it can say we are all more or less neurotic bundles of conflicting egoistic desires, but it cannot say with anything like the same conviction why we are so or why we ought not to be so. With reference to such questions the scientist sees through a glass as dark as a child's though only the greatest among them are as humble as a child about these questions.

These are only three among other interpretations that meet and clash and intermingle in our intellectual and religious confusion. They all turn up in the pulpit sooner or later in some shape. It is all the worse for the preacher if he cannot tell one from the other.

Who can say what the preacher ought to do? Who can prescribe an etiology for his use? That is his calling, his lifework. It is easier to mention some things he cannot well afford to do. He cannot preach the biblical doctrine pompously and magisterially, without bothering to marshal the evidence for his diagnosis. He cannot set an obscurant biblicism in opposition to human learning. He cannot reaffirm the old ideal of man the hero, the conqueror, the god. He cannot simply repudiate the Freudian diagnosis of man in the name of the Bible, for the Bible is more often on Freud's side than on the side of man the hero, so far as mere diagnosis goes. He cannot tinker with Freudian man in a pseudoscientific jargon that has no terms to describe man's ultimate relations with the universe of matter and spirit.

And this perhaps suggests in a general way what the preacher is called to do in our day. He can and he must rethink historical and psychological man so as to relate Freudian man with biblical doctrine. He must bring all possible knowledge to his task of interpretation. He must use all the light he can get from science, history, literature, the arts—from wherever there is light. Then, and above all, he must see sick, broken humanity in its theological dimensions, which alone furnish room for any gospel.

PRESCRIPTION

When it comes to remedies, the preacher may possibly feel that he is on safer ground. The content of theology appears as a given thing. It brings its own diagnosis, etiology, and prescription. The preacher does not have to produce a revelation of truth and a saving wisdom out of his poor resources. His is a humbler task: to explicate the church's faith in which both he and his listeners have been nurtured, to deliver a message he did not concoct, to point out a way of life he did not devise. All this he is relieved to recognize as true.

But this does not really put the preacher on safe ground. To begin with, there is the danger that he may think and speak too much about remedies and too little about anything else. It is a common fault of preachers. If good literature leans heavily on diagnosis, mediocre preaching leans just as heavily on prescription. What to do is often its starting point as well as its conclusion.

Such preaching is like doctoring symptoms. It produces religious nostrums, panaceas, like patent medicines sold over the counter. The more of them a person takes, the more hypochondriac he becomes. If he should be in a really dangerous condition, he may die with his bloodstream full of these poisons.

With the best intentions in the world, a preacher may be recommending a certain brand of religiosity for all the ailments of mankind. He wants people to attend his church's services, to join his church, to read the Bible and pray, to support the church financially, to take part in its activities, to lead morally inoffensive lives, to be baptized and married and buried in due manner, to bring up their children in the same religious pattern, and above all perhaps, not to go off on ideological tangents or cause trouble otherwise. He knows quite well that these remedies do not go to the root of human trouble. But look at his sermons for a year, ask what he is prescribing for men's ills, and you will often find that in essence it is simply this: be religious in our fashion.

That is to say, such preaching is shallow because it lacks diagnosis and etiology. Advice to read the Bible was dangerous advice to the man who, after reading it for weeks with a twisted mind, went out on the street and slaughtered seven people with a shotgun, saying that God told him to do it. Advice to pray is dangerous advice to the woman for whom prayer is an escape from reality, a form of flight from responsibilities she does not want to face. A religious pattern is a dangerous pattern when it sanctifies suburban smugness.

The comparative futility of much preaching is accounted for in this way. One-sided emphasis on what is to be done is the mark of all moralistic preaching. What I have said in Chapter 8 about teaching and about premature attempts at therapy is applicable in the relation of diagnosis to treatment. The radical cure of mankind can make sense only when it goes with a realistic description of his sickness; in the light of that diagnosis no less radical prescription makes any sense at all.

However, the danger of hasty recommendation is not the preacher's only danger, perhaps not his greatest danger at the present time. As superficial preaching is inclined to be mostly prescription, so the most thoughtful preaching of our time is inclined to be mostly diagnosis, with inadequate attention to prescription. Peter's sermon on the day of Pentecost raised the question, "Brethren, what shall we do?" It is always a pertinent question, and people too often look to their minister in vain for an answer.

There is intense preoccupation just now with man's dilemma and a dim, uncertain view of the way out. Many currents in contemporary culture strengthen this tendency. For example, not only is literature traditionally addicted to diagnosis and dubious of solutions, but a very tough and earthy, not to say coprophagous, taste for what is called realism is now the style. There is some strange satisfaction in seeing that the star character is just as vulgar as the rest of us. We embrace the heroine with less hesitation just because of the little bit of the wanton in her. In such an atmosphere a certain objectionable odor of sentimentality clings to anything that is either clean or hopeful. The man in the pulpit, too, having his own normality to demonstrate, inclines to harrow rather than to heal.

In a secular interpreter it may be a point of strength that he confines himself to diagnosis and conveys his ideals of the good life only vaguely and indirectly if at all. Such a book as Dostoevsky's *Crime and Punishment* would not be the mighty work it is if its preachment were overt. Didactic poetry is not the poetry that influences us most. An exceptional propaganda play may move us powerfully, may indeed inflame us, for the moment, but usually we draw back or resist as soon as we suspect that the author has an ax to grind. The preacher's prescription must face the same handicaps.

Moreover, the vision of good is never so clear as the palpable actualities of evil. Among the prophets, it is the mark of the true prophet of God to see wickedness and judgment, to prophesy evil, and he who prophesies good is the false prophet. Further, the prophet's images of retribution are abundant and concrete, while those of the promised salvation are less sure, and they are the more questionable the more concrete they become. Nothing could be more vividly portrayed than the hunger and blood of men and little children, the grief and shame of women, the exile and bondage of people, the lions coming out of the thicket into the streets of the city, the desolation haunted by owls and ravens. But when it came to the deliverance, even the sublime seer of the last chapters of Isaiah could describe the restoration only in terms of the national triumph of Israel, with the temple at Jerusalem as the center of the world.

Preaching is thus foredoomed, perhaps, to be more explicit in its account of evil than it can be in its description of good. Sinful failure is the actual condition beyond which we cannot see. Deliverance must take place in us before we can see its shape. It is easy to preach negation. Examples of failure and falsehood, harbingers of judgment, omens of doom, are many and near at hand. Examples of nobility, courage, goodness, faith, though they exist, are all compounded with human dross. Neither a city paved with gold in the sky nor a utopian society on earth can serve as more than a broken image of the eternal good.

Nevertheless, we cannot justify ourselves either in stopping short of prescription as the secular prophet does, or in speaking too much of evil and too little of good, or in speaking with vivid detail of evil and with nebulous generalities of good. Though no eye has seen, ear heard, or heart conceived it, we are called to preach what God has prepared for those who love him. Though the wise man, the scribe, the debater of this age, though we ourselves be made foolish along with all the world, we are given to proclaim a gospel from beyond the world. And though in the present that gospel remains an option not yet taken up, a promise not yet with all our hearts embraced, still the prescription is urgently needed: of repentance and faith before God, of obedience in love before our fellow-men. Surely we can trace the beginnings of an outline on the clouded canvas of our hope. We must not fail to trace it.

For hope is necessary to life. If I may again let Bill Hamartolos speak without breaking into dialogue with him, I think he would say something like this: "Remember, Mr. Preacher, that hope and trust and confidence of some sort are necessary to sustain the effort of living. Because they are necessary they are inevitable. And because they are inevitable, they will rest on false bases if they have no true basis. Magic and superstition betray perfectly legitimate faith. Is confidence wrong? Doesn't God intend for us to have it? Does he not provide it because it is necessary to a human being? Don't scold us for our superstitions. Don't scold us for believing anything. You play a shoddy trick on us if you do nothing but destroy our idols. The symbols of our material and social achievement are legitimate objects of devotion, if there are no better. Show us God, or don't ask us to listen!"

SUGGESTIONS

It will be well for you to supplement this chapter by a thorough reading of Read (48), in which, among many valuable things, you will meet the assertion that diagnosis should never get into the sermon. This judgment is expressed in passing, and he does not develop it or give reasons for it. You will have to draw your own conclusion as to whether he and I are thinking of diagnosis in the same way, and what are the misuses against which he is protesting.

In a sense all serious discussions of the preacher's relationship to the society in which he lives, and of what he has to say to it, involve assumptions with regard to the interpretation of life. If you have not finished Forsyth (23), you will do well to read him in this connection.

Since you need an outlook not limited by the special concerns and pressures of the immediate present, I suggest that you read some more of the older works, like Brooks (17) and Jowett (25). Balance these with some contemporary essays, like Luccock (45), Chapters I to III, pages 1-101, and Bowie (16).

CHAPTER 14

Forms of Development

> It should show nothing but its own unfolding parts:
>   Branches that thrust out by the force of its inner life
>   Sentences like leaves native to this very spray
>   True to the species
>   Not taken from alien growths
>   Illustrations like blossoms opening from inside these very twigs
>   Not brightly colored kites
>   Pulled from the wind of somebody else's thought
>   Entangled in these branches.

Up to this point of our study we have been concerned with the design of the sermon as a whole, its thought-substance apprehended in its form, its form manifesting its content. All our classification of forms, the distinction between comprehensive and contributory assertions, between organic and functional elements, between types of organic form and functional form, between types of continuity and the forms they produce—all these have to do with the total design of the sermon. They are all inherent in any sermon plan, whether noticed or not. In them is to be found the difference between good and poor design. The only way to judge or improve a sermon plan is to take note of them, deliberately or intuitively. They are meant to be used as tools in criticism and in craftsmanship.

Now we must turn to a second major phase of our study, the development of the thought in detail. The house has been designed; now we lay the bricks one after another. The drama has been conceived; now we speak the lines one after another. The symphony has been created; now we play it bar by bar.

But that does not mean that we can now forget over-all design. As the heading of this chapter indicates, the developing material, down to the minutest detail, is the very tissue, the flesh and blood of the thought-organism.

So now we have to ask a new question. How is a thought

developed? What does one do to a thought when he begins to enlarge it? Does he always do the same thing, or does he do different things to the thought from time to time? Precisely what are these different things? What forms are produced by them? Can they be named, described, illustrated separately?

In a sense there is one thing we always do in developing a thought. We always particularize it in some way. That may not help much, since the word *particularize* is about as broad as the word *develop*. But it is more descriptive of what takes place, and I think we shall see that it does help.

In the chapter on continuity (pages 174-177) we have seen what it means to go from a general to particulars and from particulars to a general. There it was said that all major movements of the mind are in one of these two directions. All the points, the structural assertions, of a well-organized sermon are particulars of the central concept. In like manner, each structural point is a generalization that contains and relates all the particulars used in its development. Or, conversely, every detail in an orderly discussion of a point is a particularizing of the point. The points are particularizations as compared with the central thought, but generalizations as compared with the detail.

Now we are studying the process of developing a thought, and are concerned with what happens when we move out into particular detail. The subject is as broad as the whole art of communication, and a single chapter can hope to do no more than stake out the ground. The first step is to draw a clear line between generals and particulars.

To begin with, the power to make generalizations is one of the most astounding faculties of the mind, the power to distil a million facts into a single meaning. Take Thoreau's, "The mass of men lead lives of quiet desperation." Take a kindred generalization, Blaise Pascal's, describing life in the face of misery and death: "It is enough, without examining particular occupations, to group them all under the heading of diversion." Take Shakespeare's, "We are such stuff as dreams are made on, and our little life is rounded with a sleep." Take any household word or memorable saying; they are all generalizations. This condensation of much in little is the mark of all great poetry and art. The ability to make significant generalizations is the test of intellectual power. The labor of trying to make them is the most constructive of all mental disciplines.

As another example, the American historian, Charles A. Beard, was once asked if he could sum up the lessons of history in a short book. He replied that he could do it in four sentences, and he chose four familiar generalizations. History teaches that:

1. Whom the gods would destroy, they first make mad with power.

2. The mills of God grind slowly, yet they grind exceeding small.

3. The bee fertilizes the flower it robs.

4. When it is dark enough you can see the stars.

"All great thoughts are general," says Samuel Johnson, Boswell's Doctor Johnson, in his *The Lives of the Poets,* in a passage discussing the metaphysical poets, Donne, Crashaw, and the rest. I quote it for the light it throws on the different effect produced by generals and particulars.

They never attempted that comprehension and expanse of thought which at once fills the whole mind, and of which the first effect is sudden astonishment, and the second rational admiration. Sublimity is produced by aggregation, and littleness by dispersion. Great thoughts are always general, and consist in positions not limited by exceptions, and in descriptions not descending to minuteness. Those writers who lay on the watch for novelty could have little hope of greatness; for great things cannot have escaped former observation.

There is much here which the student of preaching should take to heart. Johnson says that the effect of a good generalization is first astonishment and then admiration. He says that sublimity, exaltation of thought, is produced by aggregation, by adding up, that is. by generalization; and that dispersion, scattering attention over many particular things, produces an effect of littleness. He says that great general thoughts are broad, that is, each such thought embraces a large expanse of thought, furnishes a comprehensive view of a wide field of facts, or of truth, or of experience.

This passage explains the tiresome mediocrity of much preaching. The anecdotal sermon goes from one human interest item to another without adequate generalizations. It never attempts "that comprehension and expanse of thought which at once fills the whole mind." The sermon which strives for novelty and originality is sure to deal in trifles, because such novelties are not great. Certainly the great Christian thoughts are open secrets accessible to all believers in all time. If a man is dealing with such a thought, he will not be the first to have discovered it.

A generalization, then, has its own proper function to perform. It condenses a broad area of experience into a single statement, sees a large truth in a single glance. Its purpose is to pull together and unify a multitude of concrete but otherwise unrelated facts, incidents, fragments of life, and to hold them together as a unit of meaning. Its purpose is to achieve understanding, breadth and grasp of thought, to reveal and illuminate a large expanse of view in perspective.

Without clearly apprehended generalizations, a sermon will always seem to be dealing with trivialities, fragments, scraps of life, and the more interesting these particular details are, the more confusing they will be. That is what has happened when we wonder what the man is driving at. He has failed to pull his material together and make a general statement about it. For it is the generalizations that organize the material.

Thus the art of generalization is of primary importance to the preacher. The power of a generalization is proportionate to the weight of what it says and the lucidity with which it says it. Here again, as everywhere in expression, the secret is a perfect union of right content and right form. As to form, the art of generalization is to have all the essential words right, and all the dispensable words absent. Having the dispensable words absent is just as necessary as having the essential words right. Every word that can be spared is in the way, blurs the line, overloads the attention.

For this reason, the better a generalization is, the more it is likely to sound like an aphorism, to take on the style of a familiar proverb. Here is one from the Book of Proverbs, the text of one of my earliest sermons: "Keep thy heart with all diligence, for out of it are the issues of life." And here is another from Proverbs: "As in water face answereth to face, so the heart of man, to man."

But if it is true that no good sermon can exist without adequate generalizations, it is equally true that no sermon can be good without particulars. Generals and particulars do not have the same function in communication. Each has its own separate function, and each is important. We cannot say that one is more important than the other. Each is indispensable in its place.

Summed up in a single word, the function of generals is to convey understanding. We may say that in a sermon the purpose of a generalization is to cause our hearer to understand some phase of reality. On the other hand, the function of particulars is to present concrete details of that phase of reality in such a way as to cause our hearer to experience that reality for himself. The particulars are for the purpose of giving back to our hearer, through his memory and imagination, that area of experience from which the general was abstracted in the first place. Generalization interprets reality, comprehends it in large masses, while particularity evokes reality by means of concrete details.

Thus all art deals in particulars, in "evocative particularity," as someone has called it. A skyscraper is a particular shape like no other against the skyline, and it rises at a particular spot from among the other shapes around it. Schubert begins a symphony which he never finishes, but he starts with a particular voice, the solitary voice of the cello low down in the minor mode. That melody is like itself and like no other. The painter chooses a certain tree with a character and a history of its own to put on his particular hillside. Or if it is Modigliani, he chooses the image of a particular woman of a certain type (the type is his generalization) with a long neck and a long face, and with a withdrawn sadness about her. Or if it is a picture of Jesus meant to look like a real person, it will be some particular person seen or imagined, with the individual differences that distinguish him from all other persons on earth—and so, of course, it will not be Jesus but some other particular human being!

Poor preaching may fall into either of two opposite faults. It may move too exclusively among particulars and never tie the particulars together into adequate generalizations. Conversely, it may consist too exclusively of generalities, not glittering generalities, just vague, fuzzy generalities—one general assertion after another, from which nothing stands out as more important than the rest.

Good thinking moves in both directions. It usually begins with particulars and goes to generals, the process of induction. But good thought, especially when being communicated, never remains general for long. After it has generalized, it moves back again to particulars.

Let us see how this works. Go back to Thoreau's remark: "The mass of men lead lives of quiet desperation." The next sentence moves back to particulars:

What is called resignation is confirmed desperation. From the desperate city you go into the desperate country, and have to console yourself with the bravery of minks and muskrats. A stereotyped but unconscious despair is concealed even under what are called games and amusements of mankind. There is no play in them, for this comes after work. But it is a characteristic of wisdom not to do desperate things.

What has Thoreau done to develop his general thought? Resignation, though still general and abstract, is one particular manifestation among other signs of desperation. It therefore serves as an example of desperation, that is, it serves to illustrate desperation. The city and the country are more particular than resignation and more concrete, though still quite general illustrations of desperation The country people are as desperate as the city people. Only the nonhuman creatures are brave instead of desperate.

But minks and muskrats are far more particular and concrete than nature or nonhuman creatures. Minks and muskrats are concrete illustrations, not of desperation but of its opposite, bravery. The games and amusements of mankind serve as a further illustration of desperation, similar to resignation, but somewhat more particular. Play, as Thoreau conceives it, is an example of bravery, incompatible with desperation. The last sentence is a new generalization of equal rank with the first. In a word, Thoreau develops his thought by particularizing it. There are eight particulars in this short paragraph.

Let us also follow Pascal a little way in the development of his general remark that all the pursuits of man are diversions. His generalization is similar to Thoreau's, but more profound, being not only diagnosis but etiology as well. He says that he has found one very good reason why this is so, namely, that our mortal condition is so miserable that nothing can comfort us when we think of it closely. This he particularizes in numerous passages, of which a few follow:

Hence it comes that play and the society of women, war, and high post, are so sought after. Not that there is in fact any happiness in them, or that men imagine true bliss to consist in money won at play, or in the hare which they hunt; we would not take these as a gift.

The king is surrounded by persons whose only thought is to divert the king and to prevent his thinking of self. For he is unhappy, king though he be, if he think of himself.

How does it happen that this man, so distressed at the death of his wife and only son, or who has some great lawsuit which annoys him, is not at the moment sad? We need not wonder; for a ball has just been served him, and he must return it to his companion.

This man, born to know the universe, to judge all causes, to govern a whole state, is altogether occupied and taken up with the business of catching a hare.

Pascal has caught up in a few words the restless activity and the obviously insatiable desires of human beings: "The pursuits of mankind are all diversions from his ignorance, misery, mortality." His generalization conveys an understanding of a broad aspect of existence. He develops it through particulars: women, war, office,

the gambler, the king, the tennis player, the hunter, and so on.
All these particulars are examples of his meaning, illustrations of
his point. These particulars evoke the reality of which he is speaking; they make us experience it for ourselves.

Particulars are more or less concrete, more or less specific.
They are graded in almost infinite degrees of concreteness and
specificity. When the psalmist in Psalm 8 turns with astonishment
from the greatness of God's creation to the littleness of man, he
generalizes: "Yet thou hast made him little less than God, and
dost crown him with glory and honor." When in the next verse
he says, "Thou hast given him dominion over the works of thy
hands; thou hast put all things under his feet," that is still generalization. But dominion is more specific than glory, and "under his
feet," though its sense is figurative, is both specific and concrete.
And when he further says, "All sheep and oxen, and also the
beasts of the field, the birds of the air, and the fish of the sea,"
these are really concrete particulars, though not very particular
particulars if I may so speak. They are still fairly general particulars. "The beasts of the field" is a general term; "minks and
muskrats" would be more specific. But "beasts of the field" is
particular as compared with "all things."

Thus "All sheep and oxen, and also the beasts of the field, the
birds of the air, and the fish of the sea," presents five illustrations
of "the works of thy hands." They are general illustrations, several
degrees removed from being quite specific. "Fowls of the air"
is less specific than "the young ravens," or robins, or mallards.
But if I wish to be quite specific, I shall speak of the gray and
brown female pigeon which nests every year on the administration
building at our school. So the particulars that develop the
psalmist's thought are concrete, but general rather than specific,
yet they are particular enough to present the reality of which he
is speaking.

The perfect union of thought-substance and expressive form is a
sensuous image, a figure of speech. Shakespeare is a consummate
master at expressing a general thought by means of particularized

images. In Act IV, Scene 1 of *The Tempest*, Prospero, who may be taken as an image of Shakespeare himself, is giving his daughter Miranda in marriage to Ferdinand. To express the incalculable price of that gift, he says, "I have given you here a third of mine own life." Why a third? Because one third of Shakespeare's life is Ariel, the image of his creative genius, another and darker third is Caliban, the image of Shakespeare's gross animal self, and thus the other third is Miranda, the image of Shakespeare the man and father. In this way the general concept of self gets expressed in particular images.

Prospero tells the pair that if they consummate their love before marriage it will curse them both. But note the sensuous images, the evocative particulars in which he unfolds this general thought:

> If thou dost break her virgin knot before
> All sanctimonious ceremonies may
> With full and holy rite be ministered,
> No sweet aspersion shall the heavens let fall
> To make this contract grow; but barren hate,
> Sour-eyed disdain and discord shall bestrew
> The union of your beds with weeds so loathly
> That you shall hate it both.

It is nearly impossible to stop quoting short of every line! Ferdinand vows: no temptation shall ever "melt mine honor into lust." Prospero warns: "the strongest oaths are straw To the fire i' the blood." Ferdinand protests: "I warrant you, sir; The white cold virgin snow upon my heart Abates the ardour of my liver." There is a pedestrian generalization behind each of these speeches. Ferdinand might have said, and indeed with more accuracy, "My self-respect is stronger than my sexual desire." The way the thing is said makes a difference, and the difference is mainly concreteness and particularity.

To endow Miranda and Ferdinand with happiness and good fortune, Prospero creates through Ariel, his art, a pageant of spirits of the earth, the sky, and high heaven, celebrating the union and pronouncing their blessings. The pageant occurs near the hour when Caliban has planned to kill Prospero, and the vision is shattered when Prospero remembers the plot with sudden anger.

These are all images of abstract thought. In the middle of his play Shakespeare remembers what he is doing. He has created them all out of his head, Prospero, Caliban, Ariel, Ferdinand, all the characters, the shipwreck, and the island too. He is making everything happen just as he wants it to. It is all unreal. And life itself is just as unreal and impermanent. Several times in his works Shakespeare has called life a play on a stage. Life itself will disappear, as the play disappears when it is over.

But all this Shakespeare says in concrete images, and when he says it in words, the words and figures are so sensuous that our mind's eye opens wide and its nostrils dilate, for we can see all the world's cities wreathed in cloud-rack against the sky, and we can fairly smell the dissolving vapors.

The magical scene has just ended, when the dancing nymphs and reapers, at an abrupt word from Prospero, suddenly disappear with a hollow roar. Then Prospero speaks to quiet the astonished Ferdinand:

> You do look, my son, in a moved sort,
> As if you were dismayed: be cheerful, sir:
> Our revels now are ended. These our actors,
> As I foretold you, were all spirits and
> Are melted into air, into thin air:
> And, like the baseless fabric of this vision,
> The cloud-capped towers, the gorgeous palaces,
> The solemn temples, the great globe itself,
> Yea, all which it inherit, shall dissolve
> And, like this insubstantial pageant faded,
> Leave not a rack behind. We are such stuff
> As dreams are made on, and our little life
> Is rounded with a sleep.

It is insufferable to comment on that, I know. But Shakespeare showed himself so keenly interested in the craft of writing and speech that I feel sure he would not mind my saying again how he moves through particulars to generalization, from the vanishing Iris and Ceres and Juno and the nymphs and reapers, through the melting of towers, palaces, temples, and the earth itself with everything upon it, and then calls time on our frantic little parade, which ends so suddenly that no curtain is needed.

Granted that Shakespeare is a supreme artist in expression and that his masterpieces leave us in despair of emulation. We are nevertheless attempting to do the same thing he did, to communicate something more than formless rational meaning, to catch the disembodied thought and give it a local habitation and a name. To give over this task before it is begun, to neglect study of how it is accomplished, is a thing worse than false modesty; it is to rationalize our laziness. The racy expressiveness of our people's very slang rebukes us.

The question before us is: What happens to a thought when it is developed? Are there forms which the development and support of a thought takes, special forms of particularity, which can be identified, named, illustrated? The answer is that there are, and every one of them when understood becomes a useful assistant in the task of communication.

GENERAL ILLUSTRATION

One of these forms we have already identified, *general illustration*. We have seen it at work. It is the commonest and most important kind of illustration.

A good deal of confusion exists as a result of a superficial notion of what a sermon "illustration" is. In popular use, an illustration is always a special incident, an illustrative story. I have called it an anecdote, perhaps with more disrespect than it deserves. Such an anecdote has its use, an important use, as we shall soon see. But the fact is that an illustration is simply a concrete example in support of a general assertion, and hence any concrete example is an illustration.

Cyprian says, "How great is the patience of God!" Then, realizing that the patience of God will not be conceived from these words, he develops the thought by means of general illustrations:

How great is the patience of God! . . . We see that with undistinguishing equality of patience, at God's behest, the seasons minister to the guilty and the guiltless, the religious and the impious, those who give thanks and the unthankful;

The guilty and the guiltless, the religious and irreligious, the thankful and the thankless are general illustrations of God's patience, since he gives to them all alike. Then with more concrete particulars of "the seasons minister" he continues:

The elements wait on them; the winds blow, the fountains flow, the abundance of the harvests increases, the fruits of the vineyards ripen, the trees are loaded with apples, the groves put on their leaves, the meadows their verdure;

Then he turns to a form I think had better be called *explanation* of God's patience rather than illustration, continuing:

And while God is provoked with frequent, yea, with continual offences, he softens his indignation, and in patience waits for the day of retribution, once for all determined; and although he has revenge in his power, he prefers to keep patience for a long while, bearing, that is to say, mercifully, and putting off, so that, if it might be possible, the long protracted mischief may sometime be changed, and man, involved in the contagion of errors and crimes, may even though late be converted to God.[1]

Illustration is thus a broad principle. Such evocative but seemingly natural illustrations as these constitute a prominent element in any good communication of thought. The great value of general illustrations is that they always lie at hand and can be quickly multiplied to produce cumulation of evidence, and that they seem to unfold naturally like blossoms opening from inside this very twig of thought. They do not call attention to themselves as something added, extrinsic, artificial. They give reality to the thought itself.

None of us is so lowly as not to do this kind of thing. On the first page of this book I had to try to develop a crucial but extremely abstruse thought: that life is always found in a union of substance and form. Nothing but examples could show what this means. The first example is a general illustration, a plant, any plant that is complete with root, stem, leaf, flower, and fruit.

[1] *Ante-Nicene Fathers*, vol. V, p. 485.

After some details concerning the plant, two other general illustrations are briefly introduced, the cell and the animal. A thought so abstract as this can have no meaning apart from examples; the illustrations are part of the very tissue of the thought.

SPECIFIC ILLUSTRATIONS

We have seen also that these natural illustrations range through many degrees of specificity. They can be concrete but very general. They can be quite specific. Every simile, every metaphor is an illustration of some more general thought. "Like blossoms opening" is a general illustration because it includes all blossoms, any kind of blossom.

But thought, or especially a painful emotion like grief, can be as specific as a certain pair of shoes. Someone who knows nothing about Niobe can still feel the last definitive touch of Hamlet's grief when he says:

> A little month; or ere those shoes were old
> With which she followed my poor father's body,
> Like Niobe, all tears;

It takes a Shakespeare to do it that way. But we all do it sometimes, if not as carefully or as well as we could. On page 13 I had to develop the thought that a busy life does not prevent a man's doing fine work. I could have said that the world's greatest musicians, writers, and preachers have done their work in busy and crowded lives. Those would have been general illustrations. But rightly or wrongly—I of course think rightly!—it seemed to me that only the mention of certain specific instances, particular men, could bring out the real force of the point. And so William Faulkner, Bach, Mozart, Luther, and Calvin became specific illustrations of great work done by men as busy as the busiest preacher of our day.

Simile, metaphor, comparison—these are illustrations. We need not trouble ourselves about sharp distinctions between general and specific illustrations. We do need a keen sense of what is concrete, what is evocative in its particularity. No matter whether *bed* and *grave* in the following are general or specific. They are sharp and vivid in their particularity, and Lazarus at least is specific.

I have a bed of sin; delight in sin is a bed: I have a grave of sin; sense-lessness of sin is a grave: and where Lazarus had been four days, I have been for fifty years in this putrefaction; why dost thou not call me, as thou didst him, with a loud voice, since my soul is as dead as his body was? I need thy thunder, O my God; thy music will not serve me.[2]

On the basis of this passage alone we might defend Donne against Johnson's charge that he lacked comprehensiveness and expanse of thought. Bed, grave, loud voice, thunder, music—these are concrete images, metaphors, illustrations. The generalization behind them is no less comprehensive than this: that our present existence is a state of death from which only God can raise us. The illustrations are not images added, extrinsic; they are the fabric of the thought itself. They can seem artificial only to a mind enslaved by an old vice: pride in abstract thought. Such images are not peculiar to poets either. Many a vindictive mother has said to her daughter, "You've made your bed; now lie in it."

Several things should be remembered about the principle of illustration. First, an illustration to be effective must be an example clarifying or supporting some definite point that is being made. *Illustrate* is a transitive verb. We do not simply illustrate; we illustrate something. There is no such thing as a "sermon illustration." There is only an illustration of some special assertion or thought in a sermon. There is no "good illustration." There is only a good illustration of—this or that.

Secondly, an illustration is valuable only to the degree in which it centers attention on the point being made, not on itself. Consequently a natural illustration, one that does not claim attention for its own sake, one that seems a part of the thought itself, is the most valuable of all. If it claims attention to itself for its own sake, an illustration disrupts rather than assists the communication of thought.

[2] John Donne, "Expostulation" in No. XXI of his *Devotions*.

Thirdly, other things being equal, the more specific and the more concrete an illustration is, the more powerful it is. This is the value of a highly specific illustration when it is exactly right and when it is used in precisely the right way, that is, to reinforce its definite point. But this also is the danger of a specific illustration if its power is not controlled with perfect mastery. The more power the illustration has, the more damage it does if it is not perfectly controlled.

Nothing therefore could be more intrinsically powerful, interesting, suggestive, than an incident, a story involving specific persons and their actions and words. Theoretically, such a story is the best kind of illustration because of its force. I do not discount its force, and I certainly do not advise against its use. Rather, just because an illustrative story is a sort of dynamite, it must be used with skill, discrimination, caution, or it may demolish more than it builds.

The danger, of course, is that the anecdote is too often used for its own sake, for its intrinsic interest, and it claims attention for itself and not for the point it ought to illustrate. It is heard simply as a story; it is "a good illustration," but not an illustration of anything in particular.

For a human incident or a person contains many meanings, never just one, and the impression it makes on the hearer may not be that which the preacher intends. And if to the hearer it suggests something other than the preacher intends, it competes with the preacher's thought, and competes with all the advantage of its innate power. In fact, an "illustration" taken from a book or another preacher may be used to support a half-dozen different points—a certain proof that it is not the perfect illustration for any.

The clichés concerning "sermon illustrations" are several. It is argued that illustrative stories are necessary as windows to see through. But such windows cannot be necessary unless the walls of the thought are opaque. If the thought of my sermon is opaque, the story is all the more liable to be heard as a thing added but not assimilated. Besides, to cut a window is not the only way and not the best way to let in the light. It would be even better to make the walls of thought luminous.

Again it is contended that illustrative stories are necessary to supply interest, to give the human touch, and to make the message relevant to concrete human situations. The answer is the same. What does this imply concerning the texture of the thought before and after the story? It is true that if the preacher allows himself to talk in unrelieved abstractions, hazy general statements without natural illustrations, without concrete examples such as we have examined above, then his sermon will indeed need to be made interesting and human. But it is fallacious to suppose that a few stories can salvage a discourse of that character. If the preacher has something relevant to say, and if the fabric of his thought is a woof of particulars on a warp of clear generalizations, his sermon will need no artificial adornments to make it interesting.

Further it is said that illustrative stories are needed to supply pauses and resting places for listeners in the progress of the sermon's movement. This is by all odds the most valid claim made for them, in my opinion. That they are necessary in the contemporary sermon, however, is a dubious argument. Twenty-five minutes of concentrated listening, following the uninterrupted progress of a compelling thought, is not an insupportable ordeal. A three-hour tragedy needs the lighter scenes for relief, but a serious one-act play can scarcely assimilate such a scene.

In short, the second-hand story, bought, stolen, and bandied about, is usually a device to compensate for the inferior quality of the sermon's material, and for the preacher's listless effort to express his own thought well. The shopworn apocryphal story, not the specific instance gathered from a man's own observation or reading, is the target of my criticism. A story can be safely used only if it has become an integral part of the preacher's own thought, and if it is presented in unmistakable connection with the general thought it exemplifies. When so used, it is one of the keenest weapons in the preacher's arsenal.

But the faulty form and style of much preaching is not due to the neglect or careless use of the illustrative story. The fault is rather that preachers, and some writers on the craft of preaching, talk and act as if an anecdote were the only illustration, and as if illustration were the only form which a lucid development of thought can take. Other forms, as old as communication itself, as tried and true as the story, are ignored by contemporary preachers as if they did not exist. Preachers of course use them, but by accident as it were, not with purposeful discrimination.

EXPLANATION

Cyprian has supplied our first example of the development of a thought by means of explanation (pp. 252-3). He explains the patience of God by pointing out what that patience involves; first, that though God has both cause and power to punish, he long forbears; second, that man is thus given a continuing opportunity to repent.

This is the character of explanation. A thought is explained by indicating in greater particularity its meaning and implications, the terms used to express it, its relation to kindred thoughts, what it actually signifies, or what its primary consequences are. Explanation may or may not use illustrations in doing this. If illustrations become conspicuous, it should be called illustration rather than explanation. But there are many passages in sermons which merely talk about the point in an explanatory way.

Joseph Sittler in his sermon on "The Cruciform Character of Human Existence" (page 148) explains his use of the word *time,* and by means of explanation develops his assertion that we experience time as loss:

There is an understanding of time with which we are at the moment not primarily concerned—time, that is, as mensurable successiveness, as mere duration. We refer here, rather, to time as experienced passingness, mutability, irreversibleness. Time so realized imparts a sense not of something past but of something lost.

Lincoln develops one of the deathless affirmations of the Gettysburg Address by a more particular statement of its meaning:

But in a larger sense, we cannot dedicate—we cannot consecrate—we cannot hallow—this ground. The brave men, living and dead, who struggled here have consecrated it, far above our poor power to add or detract.

Lincoln's next sentence is a restatement of the last, but still by way of explanation. He continues:

The world will little note, nor long remember what we say here, but it can never forget what they did here.

RESTATEMENT

Good development makes a large use of restatement, especially in oral communication. An important thought is stated; then it is stated again, not a new thought but the same thought in other and more particular words. It may be stated several times, each restatement bringing to light some new aspect of the thought. Restatement is not repetition; it is making the same point over in a different way. It may be mainly illustrative, and so may merge with illustration. It may be mainly explanatory. Or it may be mainly corroborative, merging with argument.

Joseph Sittler, now speaking of time as contradiction as well as loss, states the point six times, with increasing particularity:

Time, so realized, carries within itself a contradiction. The days of our years are both promise and denial. Time unfolds itself both as illimitable aspiration and as inevitable limitation. That which is brought into existence within the rhythm of time is choked out of existence by the same time. We are born into time whose hands are full of promise; we come to our last hour with the clutch of time about our throats. Across the upthrust of that line of seeming endless time with which we are endowed as children and whose infinite promise constitutes the dream-stuff of our younger years—across that there runs the cross line of lostness, denial, and all ambiguity.

The prophet Ezekiel (chapter 34) piles up God's judgment of the pastors of his people, in restatements not without sobering import to our ministry today:

Ho, shepherds of Israel who have been feeding yourselves! Should not shepherds feed the sheep? You eat the fat, you clothe yourselves with the wool, you slaughter the fatlings; but you do not feed the sheep

The weak you have not strengthened, the sick you have not healed, the crippled you have not bound up, the strayed you have not brought back, the lost you have not sought, and with force and harshness you have ruled them. So they were scattered, because there was no shepherd; and they became food for all the wild beasts. My sheep were scattered, they wandered over all the mountains and on every high hill; my sheep were scattered over all the face of the earth, with none to search or seek for them.

Macbeth asks his question in four forms before he stops, and it becomes a heavier question with each restatement:

> Canst thou not minister to a mind diseased,
> Pluck from the memory a rooted sorrow,
> Raze out the written troubles of the brain,
> And with some sweet oblivious antidote
> Cleanse the stuffed bosom of that perilous stuff
> Which weighs upon the heart?

In all the preceding examples, restatement is used to impress the point, to make it more deeply felt. But restatement is equally useful, not to say necessary, in quite ordinary communication, where it serves the purpose of clarity. On page 246, for instance, I was making the point that generals and particulars have different functions in speech. Without plan or deliberate intention to do so, I wrote a paragraph of five sentences, of which the two first are a statement and a restatement of the function of generalization:

Summed up in a single word, the function of generals is to convey understanding. We may say that in a sermon the purpose of a generalization is to cause our hearer to understand some phase of reality.

The next two sentences are a statement and a restatement of the function of particulars:

On the other hand, the function of particulars is to present concrete details of that phase of reality in such a way as to cause our hearer to experience that reality for himself. The particulars are for the purpose of giving back to our hearer, through his memory and imagination, that area of experience from which the general was abstracted in the first place.

The last sentence in the paragraph again restates the function of both, in co-ordinate clauses:

Generalization interprets reality, comprehends it in large masses, while particularity evokes reality by means of concrete details.

TESTIMONY

A point may be developed by bringing the thought and words of others to its clarification or support. Primarily this means quotation.

As already indicated, there is a faulty use of quotations, namely, stringing together one after another, so that the quotations become the actual structure of the sermon, and the preacher simply chases them without making adequate generalizations of his own. This method produces the all-too-familiar scissors-and-paste sermon.

There are, however, two good reasons for quoting from time to time. They are not good reasons for quoting continually. Continual quotation soon destroys all the value of quotations, and creates the impression that the preacher has no ideas of his own.

The first reason is that I may find myself saying a thing which someone else has said far better than I can say it. Then I should quote him if I can, and if I use more than a few of his words, I should call his name and give him credit. The name stands for a person, is interesting, and will increase interest in the thought. If I don't know whose words I am using, I should still indicate in some way that I am quoting, if it is more than a brief phrase. I should not pretend that they are my words. I am free to use anyone's thought in my own words, but not free to palm off another's words as my own.

The second reason for quoting is that the thought I am expressing may have been expressed by someone whose opinion carries an influence or authority greater than mine. Then I should quote him if I can. And certainly in this case I should not omit his name, for the name is the chief strength of his support.

Joseph Sittler continues, after the passage quoted under "Explanation" above, as follows:

Time so realized imparts a sense not of something past but of something lost. There are few themes common to all human reflection which have been so widely or so poignantly celebrated in poetry. From Milton's verses one recalls the line:

Nymphs and shepherds dance no more

and from one of the Shakespeare sonnets the moment in which the poet regards the gaunt trees in wintertime, whose branches erstwhile were green and leafy against the summer sky, and sings:

That time of year thou mayst in me behold
When yellow leaves, or none, or few, do hang
Upon those boughs which shake against the cold,
Bare ruined choirs, where late the sweet birds sang.

These quotations serve a double purpose. They not only say with beauty and power what the preacher is saying, but they also support the point that the sense of time as loss is widely and poignantly celebrated in literature.

The testimony of an authority is used in a recent sermon of mine. I shall give the development of the whole point in order to show testimony being used as a support of the preacher's own generalizations, not as a substitute for them:

It is true that knowledge is power—of a kind. It is true that men, through knowledge, can dream of doing things heretofore unimagined, like penetrating space, launching new satellites of the earth, or, according to the very latest reports, exploding Jupiter to make new planets to order. All this is true—but not to the unclouded glory of mankind. It is only half the truth, the flattering half. The dark truth about us is that we cannot be trusted with the power we actually have in our hands. We cannot be relied on to use our power for good and not for our own destruction.

Did you hear Dr. William Pollard speaking to the Sunday Evening Club? He is an atomic scientist, executive director of the Oak Ridge Institute of Nuclear Studies in Tennessee. He said that "we may do irreparable damage," that "events never turn out as we expected them to beforehand." He said that "the laws of nature do not control history." He means that will controls history. And he means that our blind and blundering will may precipitate disaster.

Professor Sittler's exposition of the broken and contradictory character of human existence ends in a passage that sets the words of Paul at the climactic point of the sermon:

When, therefore, in the areas of time, of moral reflection, and of self-realization we confront central pronouncements of the gospel, we arrive at the knowledge that something is here said which is startlingly relevant. It was a man who knew time in all of the fulness of its inner ambiguity, who, caught up in the deed of Christ, was able to say "We that love the Lord have passed from death to life . . . old things have passed away, all things are become new." And it was the same man who cried, not because he was ignorant of the Greek hope of immortality but in full consciousness of it, "Now unto the Blessed and only Potentate, King of Kings, Lord of Lords, *Who only hath immortality.* . . ." [3]

Paul himself, in the fifteenth chapter of Romans, uses a series of quotations from the Old Testament to develop his point that God's promise included the Gentiles:

For I tell you that Christ became a servant to the circumcised to show God's truthfulness, in order to confirm the promises given to the patriarchs, and in order that the Gentiles might glorify God for his mercy. As it is written,
> "Therefore I will praise thee among the Gentiles,
> and sing to thy name":
and again it is said,
> "Rejoice, O Gentiles, with his people";
and again,
> "Praise the Lord, all Gentiles,
> and let all the peoples praise him";
and further Isaiah says,
> "The root of Jesse shall come,
> he who rises to rule the Gentiles;
> in him shall the Gentiles hope."

We shall stop here, though other forms of development could be identified. A thought may be developed by logical reasoning in its support. A thought may be developed simply by a considered statement of the preacher's personal reaction to it, his emotional reaction or his value judgment. And so on.

Natural illustrations, general and specific, explanation, restatement, and testimony—used singly or in combination—these are the important but neglected forms of development. If a man were as diligent in trying to improve his use of them as the average preacher is in pirating anecdotes, his preaching would be revolutionized.

[3] The Chicago Lutheran Seminary *Record,* Vol. 54, No. 4, October, 1949. Quoted by permission.

SUGGESTIONS

You can do one thing in connection with this chapter which will be worth more to you than anything else. Look through a sermon or other writing of your own and pick out a sentence in which you are saying something significant but too big to be obvious. Then set yourself deliberately to write several restatements of it, explanatory and corroborative. Next provide this thought with natural illustrations, explanations, and so on.

The next most valuable thing you can do is to study the sermons of men who speak in a good oral style, not too literary. Study them to see how they use these five forms of development—for nothing else but that. For this purpose I suggest the sermons of George Buttrick and Fulton Sheen, of Harry Emerson Fosdick and Charles R. Brown. I suggest them for the virile prose they use.

I can suggest no better description of these forms and their use than that in Phillips (62). Homiletical writings do not give them much attention, but Farmer's (22) Chapter IV on "The Need for Concreteness" is much to the point of what preaching should be in this respect, though, as he states several times, he has no very definite suggestions as to how it may be done. Brown (5), Chapter V, "The Lighter Elements of the Sermon," pages 123-154, is also to the point.

Plenty of attention is given in the literature to the use of the illustrative story or incident. Consult any index under "Illustrations." It is here that Sangster's book (13) belongs.

I strongly recommend that you get acquainted with some books on reading aloud, for the sense of living speech they can give you. The expository sections in all chapters of Parrish (61) are excellent. The "Introduction" on pages 1-38 in Tassin (66) is worth close study. Crocker (53) and Woolbert-Nelson (69) contain only brief suggestions for the study of their many selections, but their suggestions go to the heart of the matter. All this is about reading material that is already written. Your job is to turn it around, to learn what this can teach you about writing in a good oral style.

CHAPTER 15

Writing for the Ear

For last year's words belong to last year's language
And next year's words await another voice.
                                                    T. S. Eliot[1]

The basic problem of this chapter was stated in Chapter 10 (pages 163-168), when we were thinking about the hearing situation. That discussion should be reviewed at this point. Briefly, I said that the test of good writing is permanence, and the test of good speech is immediacy of apprehension and response.

This distinction puts meaning into the saying that good speech differs from good writing, that what is good when read may not be good when heard, and conversely. I shall not repeat here the reasons why in the hearing situation the language must communicate immediately or not at all, but only say that until we know why good writing and good speech differ the saying is of no use to us.

When I began a comprehensive study of homiletical literature, I found that everybody said good speech differs from good writing, but nobody said why or how they differ, beyond repeating the adage that sentences should be short and clear, and that words should be plain and familiar. These remarks helped me as a teacher no more than they had helped me as a preacher, which was little enough.

This matter could not be neglected, for the words and sentences obviously constitute the form and determine the effect of everything, simply everything that a man says, from first to last. It became clear to me that if I was to give any real help to my students, I would have to find out the facts for myself by a thorough examination of exactly what good speech does and what it does not do.

And now, after more work at this than I care to think of, I find

[1] "Little Gidding," in *Four Quartets* (New York: Harcourt, Brace, 1943).

myself about to commit the same fault I have blamed in other writers, to discuss in general statements what is particular, without being able to develop the facts with that fulness, or illustrate them with that detail, which they deserve. At least I shall devote a chapter to it, not a paragraph or two. But there are so many things to say that it would take another book to develop them properly. For oral communication is a great art, worth a lifetime devotion; if I include all I have found important, I can only sketch them.

Perhaps the truth is that the student, every man, will have to do this for himself as I did, that this is something which one man simply cannot do for another. At the very least, I can show the reader some things to look for as he examines the texture of good writing for the ear. And who knows? It may be that someday he will be the one to write the book.

Models of language for the ear should be drawn from wide sources. Sermons are not enough, may not indeed be the best sources, and surely ought not to be the only sources. Speech to the ear rather than to the eye is practiced on radio and television, as well as by ourselves in talk with one another. Excellent examples are the speeches of Churchill, Roosevelt, and other public men whose words influence multitudes of people. All playwrights write for the ear; stage and screen have much to teach us besides the newest fashions in romance.

We must not neglect the old sources, classical, immortal language addressed to the ears of men. Shakespeare's words, which I have used so often, were not written as literature to be read. They were written for the ears of the mixed crowds in the Globe Theater, and the language had to communicate or the play failed. Paul's letters were written to be heard when read aloud in the Christian assembly. The Old Testament prophecies were spoken addresses. The Greek drama, like all ancient literature, was meant to be read aloud and heard, not to be silently read.

If these facts throw a new light on the language proper to the pulpit, if they raise our estimate of people's ability to understand noble speech, if they make our condescension to a supposed child's intelligence seem as mistakenly snobbish as it is, that is well. We do not have to talk in monosyllables or think superficially in order to be understood. We need only see to it that, however profound the thing we are saying, we say it clearly and well.

By way of getting down to the subject, perhaps the first thing to say is that, in spite of the fact that speech aims at immediacy and writing at permanence, good speech differs from good writing in only a limited sense. The standards of good language are the same for both. Language that is bad when spoken is bad when written. A passage which brings to finality and permanence of statement some great thought, which requires many readings to appreciate it fully, and is richer at the fiftieth reading than it is at the first—that passage none the less uses language that is good when spoken or read aloud.

It must be so, for language is speech. Written language is an arrangement of visible symbols for sounds that are heard only in speech, and meaning attaches primarily to the sounds. That is the way it has been in the experience of the race, at any rate. Languages were employed for ages before they were ever written, and many living languages of today have never been written. That is the way it was also in the childhood of every one of us, and that is the way it still is deep down where we are always children.

Reading and writing, therefore, if they are not vicious habits themselves, may foster vicious habits in us by long and harassed use. For speed and other purposes, in our pride of intellect, we learn to read with our eyes alone, suppressing the sounds of speech. Then when we write we sometimes write with our eyes alone, still oblivious to the sounds of heard language. As a result, what we write is so denatured as to lose the character of an instrument for actual communication.

This will not do. Or, rather, it may do for the scientist describing a new discovery or experiment—but will not do for the same man when he is writing a letter to his wife and children. It may do for a recipe in a cookbook, a legal document, any work whose purpose is only to supply information. It will not do for a work that hopes to communicate on any level deeper than the surface of the mind. It will not do, then, for the preacher. On the contrary, the serious writer, the poet, and the preacher must write for the ear, not simply for the eye.

When he is wording his theme or message, when he is composing his structural assertions, when he is writing his sketch or the sentences and paragraphs of the sermon, when he sets down any words whatever, the preacher must hear how they sound when spoken, each combination of syllables, each phrase when joined with other phrases to make a sentence, each sentence when joined with others to create the movement of language. His experience and training as a student will not have prepared him for this kind of writing, may even have made it harder. But there is no help for it. He must lay on himself the discipline of listening to his language as he writes until it has become second nature. Like the deaf Beethoven, he must write a music of language heard by his inner ear.

The preacher's education and training ought to have prepared him to use language well, ought to have given him some mastery of words and sentences. If it has not done this, he is deficient in one of the essential skills of an educated man, and he will have to supply his deficiency the hard way. It can be done; he can do it, as many a man before him has done it, but he will have to make the necessary effort. With respect to the use of language the case is the same as with theology and exegesis; a book on preaching cannot be depended on to teach him. It is never too late to learn, but now the responsibility is his alone.

WORDS

If he is to write for the ear:

1. The preacher should learn to express himself in *as few words as possible*. Unneeded words are in the way. The average casually written sentence can be improved in clearness and force

by omitting one-fourth of its words. Often half the words will say it better still. "We form our opinions and judgments upon the basis of what we have known,"—fourteen words. "We think as we have known,"—six words. "These judgments and opinions then become the basis of our assertions and our activities,"—fourteen words. "We speak and act as we think,"—seven words.

"We who are within the ranks of those who are standing by the missionary enterprise, must make good our claim that our religion possesses something which cannot be supplied by other religions." That is thirty-two words, and they are printed in a book. "We who support missions must show that our faith gives what no other can." That is fourteen words, and they show the difference between verbosity and force.

Good writing also avoids verbosity, of course, and the above is bad writing. But in speech the necessity of condensation is more nearly absolute. Superfluous words have less excuse in speech, for both the voice and the person communicate in speech. The chief quality of personal communication is that it says a great deal, and suggests more, in a very few words. Excess words therefore destroy its chief quality. The thing is said all the better because the words are few, whereas the same few words written, unaided by the voice and person, may not say the thing at all. To write the same thing unambiguously often requires a great many more words.

2. He should learn to use *words that sound well together*. If he cannot make music, he must avoid making harsh dissonances. The first approach is usually this negative one.

The unit of speech is the phrase, not the word. "In an inextricable predicament" is nearly impossible to pronounce, but if one is not listening, he may write it. "Men in positions of power show themselves irresponsible in evading giving proper account of themselves." Only a temporarily deaf man could write "irresponsible in evading giving."

"Only comparatively recently was this distinctly seen"—that is the -ly jingle. The following -ity jingle was spoken in my classroom.

The fact about individuality, the fact that each of us holds some private talent or gift, is an opportunity for our own egocentricity. The esthetic gift is an opportunity for the discovery in one's individuality of a just basis of superiority. To take advantage of the opportunity is to make a community disintegrate. Yet it is in this very individuality that the possibility of collective unity resides.

"To deal with life at first hand, to act without the paralysis of too much analysis"—the rhyme in prose is called a hidden rhyme, possibly because it is so conspicuous it cannot be missed except by a deaf man. It has comic value. Louis Bromfield can say, "There is a perkiness, a jerkiness, about him" (the prairie dog), and it is pleasing. For the hidden rhyme belongs to fanciful good humor such as this, not to serious discourse.

Granting that we cannot all be Beethovens with words, we can still avoid sounds that make the difference between euphony and cacophony.

3. He should cultivate a preference for *short, strong, clear, familiar words*. This is, of course, a requirement for good writing too. In writing, as well as in speaking, it is better to say "we ought" instead of "it behooves us," to say "everyone" instead of "every individual" (if one simply means everybody), to say "we can see" instead of "we are able to visualize," to say "we know that" instead of "we are cognizant of the fact that."

Not that one should always use the shorter word, or even the more familiar word. There are times when the longer and more uncommon word is the only right word. Lincoln's "Fourscore and seven years ago" is right and "Eighty-seven years ago" would be wrong. Though the denotation is the same the connotation is different. "Our fathers brought forth" is right and "our fathers established" would be wrong. Here the simpler word is right, though not because it is simpler. "On this continent" is right and "in this country" would not do at all, though it is simpler. "Continent" denotes North America, but it connotes a new-found world that cradles mankind's new hope, his last, best hope. The words Lincoln chose connote the generations of men in the Bible's perspective of history, begetting, conceiving, and bringing forth, not fabricating, a new nation.

So this does not mean that the preacher should try to put everything he says in childish monosyllables (What a slander of the child! He loves mouth-filling words—the bigger the better). It means that a man should cultivate a taste, a preference for the short, familiar word when a longer or more exact word is not definitely needed. He should use these plain words where they will serve, so that the hearer does not notice the words but only what they say. Then when a special word is needed—usually it is a Latin or Greek word—it will justify its use by doing its proper work, by conveying the meaning more exactly.

The Anglo-Saxon words in our vocabulary are without a doubt nearer to the heart. The Greek and Latin words, with equal certainty, are more discriminating. Both elements are needed. Both came into the language because they were needed. But another look at the quotations under 2 above will show that "Love of the long word" is a common vice. A man must overcome it if he is to write for the ear.

4. He should cultivate a preference for *sensuous rather than abstract, and specific rather than general words.* Sensuous words are words that are close to the five senses, suggesting pictures the mind can see, sounds it can hear, things it can touch, taste, smell. Specific words designate particular things rather than groups or classes of things.

Here we are not dealing with mere technical tricks in the choice of words. The two columns below represent two entirely different modes of awareness. To cultivate a preference for the second class of words means to cultivate a certain quality in the apprehension of reality. A man uses specific words because he sees things where another sees only generalities.

General	*Specific*
Flowers	Apple blossoms
Ignorant savages	Pygmies from the center of Africa
	(Harry Emerson Fosdick)

A great English poet	John Milton
A dirty animal	A pig
Extreme suffering	Blood, toil, tears and sweat (Churchill)

A man uses sensuous words because his five senses participate in his experience of life and truth. Peter Marshall apprehended the reality of Jesus' death and resurrection in this manner. He heard, saw, touched, tasted, and smelled that reality when preaching on "The Grave in the Garden." [1] Those who cannot emulate him —and therefore envy him—find fault with him for doing it.

Abstract	*Sensuous*
The alarm	The roar of the siren
He criticized them severely	He blistered them with words (Fulton Sheen)
We avoid thinking of death	We disguise death with flowers (Peter Marshall)
Young people enjoy life	Life is sweet on the tongue of youth
The spot where Jesus lay	The cold stone slab (Marshall)
The odors in Jesus' tomb	Strange scents of linen and bandages, and spices, and close air and blood (Marshall)

The sensuous and specific quality of words brings us close to the figure of speech, for the best words are metaphors, that is, they contain sensory images—though we are so callous to life that we commonly ignore them. But ability to use sensory images is of the greatest importance in writing for the ear. Abstract thought that might be lost is quickly and vividly apprehended when Professor Sittler says, "We are born into time whose hands are full of promise; we come to our last hour with the clutch of time about our throats," or when Augustine says, "Of what use to us is a golden key, if it is unable to open what we desire?" or when Christopher Morley says, "Life is a foreign language; all men mispronounce it." The difference is sensuous and specific words and the images they evoke.

5. He should rely on *strong nouns and verbs* to carry the weight of his thought. Nouns are names of things, and should be concrete when possible. Verbs are symbols of actions, and should

[1] *Mr. Jones, Meet the Master,* p. 104f.

be in the active voice when possible. Adjectives and adverbs mark only qualities of the things and actions signified by the nouns and verbs, and adjectives and adverbs should be used sparingly. They cannot convey thought; they can only color it.

Here is a thought weighed down with abstract nouns and qualifying phrases, most of which are superfluous. Its verb, though in the active voice, is also a dim abstraction. "One of the considerable benefits accruing from the widespread or universal observance of courtesy in our contacts with one another, is that it minimizes the hazards of living." Here is the same thought in two nouns and a verb on the back of a truck: "Courtesy saves lives."

Bishop Berggrav is speaking in London about the Bible in wartime Norway. With the little verb *was,* three nouns, and no adjectives, he says this: "The Bible was the weapon of our souls." The strength of the next passage is due to five active verbs: "It was with us in suffering, it fought for us, and our foes feared it. And why did they hate that very old book? For the same reason we ourselves loved it." He has used only two adjectives, *very old* and *same.* Later on, still relying on nouns and verbs, he reaches a place where the single adjective *dangerous* speaks volumes: "The Bible was in the war, and being in the war was fought against by those who recognized its dangerous power."

Every one of these principles in the use of words applies to writing as well as to speech. Good speech simply does not differ from good writing in the kind of language it uses, except that it can afford to be more informal—though this too has its peril. The difference is not in form but in function. Good speech, good writing for the ear, is that which most immediately and with strictest economy of words achieves—through sound, voice, bodily expression alone—a clear realization of the thought plus a genuine response to it in imagination and feeling. Good writing for the eye is that which, without the help of voice, gesture, physical presence, clearly sets forth and permanently holds the thought in all its full significance.

Even so brief a statement about words must not end without a warning that these are not tricks of language which a man can use to manipulate people for his own ends without himself being involved in the expensive venture of living. He can hear a striking figure like "the shadow of death," can like it, can steal and use it, but not for long. It is soon worn out and means nothing either to him or his hearers. He must first sense the reality of existence for himself, then put his own words together to make his own images. There is no escape. There is no handier or less costly way. The more vivid a phrase was when fresh, the more false it sounds when it has become jargon.

SENTENCES

This book ends where it began, with a subject joined to a predicate to make a thought, a sentence. In communication we do not advance beyond that, whatever we do in dreams. It might seem that we do not need to study sentences, since we use them all the time. But that is just why we must think of them. Because we always speak in them, we do not discriminate between good, bad, and indifferent sentences.

The sentence that concerns us here is the heard sentence. Rules for constructing and punctuating a sentence for the eye will not help us. For the heard sentence is simply the form a thought takes in the course of getting spoken, is simply the way one says what he thinks. The books on writing, of which there are many good ones, can help us much. Unfortunately, at every point where writing for the ear may differ from writing for the eye, the books go in the direction of writing for the eye. Regarding the ways in which the good spoken sentence is like the good written sentence— that is most ways—the books are helpful. At every point of difference, where we most need help, they either fail us or take us in the wrong direction.

The often-repeated rule that spoken sentences should be clear and short does not help us much. Clear they should certainly be, but this holds good for writing as well as for speech. If speech requires any special attention to clarity, we have to ask what it is that makes a sentence clear to the ear, regardless of how it looks on paper. And writing for the ear means listening to the sound of whole sentences, as well as to words and phrases.

But an unqualified rule of shortness will not do. The notion that good speech invariably uses shorter sentences than does good writing is simply not true. I started out believing it, but extensive research has forced me to revise and qualify this conclusion. Good writing also tends to shorter sentences in our day, and the prevailing styles in editing and printing strengthen the tendency. Many a sequence of short sentences beginning with *ands* and *fors* and *buts* would a hundred years ago have been written and printed as one sentence. The difference is mainly in the way it looks, not in the way it sounds when spoken.

It was the tape recorder which finally removed all lingering doubt and hesitation about this heretical conclusion of mine. Like everyone else I had for years listened to discourse in person and over the radio, thinking almost exclusively of content and paying little or no attention to form. What little I could gather about sentences was only sketchy impressions subject to the uncertainty and inaccuracy of memory. I never learned shorthand so as to preserve every word and sentence as it fell.

Then I began to record sermons and afterwards to transcribe them word for word on the typewriter. Call me a fool for work, or say that I was unusually curious to know exactly what goes on in speech—I do not care which. Anyhow, I learned things in this process. In general I learned for the first time—believe it or not—the real significance of a simple fact: there is no visible punctuation in speech, no punctuation at all except what you can hear.

And in particular I learned for sure two things I had not been sure of before. First, it became clear that there are long sentences in good speech, in clear and moving speech. I transcribed many a passage which could not be punctuated as short sentences without leaving them ungrammatical fragments. The long sentence was there, it had actually been spoken, and sometimes it was really long. The speaker may have written it as a sequence of shorter sentences—I do not know. He would almost certainly make short sentences of it if he prepared it for the printer. But he spoke it as a long sentence, and far from finding it hard to listen to, nobody noticed its being long. It had required a tape recorder to reveal the fact that it was long.

The second thing I learned is that effective speech is not heard as sentences, separate sentences, at all. Speech is heard as larger and more complex units of thought. If it cannot be fitted together into larger units, it cannot be taken in. And we not only hear in larger units, we speak in larger units when we talk naturally.

It is nothing unusual for a man to utter what must be six or eight written sentences in one sustained flow of speech, even in tempo and volume and with no breaks other than oratorical pauses, so that when transcribing I cannot tell whether to punctuate the passage as a number of sentences or as one extremely long one. Many a sequence of short sentences will be taken in by the listener as a single unit of thought, consisting of several parts that cohere, and he would hear it just the same if it were written as one long sentence. The short sentences are more help to the eye in rapid reading than to the ear in listening.

As a brief example, my last sentence but one might have been written as three:

Many a sequence of short sentences will be taken in by the listener as a single unit of thought. Such a unit of thought consists of several parts that cohere. A listener, however, would hear it just the same if it were written as one long sentence.

This might be easier to read rapidly. But it is easier to hear it as it was first written, if the sentence is well spoken. Oral communication is just as hospitable to a long sentence as modern writing is, as long as the sentence meets certain standards of clarity. If there is any difference, speech is more hospitable to long sentences than is writing.

Much more reliable than the rule of shortness is the rule that good writing for either the ear or the eye uses a mixture of short and longer sentences. A sequence of longer sentences should be broken by a short sentence. A sequence of short sentences should not continue long without introducing a longer sentence. But this is no blind rule to follow without good reason. We have to ask why there should be this mixture of short and longer sentences.

The reason is to be found in function rather than form. The short sentence has one purpose, and the longer sentence has another and quite different purpose. Short and long sentences have different functions and produce different effects. The virtues and vices of the short sentence are not the same as the virtues and vices of the longer sentence, and if we are to study them intelligently, we shall have to treat them separately.

The Short Sentence

The purpose and effect of the short sentence is to accent what it says, to emphasize the thought it expresses, to give it clarity, distinctness, sharpness. Out of this fact grow the virtues and the vices of the short sentence.

The purpose and effect of a long sentence is just the opposite: to give a sweep and perspective of thought, to bring the several parts of a complex thought together in relation to one another, to make some parts stand out and to subordinate others, and at the same time to build them into one thought. As with the short sentence, both its virtues and vices spring from this.

The working principle governing a successful use of long and short sentences is based on this difference in function. If I wish to accent a certain thought or part of a thought, I put it in a short sentence all by itself. The vicious converse is that when I put a thought or part of a thought in a short sentence all by itself, I emphasize it, whether I wish to or not. If each constituent of a complex thought is put in a short sentence of its own, every constituent is accented equally. There is no possible way either to stress it or subordinate it. There is no way to show its relation to other fragments of the larger thought except by beginning these short sentences with *ands* and *buts* and *fors*.

A short sentence is like the accent in music, like the high light in a picture. If I accent every note I accent no note. If I use only high lights I get a glare but no picture. In a succession of short sentences every detail stands out sharp and stiff, and the passage stamps and pounds in the ear.

When every detail is equally important, equally deserves to be stressed, then a succession of short sentences is effective. But if some parts of a large thought are more important than others, which is nearly always the case, then to put a secondary part in a sentence by itself is to make a false claim for it, to give it an emphasis it does not deserve. A series of short sentences is incapable of perspective. Only in a longer sentence can we put one thing higher or lower than another, set one thing nearer to us and another farther off.

There are times when such a succession of short sentences is natural and right. One such time is when there are only a few things to be said, each equally urgent, each deeply felt. This accounts for the fact, confirmed in great literature, that though a person may grow voluble under the stress of a common passion like anger, there is a degree of emotion, perplexing, overwhelming, or crushing, in which his sentences are likely to be short. George Buttrick, when he is speaking most earnestly, often uses a succession of short sentences. His sermons furnish good examples of how such a succession imparts a strong emotional force to what he is saying.

Another occasion that calls for short sentences is when one is striving for clarity. Short sentences can make clear the chief features of a complicated thought, one at a time. When they do this, it is sharpness of thought rather than force of feeling that characterizes them. Thus above, for example, my effort to make clear the special function of a short sentence might justify a longer succession of short sentences:

A short sentence is like the accent in music. It is like the high light in a picture. If I accent every note I accent no note. If I use only high lights I get a glare but no picture. In a succession of short sentences every detail stands out sharp and stiff. The passage stamps and pounds in the ear.

But it is clear that even with the best of reasons this sort of thing cannot go on long without boredom. These sentences would never offend the eye, but the ear cannot long bear them without pain.

Furthermore, short sentences are useful when we need to make swift progress across a level field of thought where the going is easy. Each sentence becomes a step in advance of the previous one. We must of course be sure that our listener will be able to take the step as easily as we do without stumbling. It should therefore be a field so familiar that it needs no mapping, so smooth that it contains no obstacles. Or it may be a field which has just been worked over and leveled, so that the sentences become steps that can now be taken easily. This paragraph is an example of rather quick steppingstone sentences, and here is another I wrote on page 271.

The Anglo-Saxon words in our vocabulary are without a doubt nearer to the heart. The Greek and Latin words, with equal certainty, are more discriminating. Both elements are needed. Both came into the language because they were needed. But another look at the quotations under 2 above will show that "Love of the long word" is a common vice. A man must overcome it if he is to write for the ear.

These, then—force, clarity, swiftness—are the most important purposes of a series of short sentences.

A single short sentence, used not in a series but alone, serves at once to summarize and to emphasize a thought. Coming after one or more longer sentences, as a brief restatement, it satisfies both ear and mind, puts the hearer in firm possession of a large truth whose parts have already been seen. The process is induction.

Coming before one or more longer sentences, a short sentence can serve to introduce in a few words a larger thought whose parts are about to be presented. The process is deduction, moving from generalization to particularity. Without bothering to look for better examples, here is a paragraph from page 267 which contains both uses. The two short sentences in the middle say the same thing, the second restating the first.

By way of getting down to the subject, perhaps the first thing to say is that, in spite of the fact that speech aims at immediacy and writing at permanence, good speech differs from good writing in only a limited sense. The standards of good language are the same for both. Language that is bad when spoken is bad when written. A passage which brings to finality and permanence of statement some great thought, which requires many readings to appreciate it fully, and is richer at the fiftieth reading than it is at the first—that passage nonetheless uses language that is good when spoken or read aloud.

What in writing is called the topical sentence of a paragraph becomes even more important, if that is possible, when writing for the ear. That sentence is in fact the general statement of the point in a short sentence. It may begin the development as it often begins the paragraph. It may come in the middle or it may come at the end of the development. In speech it can hardly come too often, if it is restated at each occurrence. The ear is far more tolerant than the eye of reiteration, so long as it is not deadly repetition. A short sentence restating the point can come at the beginning, in the middle, and again at the end, with no offense, provided the development is interesting. This last use of the short sentence, as a generalization of the point, is undoubtedly one of its most important functions when writing for the ear.

The shortest sentence has two parts or elements: the subject, the thing or person element, and the predicate, the action or state element. It may have a third element: the complement, the object of the action, direct or indirect, or the consequence of the action or state. There is a fourth element common even in the short sentence: the adverbial element, the element of time, place, or condition. These are the factors that must be handled properly in writing for the ear.

The normal English order is: subject—predicate—complement. If there is an adverbial element it commonly comes first, before the subject, as in "First I must know what to say," or in "Sometimes a man does not know what to say."

A change in the order of parts makes a change in the distribution of emphasis. It is calamitous if a man supposes that the way a sentence happens to get down on paper as he writes is the best way it could be said.

Speaking of the persons who confronted Jesus in the Gospel story, I once said, "Commonplace those men and women were for the most part." The normal order would be, "Those men and women were commonplace for the most part," or, putting the adverbial element first, "For the most part those men and women were commonplace."

To understand the different force produced by these arrangements, we must remember that every sentence has two positions of natural strength, the beginning and the end. That means that if I wish to emphasize one part I must put it first or last. To put it in the middle de-emphasizes it whether I will or no. It means that what comes last is also emphasized.

If I wish to stress the commonplaceness of those people, to suggest that they are like ourselves, I must put the commonplaceness first or last. But one normal order would put it last, and an unusual order is more emphatic than the normal order. This accounts for the effect of, "Commonplace those men and women were for the most part." We must hear the sound in order to feel the difference in force.

> Those men and women were commonplace for the most part.
> Those men and women were for the most part commonplace.
> For the most part those were commonplace men and women.
> Commonplace those men and women were for the most part.
> Commonplace for the most part those men and women were.

I cannot resist giving another example. "I will gladly do this for you, my dearest friend." The person element is "I." The action element is "will do." The direct object is "this," and the indirect object is "for you." The adverbial element is "gladly." "My dearest friend" is appositional to "you." That makes six parts. A better mathematician that I am would know how many combinations of these six elements are possible. I have before me a list of nearly forty ways, some good and some terrible, in which

I have written this sentence without exhausting the possibilities. I will inflict only a few on my reader.

> I will do this gladly for you, my dearest friend.
> I will do this for you, my dearest friend, gladly.
> For you, my dearest friend, I will do this gladly.
> For you, my dearest friend, I will gladly do this.
> This will I do gladly for you, my dearest friend.
> This will I gladly do, my dearest friend, for you.
> My dearest friend, I will do this gladly for you.
> My dearest friend, I will do this for you gladly.
> My dearest friend, gladly will I do this for you.
> Gladly will I do this for you, my dearest friend.
> Gladly, my dearest friend, I will do this for you.
> Gladly for you, my dearest friend, will I do this.

The Longer Sentence

The function of a longer sentence is to give breadth and perspective to a field of thought, to combine parts so as to raise some and lower others, to bring some nearer and set others farther off, to accent some and subdue others. The value of a longer sentence is that it can do all this.

The disadvantage is that while the longer sentence can relate numerous parts to a larger whole, it cannot emphasize any one of those parts as strongly as a short sentence can. Consequently, when longer sentences are used in sequence the effect is to dull somewhat the sharpness of all details. The thoughts become fuller and the general level of force may be raised, but nothing in particular stands out. We take in the whole forest, but we see no individual tree. As the effect of a series of short sentences is to split the thought into sharp splinters, so the effect of a series of long sentences is to dull all points of the thought.

The vices of the long sentence result from the fact that it gives a birdseye view of the whole forest. There is in the long sentence more woodland, much darker and denser woods, for the thought to get lost in than there is in the short sentence. Thus the principles governing the right use of the long sentence are not the same as those for a short sentence.

As we aim to write for the ear, we are concerned only with the sentence as it is heard, not as it is seen. It makes no difference to the listener whether at a given place there is a period, a semicolon or colon, a comma, a dash, a capital letter, or nothing at all. He hears nothing but the variations in the sound. We need to be clear about this. Language, the sound heard, cannot be written on paper at all. The convention of printed marks gives only an illusion of language, and the things most essential to communication are not even indicated by these marks.

The language of sound, the things essential to communication, must be sharply distinguished from the look of the sentence. In speech the necessary things are not the visible letters but the sound of vowels and consonants, the variations of the voice in pitch and volume, stress, inflection, intonation, melody, the hundred subtly different ways the voice can fall or avoid falling at the pauses, the length of the pauses, changes of syllabic speed, the timing in general. These are the essentials of speech, and these are precisely the things writing cannot possibly indicate.

Not to suggest that new ways of writing can indicate the sound of speech, but to remind us of visible symbols which are not heard, to show how nearly everything must be supplied by the voice alone, let me give the bare words of a paragraph I wrote on page 267.

this will not do—or rather—it may do for the scientist describing a new discovery—or experiment—but will not do for the same man— when he is writing a letter—to his wife and children—it may do for a recipe in a cookbook—a legal document—any work whose purpose is only to supply information—it will not do—for a work that hopes to communicate—on any level deeper than the surface of the mind— it will not do then—for the preacher—on the contrary—the serious writer—the poet—and the preacher—must write for the ear—not simply for the eye

The average speaker lets his voice fall not only at periods but also sometimes at commas, and just as often at an oratorical pause not marked by any punctuation. It matters not at all to the listener how the above paragraph is punctuated, whether as short sentences, or some longer and some shorter, or as a single long sentence. If it is properly spoken he will hear it as one unit.

All I shall say about the longer sentence, then, concerns the heard sentence alone. And I am not suggesting that the reader scorn or neglect the form of good writing, nor that he invent some strange new format which will be as impotent to make speech visible as are conventional forms. My experiments in suggesting how language is heard are aimed at his ear and his brain.

Now the successful use of longer sentences depends on the observance of certain basic principles. Every one of them applies to good writing as well as good speech, for the good writer hears what he writes. The difference is mainly of degree. The requirements are more rigid for immediate communication than for permanent statement, because to fail of immediate clarity is to fail irretrievably.

1. The first factor is the *skeletal structure* of the sentence. The basic structure of the good longer sentence is logical, uncluttered, obvious. At its simplest this means that every good longer sentence can be reduced to a good short sentence with subject, predicate, complement, and possibly also an adverbial element, all in clearly ordered relation. The long sentence contains this short sentence, is in fact nothing but the elaboration of this short sentence by means of particulars added to its various parts, or by doubling and redoubling one or more of these parts. The long sentence is heard as an ampler statement of the thought contained in the short sentence.

For example, on page 268 I wrote this sentence:

When he is wording his theme or message, when he is composing his structural assertions, when he is writing his sketch or the sentences and paragraphs of the sermon, when he sets down any words whatever, the preacher must hear how they sound when spoken, each combination of syllables, each phrase when joined with other phrases to make a sentence, each sentence when joined with others to create the movement of language.

The basic sentence is, "When writing he must hear what he writes." In order to show how this applies to the entire task of designing a sermon, I wanted to particularize two elements, the act of writing and what is written. The four "whens" supply four phases of writing and keep the act of writing in clear focus until we come to the subject and predicate, "the preacher must hear." After that the sound of what he writes is given particularity and kept in focus by the "eaches." The structure of the sentence is: "When— when—the preacher must hear how they sound—each—each—." The ear will follow a logical, ordered procedure of this kind, but not a procedure that is confused.

All this is as true of a great sentence as of mine. The Lord speaks to Job (38:25) as follows:

> Who has cleft a channel for the torrents of rain,
> and a way for the thunderbolt,
> to bring rain on a land where no man is,
> on the desert in which there is no man;
> to satisfy the waste and desolate land,
> and to make the ground put forth grass?

So it is with all good long sentences; they are clearly con- structed. The longer sentence tends to move as a good short sentence moves, from adverbial element to subject, to predicate, to complement, or in some other logical order. Any or all of these elements may be elaborated, but usually it is only one or two. Clearness requires that one be finished before the next is begun, that there be no return to an element once it has been left, and that the transitions be clearly marked.

2. A second factor, *connecting words,* is closely related to the first. The connecting words show the relation between structural parts of the sentence and mark the transition from one to another. They also mark the relation between smaller fragments, words and phrases, within each part. One virtue in a good long sentence is scrupulous care in the use of connectives.

This has already been illustrated in the previous examples. In- deed it is impossible to show the basic structure of a sentence without using its connecting words, for it is these words which articulate the sentence, furnish its joints and ligaments. Thus the "when—when" and the "each—each" of my sentence and the "a channel—and a way—to bring—to satisfy" in the sentence from Job are connecting words.

Such words are for the ear what commas and semicolons and dashes are for the eye. They are the audible punctuation of the sentence. For this reason, when we are writing for the ear we cannot safely omit them. A multiplication of such words, an insistence upon them, which would look labored and artificial on paper, will be no offense to the ear, but will make for ease and clarity in listening.

Even within constituent clauses of the sentence, connecting words are needed as punctuation of the thought. It is not considerate to our listener to say "We are not cold, and we are not hot either" if we mean only to say "We are neither cold nor hot." Think what a word like "neither" does to our mind when we hear it. "Neither the innocence of girlhood. . . ." We are all ears to hear more!

Good speech makes a more lavish use of such connectives than good writing. I have before me a wartime speech of President Roosevelt in which a hasty check shows him to have used at least a dozen different connective combinations of the kind in which the English language is so rich. It shows not only how often he used them but also the skill with which he adapted them to his purpose. Some of them are in the following list, which is meant only to suggest a few of the unlimited possibilities.

Almost always . . . but
    sometimes
even if . . . still
if . . . much more (less)
good . . . better . . . best of
    all
important . . . more
    important . . .
  most important of all
in contrast with . . . there is
one . . . another .. . still
    another

either . . . or
both . . . and
when . . . then
not . . . but rather (but only)
not merely . . . but also . . . and then
though . . . yet (nevertheless)
on the one hand . . . on the other hand
not . . . nor . . . far less (how much less)

But to return to connectives that mark the structure of the whole sentence, think what power the word *if* has to hold a long sentence suspended while we wait for its resolution. "If in the last hundred years the race of man has acquired such power as makes him dream of extending his dominion to include the planets of the solar system. . . ." Think of the cumulative suspense created by a series of *ifs:* "If (this)—if (that)—if (these)—if (those) . . ." and what force it gives to the final "then (this)." Here is Job speaking (31:16-22):

> If I have withheld anything that the poor desired,
> > or have caused the eyes of the widow to fail,
> > or have eaten my morsel alone,
> > and the fatherless has not eaten of it . . .
> if I have seen anyone perish for lack of clothing,
> > or a poor man without covering;
> if his loins have not blessed me,
> > and if he was not warmed with the fleece of my sheep;
> if I have raised my hand against the fatherless,
> > because I saw help in the gate;
> then let my shoulder blade fall from my shoulder,
> > and let my arm be broken from its socket.

Many good long sentences are held together by the force of such connective words. Here are a few examples:

They intend not only to . . . , but also to . . . , and then to. . . .

If we would find him, we should seek him not in . . . , not in . . . not in . . . ; we should seek him rather in . . . , in . . . , in. . . .

We in our day, partly because . . . , partly because . . . , but chiefly because . . . , have come to believe that . . . , and that. . . .

When we consider how . . . , how . . . , how . . . , we might think that . . . , that . . . , that . . . , and that. . . .

Paul puts his elaboration after the subject and predicate:

> You put up with fools gladly, being yourselves so wise!
> You put up with it if a man makes slaves of you,
> > if a man devours you,
> > if a man dupes you,
> > if a man exalts himself,
> > if a man slaps you in the face.
> To my shame, I must admit, I was too weak for that![2]

II Corinthians 11:19-21. Version composite.

3. A third factor is *correspondence of parts,* of the phrases within a clause and of the clauses within the sentence. This means parallel construction and repeated construction.

Parallel construction means a harmony, a correspondence short of identity, in the words, phrases, and clauses of the sentence. It means verbs after verbs, nouns after nouns, adjectives, adverbs, participles, or infinitives following one another consistently. Repeated construction means the recurrence of an identical construction in the same form of words. The preamble to the American Constitution is an example of parallel construction, not so mathematically regular as to be monotonous:

```
We the People of the United States, in Order to
    form        a more perfect   Union,
    establish                     Justice,
    insure              domestic  Tranquility,
    provide for the     common    defence,
    promote     the     general   Welfare, and
    secure   the Blessings of      Liberty
            to ourselves and our  Posterity,
    do ordain and establish this Constitution
            for the United States of America.
```

Abraham Lincoln's Second Inaugural Address will supply us with all the further examples we shall need of both parallel and repeated construction.

```
        Fondly    do we hope
        Fervently do we pray
```

The ear can hear this correspondence, if the words are well spoken, more plainly than the eye can see it.

Both parties deprecated war; but one of them would make war rather than let the nation survive; and the other would accept war rather than let it perish. . . .

Let us strive on—to finish the work we are in—to bind up the nation's wounds—to care for him who shall have borne the battle   and for his widow   and his orphan—to do all which may achieve and cherish a just and lasting peace among ourselves   and with all nations.

Like all the other factors, parallel and repeated construction is employed in good writing for the eye. But good writing for the ear makes more frequent and more deliberate use of them. It is right that speech should use them thus, not only for clarity but also for cumulative emphasis.

4. A fourth factor is *co-ordination*. It means joining together elements of equal rank, words, phrases, and clauses, adding one to another with or without conjunctions.

However, co-ordination makes a large use of conjunctions like *and, but, for, also, therefore, because,* and their variants. The series of sentences beginning with *ands, buts,* and *fors,* to which I have referred, is an example of co-ordination.

Co-ordination is the opposite of subordination, in which one element is the principal one and the other is secondary. In "When I wake, I am still with thee" the "when I wake" could not stand alone; it is subordinate to "I am still with thee." But in "I wake, and I am still with thee" the *and* could be replaced by a period, and either clause could stand alone. "I wake. I am still with thee." The clauses are co-ordinate.

Both these processes, co-ordination and subordination, are common to all language. The point here is that the ear will welcome a larger use of co-ordination than is acceptable in the current style of literary language.

Many a good longer sentence is built up by co-ordination of otherwise independent sentences, and the ear hears many a group of independent sentences as one co-ordinated group of thoughts.

One notable achievement in co-ordination is found in Hebrew poetry. The basic principle of Hebrew poetry, the balanced sentence, requires the constant use of co-ordinated sentences, sentences built by doubling and redoubling independent statements. The colon used in printing the Psalms for liturgical use has the effect of a conjunction even if not followed by a conjunction, as it usually is.

When the psalmist says, "The snare is broken, and we are escaped," he joins two independent statements with the additive conjunction *and.* Jeremiah joins three independent statements when he says, "The harvest is past, the summer is ended, and we are not saved." The same prophet joins four independent statements:

For the pastors are become brutish, and have not sought the Lord: therefore they shall not prosper, and all their flocks shall be scattered (10:21, A.V.).

But smaller co-ordinate parts can be multiplied too:

Faith is not simply believing, nor praying, nor giving money, nor making sacrifices, nor cultivating virtues, nor doing good to others, nor striving to carry about us some nostalgic but synthetic perfume of sainthood; but faith is to entrust ourselves to God's hands, to worship him with our heart's devotion, and to live humbly and thankfully in the consciousness of his presence.

The voice is a great co-ordinator. Any man who for a long time has been trying to write for the ear will find himself putting on paper what would be acceptable to the ear if rightly spoken, but is not good for the eye. On page 7 I had first written this sentence:

The Word of God calls us to a way we would not choose to go, tells us the self we are must die that the self he wills may be born, while we struggle to preserve the self that is at any cost.

A reader said to break that up, and he was right. The voice, speaking that sentence in the pattern established by the flow of the preceding sentences, with the right inflections and pauses, would have made it clear. But its thought is too wide, and its parts too loosely related, for the eye to take it in readily. On the previous page I first wrote another sentence thus:

The truth can reach him best through its imaged forms: beauty and compassion and strength and courage and forgiveness and regret and faithfulness and love and pain and hope.

My daughter, who is a good reader, rightly objected to that string of *ands*. Yet I venture to think it would have been better for the ear than "beauty and compassion, strength and courage, forgiveness and regret," and so on. In fact, the sentence as I first wrote it made her hear me speaking it, and she knew that without the voice it would not be the same.

5. A fifth factor is the *length of inner parts* of the sentence. Here is a difference between writing for the ear and for the eye. The ear cannot manage an element within the sentence that grows too long.

The ear can take in a rather long clause that comes at the end of the sentence. The beginning can be extended considerably before the principal movement of the thought gets under way. The inner parts can be multiplied so long as they are clearly organized and kept short and general rather than particular. But an inner part cannot become much extended or be loaded with much detail without causing the listener to forget how the sentence started and in what direction it is going.

One example should be enough to show what this means. A sublime sentence in Lincoln's Second Inaugural Address reads as below. I shall display it in parts, keeping the structural words at the left-hand margin.

If we shall suppose
    that American slavery is one of those
       offenses
         which, in the providence of God, must needs come, but
         which, having continued through His appointed time,
           he now wills to remove, and
    that he gives to both North and South this terrible
      war, as the
        woe due to those by whom the offense came,
shall we discern therein any
      departure from those divine
      attributes
      which believers in a living God
        always ascribe to him?

This is a deathless sentence. It could not be altered without weakening it. Certainly it could not be split into short sentences without making it sound trivial compared to what it is now. At the fiftieth reading it is better than at the first.

But that sentence was not written for the ear, to be heard once. It was written to stand on record before God and the ages.[8] For a one-time hearing it would need a different organization, at what-

---

[8] As Lincoln wrote to Thurlow Weed on March 15, 1865: "I expect [the recent Inaugural Address] to wear as well as—perhaps better than—anything I have produced; but I believe it is not immediately popular. Men are not flattered by being shown that there is a difference between the Almighty and them." Quoted in Houston Peterson's *A Treasury of the World's Great Speeches* (New York: Simon and Schuster, 1954), p. 525.

ever sacrifice of literary quality. The two *which*-clauses following the first *that* are so extended in reach and meaning that the ear is not immediately prepared to relate the second *that* to the first.

I shall not expose myself to odious comparison. I shall only say that while the first *which*-clause is properly controlled by the first *that,* the material of the second *which*-clause would, for the ear's sake, need somehow to become a second distinct part, equal in rank with the coming of slavery before it, and with the penalty of war that follows it. The beginning, "if we shall suppose," might be repeated to introduce the removal of war. Or a second *that* might introduce it, "that it is an offense, which. . . ."

Lincoln's sentence is not the best example of an inner part that becomes too extended for the ear. Its architecture is so strong that if properly spoken it will be heard without trouble. I choose it on purpose to show that the great sentence, more than any other perhaps, reveals the difference between writing for the ear and writing for the eye.

6. A final factor is that of the *positions of natural strength* in the sentence. The strongest places in a long sentence, as in a short one, are the beginning and the end.

A long sentence has numerous constituent thoughts. The first and the last are emphasized, whether or not we intend them to be emphatic. Anything put in an inner part is de-emphasized, whether we will or no. An element of the thought which we wish to emphasize should be put first or last.

But the beginning of a long sentence is hardly ever free. It must usually be given to that part of the thought which best connects with what has gone before. Every sentence after the first one in a discourse stands in relation to everything that has gone before it. Every sentence is thus composed of two elements, the old and the new; it is partly restatement and partly fresh statement.

Consequently, the working principle for controlling a sentence's distribution of force is that the most important new assertion should be put last, at the end of the sentence. Anything secondary should be put among the inner parts of the sentence.

This matter of the distribution of force is more crucial in a long sentence than it is in a short one, for the reason that some parts of a large thought are necessarily subordinated in a long sentence, while short sentences give independent statement to every important constituent thought. Let us observe this at work. We write a sentence thus:

It is not enough to speak the truth. Your words will fall unheeded, even though they are as true as the Bible, if they are not relevant to the life of your people, and unless your voice gives them the accent of personal concern.

Why is that sentence unsatisfactory? For one thing, "if they are not" and "unless your voice" are not in parallel construction. "If your voice fails to" would be better. For another thing, "Your words will fall unheeded" is not the part that best connects with the previous sentence. "Though they may be as true as the Bible" is the part most related to what has gone before. Putting it first:

Though your words may be as true as the Bible, they will fall unheeded, if they are not relevant to the life of your people, and if your voice fails to give them the accent of personal concern.

This is better at the beginning but weak at the end, unless the use of the voice is the main thing we are talking about. If it is, we will need to reword the sentence, for the *ifs* are subordinating words, and the sentence trails off in two subordinate clauses. This makes what is technically known as a "loose sentence," and there is no objection to a loose sentence. But the principal assertion in this sentence, as it is written, is "they will fall unheeded." If that is the main new statement, we put it last, getting a "periodic sentence" as follows:

It is not enough to speak the truth. Though your words may be as true as the Bible, yet if they are not relevant to the life of your people, and if your voice fails to give them the accent of personal concern, they will still fall unheeded.

FINAL SUGGESTION

You will, I hope, have some joy as well as pain in your wrestling with language. If you come at last to read literature for language as well as for ideas, I shall not be sorry, for you will not lose but gain.

If you are not yet acquainted with Fowler's *Modern English Usage* (55), get hold of a copy and give yourself several hours to browse among its articles. You will need the hours, for you have a delightful adventure ahead of you. Nicholson (60), based on Fowler, was published after my book was finished, and is adapted to American usage.

Use—constantly—the best dictionary you can afford. Other indispensable reference books are a good dictionary of synonyms (I like Roget), a dictionary of quotations (I like Bartlett), and a handbook of composition, an old one like Century or Wooley, or a new one like Warfel, Mathews and Bushman (68).

Rhetoric! My life has been spent with Genung (56), but a good new one is Brooks and Warren (52). If you want a little from all periods from Plato down, there is Thonssen (67).

Do you like John Ruskin? "Of Kings' Treasuries," the first lecture in his *Sesame and Lilies*, is worth anybody's time. Another superb older work, Quiller-Couch's *On the Art of Writing* is out in a new edition (63). Rudolph Flesch's *The Art of Plain Talk* (54) is worth one reading, but his general theory is dubious. In the same vein, and more to my taste, is Gowers (57).

Here is my last word to you. You will not acquire mastery of words and sentences by reading books about them—though you may never acquire mastery unless you read. Mastery of language equals taking language captive, subduing it to the service of the thing you have to say. Language has no right to exist apart from the thing it says.

This is all. There isn't any more, except to pray that you may be disenthralled from last year's words, that yours may prove to be one of those voices for which next year's words are waiting.

Wednesday of Holy Week, 1956.

Bibliography

This list of books is, as far as it goes, an acknowledgment of indebtedness, since every one has contributed something to the study that led up to the writing of this volume. It does not begin to include all the works, nor even the most important works, to which I am so indebted, but only some that may be available to the reader.

A bibliography on preaching can never come to an end. It merges imperceptibly with all other fields of study, not only with theological and biblical studies, but also with history, philosophy, literature, sociology, and politics—not to mention psychology. I have tried to keep to works that can aid in the study of sermonic design.

The classification is intended to make the list more usable. But categories I-III are by no means rigid. Some works might have been put in any of them. The placing indicates the connection in which the work has seemed most significant to me.

I. On Craftsmanship

These are technical works on homiletics, but most of them include more than the craft of sermon construction. Some are formal treatises, and others are lectures or essays.

1. BAUGHMAN, HARRY F. *Preaching from the Propers.* Philadelphia: United Lutheran Board of Publication, 1949.
2. BAXTER, B. B. *The Heart of the Yale Lectures.* New York: Macmillan Co., 1947.
3. BLACKWOOD, ANDREW W. *The Preparation of Sermons.* Nashville: Abingdon-Cokesbury Press, 1948.
4. BROADUS, J. A. *On the Preparation and Delivery of Sermons.* Revised by Jesse Burton Weatherspoon. New York: Harper & Brothers, 1944.
5. BROWN, CHARLES R. *The Art of Preaching.* New York: Macmillan Co., 1922.
6. DAVIS, OZORA S. *Principles of Preaching.* Chicago: University of Chicago Press, 1924.
7. FERRIS, THEODORE P. *Go Tell the People.* New York: Charles Scribner's Sons, 1951.
8. GARVIE, A. E. *The Christian Preacher.* New York: Charles Scribner's Sons, 1937.

9. NEWTON, JOSEPH F. *If I Had Only One Sermon to Prepare.* New York: Harper & Brothers, 1932. Twenty-two preachers talk of their sermonizing.

10. PHELPS, AUSTIN. *The Theory of Preaching.* Abridged edition by F. D. Whitesell. Grand Rapids: Eerdmans, 1947.

11. REU, M. *Homiletics.* Translated by Albert Steinhaeuser. Chicago: Wartburg Publishing House, 1922.

12. SANGSTER, W. E. *The Craft of Sermon Construction.* Philadelphia: Westminster Press, 1951.

13. ————. *The Craft of Sermon Illustration.* Philadelphia: Westminster Press, 1950.

14. SMITH, DAVID. *The Art of Preaching.* London: Hodder & Stoughton, n. d.

II. On the Preaching Ministry

These are more general works on the life and work of the preaching pastor, his qualifications, his preparation, his relations, problems, and opportunities, in which the preparation of sermons is only one task, though a supremely important task. The number of lectures and essays in this category is quite staggering.

15. BLACK, JAMES. *The Mystery of Preaching.* New York: Revell, 1924.

16. BOWIE, WALTER R. *Preaching.* Nashville: Abingdon Press, 1954.

17. BROOKS, PHILLIPS. *Lectures on Preaching.* New York: E. P. Dutton, 1907.

18. BUTTRICK, GEORGE A. *Jesus Came Preaching.* New York: Charles Scribner's Sons, 1931.

19. ————, POTEAT, E. M., *et al. Preaching in These Times.* New York: Charles Scribner's Sons, 1940.

20. DARGAN, E. C. *A History of Preaching.* Two volumes. New York: Doran, 1912.

21. ————. *The Art of Preaching in the Light of Its History.* New York: Doran, 1922.

22. FARMER, H. H. *The Servant of the Word.* New York: Charles Scribner's Sons, 1942.

23. FORSYTH, P. T. *Positive Preaching and the Modern Mind.* Cincinnati: Jennings & Graham; New York: Eaton & Mains, 1907.

24. JONES, EDGAR D. *The Royalty of the Pulpit* (Lyman Beecher Lectures). New York: Harper & Brothers, 1951.

25. JOWETT, J. H. *The Preacher, His Life and Work*. New York: Doran, 1912.

26. LUCCOCK, HALFORD E. *In the Minister's Workshop*. Nashville: Abingdon-Cokesbury, 1944.

27. SANGSTER, W. E. *The Approach to Preaching*. Philadelphia: Westminster Press, 1952.

28. SCHERER, PAUL E. *For We Have This Treasure*. New York: Harper & Brothers, 1944.

29. ———. Five tape-recorded lectures on preaching, 1954. Richmond: Charles G. Reigner Library of Recorded Sermons and Addresses, Union Seminary in Virginia.

30. SOCKMAN, RALPH W. *The Highway of God*. New York: Macmillan Co., 1942.

31. STEWART. JAMES S. *Heralds of God*. New York: Charles Scribner's Sons, 1946.

32. WEBBER, F. R. *A History of Preaching in Britain and America*. Two volumes. Milwaukee: Northwestern Publishing House, 1952.

33. Volumes of the Lyman Beecher Lectures at Yale. Index in Baxter (2), in Buttrick, Poteat, *et al.* (19), and Jones (24: complete to 1949).

III. On the Christian Message

Under this head every important biblical study and every vital exposition of Christian theology has a place. This list does not include the books that have had most influence on the writer's development, and it cannot be relied on to equip the reader for his theological and biblical task. These are mostly short essays that throw light on the functional use of theological studies. The diversity of view is intentional. A preacher cannot be shielded from variable winds of doctrine. He will be blown about until he can discriminate for himself.

34. BARTH, KARL. *The Word of God and the Word of Man*. Boston: Pilgrim Press, 1928.

35. BRUNNER, EMIL. *Our Faith*. Translated by J. W. Rilling. New York: Charles Scribner's Sons, 1936.

36. DODD, C. H. *The Apostolic Preaching*. New York: Harper & Brothers, 1950.

37. ———. *Gospel and Law*. New York: Columbia University Press, 1951.

38. FLEW, N. R., DAVIES, R. E., *et al*. *The Catholicity of Protestantism*. London: Lutterworth Press, 1950, and Philadelphia: Muhlenberg Press, 1954.

39. HILDEBRANDT, FRANZ. *This Is the Message.* London: Lutterworth Press, 1944.

40. KANTONEN, T. A. *Resurgence of the Gospel.* Philadelphia: Muhlenberg Press, 1948.

41. KENNEDY, GERALD. *God's Good News.* New York: Harper & Brothers, 1955.

42. ———. *Who Speaks for God?* Nashville: Abingdon Press, 1954.

43. KERR, HUGH T. *Preaching in the Early Church.* New York· Fleming H. Revell Co., 1942.

44. LEHMANN, H. T. *Heralds of the Gospel.* Philadelphia: Muhlenberg Press, 1953.

45. LUCCOCK, HALFORD E. *Communicating the Gospel.* New York: Harper & Brothers, 1954.

46. NYGREN, ANDERS. *The Gospel of God.* Translated by L. J. Trinterud. Philadelphia: Westminster Press, 1951.

47. PIPER, OTTO A. *Reality in Preaching.* Philadelphia: Muhlenberg Press, 1942.

48. READ, DAVID H. C. *The Communication of the Gospel.* London: SCM Press, 1952.

49. THOMPSON, ERNEST T. *Changing Emphases in American Preaching.* Philadelphia: Westminster Press, 1943.

50. WATSON, PHILIP S. *Let God Be God;* An Interpretation of the Theology of Martin Luther. London: The Epworth Press, 1947; Philadelphia: Muhlenberg Press, 1948.

IV. On Speech and Writing

51. ANDERSON, VIRGIL A. *Training the Speaking Voice.* New York: Oxford University Press, 1942.

52. BROOKS, CLEANTH, and WARREN, ROBERT P. *Modern Rhetoric.* New York: Harcourt, Brace and Co., 1949.

53. CROCKER, LIONEL. *Interpretative Speech.* New York: Prentice-Hall, 1952.

54. FLESCH, RUDOLPH. *The Art of Plain Talk.* New York: Harper & Brothers, 1946.

55. FOWLER, H. W. *A Dictionary of Modern English Usage.* London: Oxford-Clarendon Press, 1940.

56. GENUNG, JOHN F. *The Working Principles of Rhetoric.* Boston: Ginn & Co., 1900.

57. GOWERS, ERNEST. *Plain Words: Their A B C.* New York: Alfred A. Knopf, 1954.

58. LEE, CHARLOTTE I. *Oral Interpretation.* New York: Houghton Mifflin, 1952.

59. MONROE, A. H. *Principles and Types of Speech.* New York: Scott, Foresman & Co., 1935.

60. NICHOLSON, MARGARET. *Dictionary of American-English Usage.* New York: Oxford University Press, 1957.

61. PARRISH, W. M. *Reading Aloud.* New York: Ronald Press, 1941.

62. PHILLIPS, ARTHUR E. *Effective Speaking.* Revised edition. Chicago: Newton Co., 1938.

63. QUILLER-COUCH, ARTHUR. *On the Art of Writing.* Revised edition. New York: G. P. Putnam's Sons, 1950.

64. SAINTSBURY, GEORGE. *A History of English Prose Rhythm.* New York: Macmillan Co., 1922.

65. SARETT, LEW R. and FOSTER, W. *Basic Principles of Speech.* Boston: Houghton Mifflin Co., 1946.

66. TASSIN, ALGERNON. *The Oral Study of Literature.* New York: Appleton-Century-Crofts, 1939.

67. THONSSEN, LESTER. *Selected Readings in Rhetoric and Public Speaking.* New York: H. W. Wilson Co., 1942.

68. WARFEL, H. R., MATHEWS, E. C., and BUSHMAN, J. C. *American College English.* A Handbook of Usage and Composition. New York: American Book Co., 1949.

69. WOOLBERT, C. H. and NELSON, S. E. *The Art of Interpretative Speech.* New York: F. S. Crofts & Co., 1946.

V. Collections of Sermons

None of the many volumes of sermons by individual preachers has been included in this list. Once we began that, there would be no end. While working with the essentials of sermonic design, there is advantage in comparing the work of different preachers. Availability has been a primary consideration in making this selection.

70. ATKINS, G. G. *Master Sermons of the Nineteenth Century.* Chicago: Willett, Clark and Co., 1940.

71. BLACKWOOD, ANDREW W. *The Protestant Pulpit.* Nashville: Abingdon-Cokesbury Press, 1947.

72. BUTLER, G. PAUL. *Best Sermons.* The annual volume of 1945 or any thereafter. New York: Macmillan Co.

73. DAVIS, OZORA S. *Principles of Preaching.* Chicago: University of Chicago Press, 1924. Eight sermons.

74. KLEISER, GRENVILLE. *The World's Great Sermons.* Ten volumes. New York: Funk and Wagnalls, 1908.

75. MACARTNEY, C. E. *Great Sermons of the World*. Boston: Stratford Co., 1926.

76. MOTTER, A. M. *Sunday Evening Sermons*. Sermons preached before the Chicago Sunday Evening Club. New York: Harper & Brothers, 1952.

77. ————. *Great Preaching Today*. More Sunday Evening Club sermons. New York: Harper & Brothers, 1955.

78. STELZLE, CHARLES. *If I Had Only One Sermon to Preach*. New York: Harper & Brothers, 1927.

79. Tape and disk recordings. The student today cannot afford to neglect to study preaching in the accents of the living voice. The most extensive source is the catalog of the Charles G. Reigner Library of (tape) Recorded Sermons and Addresses, at Union Seminary, Richmond 27, Virginia. Union Seminary in New York has important disk recordings, and recordings can no doubt be found at other theological schools. See also the "Spoken and Miscellaneous" section in Schwann's catalog of long-playing records.

Index